'In this lively, eclectic and consistently stimulating book, Tom Vine identifies the remarkable prevalence of paradox in human life and offers a spirited defence of embracing its peculiar logic. Against the conventional wisdom of means-ends reasoning and calculative rationality, Vine argues that paradox reveals fractures in our common-sense that we would do well to explore and exacerbate rather than eradicate or resolve. Taking an ethnographic, transdisciplinary, wide angle view, Vine's primary focus is the lived experience of paradox: our counterintuitive tendency to embrace contrary positions and the unfathomable longing to act against our own best interests. In a world that is being re-contoured by rapid advances in artificial intelligence and information technology, Tom Vine's book is an ardent appeal to the humanising power of paradox.'

Jill Marsden, *Professor of Literature and Philosophy,*
University of Bolton, UK

'This book represents the active and loving embrace of paradox in art, society, organization, nature and ontology but it also (paradoxically) describes the relationship between author and textual material as grappling, staggering, discombobulating and thorny. Take paradox away from the thinker and you have the tame professor yet (paradoxically) to outwit paradox would be accepting a Faustian pact. Paradox is a vague rule of sociology wherein (paradoxically) there is no universally accepted rule book on anything. Vine has produced a text that is both broad and deep, where we are allowed to see paradox at work, everywhere and at every time. It forcibly opens our eyes just as the reader might want to blink and slink back into a less-pressing, logical and linear comfortableness. It is to be highly commended for its smooth disruptiveness.'

Gibson Burrell, *Professor of Organization Theory,*
University of Manchester, UK

'In this important and wide-ranging book Tom Vine makes a strong case for the unique human capacity to entertain one thing and its opposite at the same time. He demonstrates how this is not a result of flawed thinking, but is crucial for exploring complex experience. Vine shows us how paradoxical thinking manifests in the full range of human activity; from art to science, and from pedagogy to the ethics involved in navigating between competing goods.'

Christopher Mowles, *Professor of Complexity and Management,*
University of Hertfordshire, UK

T0362262

Acclaim for Vine's 2021 book, *Bureaucracy: A Key Idea for Business and Society*

'This book is both stimulatingly provocative and deeply questioning of much of the literature on the bureaucratic phenomenon. Tom Vine advances a Deleuzian perspective on bureaucracy as an "emergent and immanent force" in late modernism. Repetitive and recurrent "differences" within and across its operational planes require life-skills in their positive resolution. In presenting his arguments he draws from a wide range of alternative perspectives.'

Ray Loveridge, *Professor Emeritus, Aston University, UK*

'Tom Vine's erudite and engagingly personal reexamination of bureaucracy offers compelling alternatives to the familiar debate on "post-bureaucracy" and the pejorative caricatures of bureaucracy in popular management literature. Rather than arguing for or against bureaucracy, Dr. Vine's unique approach is to ask how people in organisations experience, navigate and make sense of this phenomenon. He combines autoethnography, literary criticism and expansive scholarship to develop a phenomenology of bureaucracy. Written with refreshing style and a colourful wit, his book offers invaluable insights for the critical study of contemporary organisations.'

Dr. Samuel Mansell, *University of St Andrews, UK*

PARADOX

History reveals countless attempts by great minds to solve life's paradoxes. But what if these attempts miss the point? What if paradox *is* life?

Contrary to the supposedly sublime linear logic that underpins our prevalent modes of theoretical and empirical enquiry, in this fascinating book, organizational anthropologist Tom Vine charts the pervasiveness of paradox across the academy: from arithmetic to zoology. In so doing, he reflects on the concept of paradox as a widespread existential 'pattern', a pattern which holds significant metatheoretical and pedagogical potential. Paradoxes, he argues, are not inconveniences or 'fault lines in our common-sense world' but are coded into our very existence. Paradoxes thus present their own vital logics that shape our lives: they thwart moral and ideological uniformity; they even out subjective experience between 'the haves' and 'the have nots'; and they shed light on the opaque concepts of consciousness and agency.

This book will appeal to anybody with a curious mind, particularly scholars and students with an interest in one or more of the following: complexity theory, critical pedagogies, ethnography, nonlinear dynamics, organization theory, and systems theory.

Tom Vine completed his first two degrees at the University of Warwick before moving to the University of Essex for his doctorate. He is currently Associate Professor at the University of Suffolk. When he's not grappling with Nietzsche, Tom enjoys charity shop crawls, restoring old boats, and cold water swimming in the rivers of East Anglia.

PARADOX

Towards a Metatheory

Tom Vine

 Routledge
Taylor & Francis Group

LONDON AND NEW YORK

First published 2024
by Routledge
4 Park Square, Milton Park, Abingdon, Oxon OX14 4RN

and by Routledge
605 Third Avenue, New York, NY 10158

Routledge is an imprint of the Taylor & Francis Group, an informa business

© 2024 Tom Vine

British Library Cataloguing-in-Publication Data
A catalogue record for this book is available from the British Library

Library of Congress Cataloging-in-Publication Data
Names: Vine, Tom, author.
Title: Paradox : towards a metatheory / Tom Vine.
Description: New York : Routledge, 2023. | Includes bibliographical references and index.
Identifiers: LCCN 2023026071 (print) | LCCN 2023026072 (ebook) |
ISBN 9781032066721 (hardback) | ISBN 9781032066714 (paperback) |
ISBN 9781003203339 (ebook)
Subjects: LCSH: Organizational sociology. | Paradox. | Ethnology.
Classification: LCC HM711 .V56 2023 (print) | LCC HM711 (ebook) |
DDC 302.3/5–dc23/eng/20230724
LC record available at https://lccn.loc.gov/2023026071
LC ebook record available at https://lccn.loc.gov/2023026072

ISBN: 978-1-032-06672-1 (hbk)
ISBN: 978-1-032-06671-4 (pbk)
ISBN: 978-1-003-20333-9 (ebk)

DOI: 10.4324/9781003203339

Typeset in Sabon
by Newgen Publishing UK

For Sophie.

CONTENTS

Acknowledgements   *xi*

1   Introduction   1

PART I
The Pervasiveness of Paradox   **17**

2   Paradox and Art   19

3   Paradox and Society   44

4   Paradox and Organization   80

5   Paradox and Nature   103

6   Paradox and Ontology   128

PART II
The Pedagogical Potential for Paradox   **151**

7   Pedagogical Logic I: Paradox Thwarts Moral
    Closure   153

8 Pedagogical Logic II: Paradox Elicits Egalitarian
  Inertia   169

9 Pedagogical Logic III: Paradox Augments
  Understanding of Agency   184

10 Conclusion   193

References   224
Index   241

ACKNOWLEDGEMENTS

In a transdisciplinary project of this nature, I inevitably sought counsel from colleagues beyond my native field. In addition to the unnamed experts involved in the blind review process brokered by Routledge, I remain forever grateful for the inspiration, conversation, and contributions of the following distinguished individuals: Dr. Jenny Amos (sociolinguistics), Dr. James Burridge (mathematics and physics), Dr. Samia Burridge (earth sciences and chemistry), Dr. Edzia Carvalho (political theory), Prof. Peter Cochrane OBE (engineering and technology), Dr. Charlotte Gregory (clinical psychology), Prof. Harro Höpfl (political philosophy), Dr. Rebecca Ison (clinical psychology), Dr. Sam Mansell (ethical theory), Les Stratton (mathematics and physics), Dr. Will Thomas (moral philosophy), and Dr. Luke Wainscoat (economics). Beyond the academic realm, I am immensely grateful to poet Neil Gregory, musician Luke Scurr, and genealogist Carol Stratton for their specialist advice. I would also like to express my thanks to the following for their broader support in bringing this project to fruition: Prof. David Collins (management theory), Prof. Ray Loveridge (industrial sociology), Prof. Clare Rigg (critical management education), and Prof. David Weir (organizational behaviour). I wish also to extend my deep appreciation to the various copyright holders for facilitating the reproduction of the numerous artworks, images and illustrations in this book. Finally, a particular—and heartfelt—thanks goes to Luke Scurr for sacrificing a significant amount of his own time to provide extensive commentary on a full-length draft of the manuscript. My sincere gratitude to all of these individuals notwithstanding, it does of course fall to me alone to assume responsibility for the content herewith, purulent boils and all.

1

INTRODUCTION

It is impressed upon us from a very early age to think in accordance with linear logic. In the sciences this is described as *cause-and-effect*. In the humanities it takes the form of *beginning-middle-end*. Such instruction is, we're told, a simple matter of common sense. But, on reflection, common sense is anything but common. If we are 'creatures of habit' then why is 'variety the spice of life'? If 'you're never too old to learn' then why is it 'you can't teach an old dog new tricks'? None less than celebrated theoretical physicist Albert Einstein is said to have described common sense as a set of learned prejudices (see Barnett, 1948). Even a cursory reflection, then, on the world in which we inhabit suggests common sense is problematic. And yet the linear logic it purportedly reflects unabashedly continues to shape and constrain the way we think. Upon closer scrutiny, common sense and linear logic are oversimplifications. Just ask a physicist about relativity, a psychoanalyst about repression, or a literary theorist about Shakespearian self-fulfilling prophecy. For Marsden (1993: 115), 'there can be no power without resistance because it is the relationship between A and B that causes the behaviour of both'. Candidly, we inhabit a world animated by paradox and it deserves our attention.

In this book, I advance the contentious argument that paradox is coded into our very existence. To this end I seek out and chart the extraordinary pervasiveness of paradox across art, society, organization, and nature. While cautious to avoid the Apophenian trap (a tendency to see connections between phenomena where none exist), I advance an understanding of paradox as a widespread existential 'pattern', a pattern that holds significant metatheoretical potential. I further argue that the many historical attempts to solve, resolve, or dissolve paradoxes are misplaced. To take just one example

DOI: 10.4324/9781003203339-1

of this disposition, Rappaport (1981: 1) insists that 'our tasks as researchers, scholars and professionals should be to unpack and influence contemporary resolutions to paradox'. I disagree. Our inclination to attempt to resolve paradoxes stems from the Augustinian conviction that interest in paradox is a sign of fallen reason (Sorensen, 2003: 287). Instead, readers are encouraged to consider paradox as a salient characteristic of our sensorium—our *'being-in-the-world'*. Over the course of this book I document the extraordinary degree to which paradox saturates our world; paradox is it seems etched into our being. Inevitably, this is a book which consciously and deliberately engages with a controversial subject matter and to this end invokes examples which at first glance may present as at the very least 'analytically inconvenient'. Readers are urged to suspend their assumptions.

Several good books have already been written about paradox. However, these are either written from abstruse philosophical perspectives or constitute examinations of specific paradoxes in specific fields. My objectives are different. In addition to documenting the pervasiveness of paradox (which necessitates transdisciplinary elucidation), I am interested foremost in the 'lived experience' of paradox, a distinct epistemological focus which is beginning to bear fruit (see, e.g. Pradies et al., 2021). Although entertaining, abstract paradoxes which hinge on semantics are not especially relevant to our everyday lives and so their pedagogical potential is limited. An example of this abstract species is Epimenides' liar paradox and its later derivatives. In the original paradox, Epimenides, a Cretan, states categorically that all Cretans are liars. Interesting? Yes. But is it influential in respect of our lived experience? Not really. And as Sorensen (2003) notes it is simply false, not a paradox. Inevitably, the study of abstract paradoxes such as this has a tendency to descend into platitude. Such paradoxes are, at heart, little more than deliberate 'errors' involving circular or self-referential logic; they are, in effect, self-stultifying statements (Goldstein, 1996: 304). However, paradoxes that concern our lived experience (such as social theorist George Simmel's (1955) observation that conflict is fundamental to healthy and productive human relations) are much more interesting—even if we do not routinely describe them using the vocabulary of paradox.

Unlike other texts on paradox, I advance some distinct practical corollaries for this book. First, and at its most fundamental, I demonstrate how a nuanced understanding of paradox can enhance pedagogical technique, both as a means of keeping both moral and ideological conviction in check, and in respect of critical thinking more broadly. I thus advance the concept of paradox as one which can help illuminate the concerns of critical theorists to students. In this sense, I regard paradox as something which—paradoxically—helps us understand. It is, foremost, a pedagogical device.

Second, I argue that paradox has an egalitarian inertia—a sort of 'self-correcting' mechanism trained on utility. It helps even out lived experience—in two ways. First, it evens out lived experience between fortunate and less fortunate human lives (i.e. interpersonally). Second, it evens out lived experience over the course of an individual's lifetime (i.e. intrapersonally). The pleasure paradox provides an instructive example of precisely this. In an interpersonal sense, for example, Schkade and Kahneman (1998) report that despite stereotyped preconceptions of the relationship between sunshine and happiness, Californians (who live in a sunny climate) and Midwesterners (who don't) report no difference in levels of happiness. Equally, in an intrapersonal sense, it seems significant changes in objective life circumstances (such as a tragic accident that leaves one as a paraplegic or the unexpected death of a loved one) have relatively little impact on long-term subjective wellbeing (Silver, 1982; Suh et al., 1996). This is often referred to as hedonic adaptation. It is, perhaps, no surprise that Pozzo comments thus in Samuel Beckett's 1978 play *Waiting for Godot*: 'The tears of the world are a constant quantity'. Psychoanalyst Jacques Lacan's concept of lack as prerequisite for desire (see, e.g. Lacan, 1977) is acutely relevant here, too. We cannot experience desire (ostensibly positive) without an experience of deprivation associated with lack (ostensibly negative). Upon satisfying that lack—and hence quenching that desire—we are compelled to seek out and latch on to another lack if we are to elicit a sense of desire again. I thus reason that a greater sensitivity to paradox will enable us to tackle existential discontentment more effectively. To this end, I explore the possibility of mitigating the downside of the pleasure paradox so as to re-conceptualize pain in a constructive sense. So, for example, going jogging on a rainy morning is considered the painful counterpart to the pleasure associated with the endorphin release and sense of accomplishment that the exercise elicits; however, the wet run compares favourably to the hangover and sense of regret, the painful counterparts to the pleasure associated with a night of heavy drinking. Physical exercise, even in the rain (perhaps even *especially* in the rain), is thus presented as a 'constructive' form of pain. A hangover isn't.

Third, I establish foundations for a more controversial argument: paradox enhances our understanding of consciousness, human agency, and relativism. A world without paradox could feasibly be inhabited by non-conscious life in which straightforward linear cause-and-effect reflexes maintain existential bearing. Put another way, without paradox life could feasibly be reduced to a predetermined calculus (and the concept of being-in-the-world would lose all traction). Conversely, a world characterized by paradox requires of its inhabitants an ability to maintain contradictory positions and beliefs; it necessitates existential manoeuvring, ongoing ontological readjustment, and an ability to intuit balance. These are possible only by recourse to conscious agency. Interestingly, this position also has implications for the prospects of Artificial Intelligence, an argument I have delineated elsewhere (see Vine, 2018c).

Paradox: distinguished

There is a sense of the paradoxical in the very act of definition. This is because definition typically involves distinguishing some*thing* from something *else*; and this necessitates a dependence on that something else. It is a sort of existential quantum entanglement. Before developing and defending a robust definition for paradox, it is thus sensible to consider what it is not. Over the course of conducting the research for this book, I found myself comparing paradox to numerous other analytical concepts. In some cases, it was relatively straightforward to distinguish these from paradox. Concepts such as elusiveness, irony, juxtaposition, quandary, and scepticism fall into this category and do not require further comment. However, in the case of other analytical concepts I encountered along the way, more careful elucidation was warranted. Paradox can thus be compared to, but distinguished from, *antinomies, apeiron, contradictions, dialectics, dichotomies, double-binds, dualities, fallacies, symmetries,* and *wicked problems.* Each is briefly considered, below. Readers are advised that this exercise is presented not so that we can later dismiss tensions which might be said to fall outside a narrow definition of paradox, but because discussions pertaining to definition help hone our understanding of what remains a discombobulating concept.

Antinomy contra paradox. Antinomies are a celebrated part of German philosopher Immanuel Kant's canon. Over the course of the research for this book, it became clear that antinomy is routinely used interchangeably with paradox. For example, Rappaport (1981: 2) suggests that the '[b]asic idea of paradox is the notion of antinomy'. However, we might usefully forge a subtle but significant distinction; according to the *Oxford English Dictionary* (OED), antinomy can be defined as 'a contradiction between two beliefs or conclusions that are in themselves reasonable'. For purists, this is distinguishable from a paradox which is *inherently* self-contradictory, i.e. it is only true if it is false, or false if it is true.

Aporia contra paradox. While some contributors such as Hofmann (2001) imply that aporia are a particular species (or in Hofmann's case, 'level') of paradox, more often than not they are distinguished from one another. While aporia invokes an impasse, it doesn't necessarily mean that this impasse is due to a situation which is inherently paradoxical.

Apeiron contra paradox. According to Charlton (1995), apeiron is the earliest known philosophical expression. 'Literally "without limit", it is used by Anaximander for the material out of which everything arises' (ibid.: 41). To this end, apeiron represents an attempt to intuit a universal principle, which—to some degree at least–is something this book argues for in respect of paradox. However, unlike paradoxes which are characterized by internal contradiction, rudimentary binaries such as hot/cold and dry/wet represent the principal parameters of apeiron.

Contradiction contra paradox. While it is reasonable to suggest that all true paradoxes contain contradictions, it is not the case that all contradictions are paradoxes. Paradoxes typically involve *self*-contradiction, but a conventional contradiction can involve two or more conflicting instructions. For example, the German musical collective, Enigma, released a song in the 1990s called *Silence must be heard*, and in so doing inadvertently helped us distinguish paradox from contradiction. While the song title represents a contradiction, it is an instruction rather than an observation and hence it can quite easily be reversed, i.e. silence *isn't* something that must be heard. A genuine paradox, however, cannot be reversed in this way. Furthermore, in the case of a contradiction one position may be true while another is false. In the case of paradox, each position is concurrently true *and* false.

Dialectics contra paradox. At its most rudimentary, dialectics refers to the back-and-forth dialogue between opposing or contradictory positions. In his discussion of paradox, Stent (1978: 119) intentionally builds on Marx's understanding of dialectics. For Marx, contradiction elicits progress via revolution. This is certainly an important observation, and one we explore later in this book. But while Marx's canon hinges on the observation that contradiction elicits progress, I see something very different. I note that contradiction is perennially ignored or overlooked. More pointedly, whereas dialectics implies that synthesis between opposites can be secured or that positions that transcend opposites can be discerned, I argue that such endeavours miss the point. The point is that opposites (or in our present case, paradoxes) *cannot be synthesized or resolved*, and nor should we attempt to do this because it is the paradox itself that brokers meaning. An overriding faith in the efficacy of synthesis undermines the purpose and potential of paradox. Although dialectics was clearly important for Marx, it was of course Hegel – whose work influenced Marx – who is pivotal in discussions of dialectics. 'Hegel's contention is that reality is to be understood as a *final* synthesis of all those abstract formulations which necessarily distort human understanding' (Dixon, 1980: 20, emphasis added). But to the extent that we can discern an internal logic in paradox, it is one that *doesn't* strive for a final synthesis. Indeed, synthesis is anathema to paradox. Dixon further notes that dialectics is about resolution:

> It is the universal operation of the dialectic within the historical process which allegedly allows for the resolution of the conflict between Marx's historicist and economic determinist ambition on the one hand and his utopian concepts of ultimate human realisation on the other.
>
> *(ibid.: 26)*

And—to stress again—our approach to paradox must de-emphasize resolution if it is to advance. Finally, Dixon argues that the term dialectic may be loosely employed to 'indicate interaction' (ibid.: 39). And this of course is where we are really able to distinguish paradox from dialectics. Paradox is clearly so much more than mere 'interaction'. Finally, and perhaps most importantly, Hegel's view of history was both deterministic and linear (see, e.g. Stent, 2002); paradox is very much at odds with this reflection because it encapsulates non linearity. Having said all this, Hegelian dialectics is nonetheless an important precursor to the idea that paradox is a central concept to all life (see, e.g. Singer, 2009: 13). What is, perhaps, most puzzling is that unlike dialectics which has a long conceptual history in the social sciences, the concept of paradox is woefully underrepresented. This book seeks to remedy this.

Dichotomies contra paradox. For Grayling (1995: 199), a dichotomy is 'a division of a whole into two parts, as with a class into two mutually exclusive and jointly exhaustive subclasses, or a genus into two likewise disjoint species'. There is a key semantic distinction here, then, particularly in respect of the use of verbs. A dichotomy implies a split. Paradox, meanwhile, entails no such division; rather it is a question of rival and ostensibly incompatible arguments, each of which appears to be based on infallible logic. However, this is not to say that dichotomy and paradox are not sometimes conflated. Famously, Zeno of Elea's paradox of the stadium is often referred to as 'The Dichotomy'; in this particular case, the dichotomy refers to an arithmetical or geometrical division.

Double-binds contra paradox. A double bind is 'a difficult situation in which, whatever action you take, you cannot escape unpleasant results' (Cambridge University Dictionary). Such a conclusion is, however, by no means certain in the case of paradox. The pleasure paradox is, as we shall see later in the book, a case in point.

Dualisms contra paradox. As with dichotomies, the key distinction here is language. While dichotomies rely on a vocabulary of division of a whole into competing parts, dualisms rely on distinction of one whole (as a form) and another whole (as a distinct form). Classic examples of dualisms are distinctions between material things and mental ideas. Another is the distinction between nature and nurture. In and of themselves, they are *not* paradoxical. However, as with dichotomies, this should not imply that dualisms cannot be reconfigured in such a way that they meet the contradictory characteristics unique to paradox.

Fallacies contra paradox. Sorensen (2003: 15) presents an instructive and accessible distinction between those two concepts: 'Fallacies differ from paradoxes in being clearly diagnosed errors. By "clear" I mean clear to the experts. Modern casinos are filled with people who still commit the gambler's fallacy'.

Symmetry contra paradox. Symmetry can certainly be conceptualized as a rather elegant paradox because it is, concurrently, both the same and the opposite. However, it is not the case that all paradoxes are (in the visual sense at least) symmetrical.

Wicked problems contra paradox. Like double-binds, wicked problems are those which arise in circumstances characterized by inadequate feedback loops and hence irrespective of the action you choose to take, the outcome is undesirable. Although a wicked problem might be legitimately presented as paradoxical, it does not make wicked problems, by definition, paradoxes. This is because paradox does not necessarily imply undesirable ends.

In the case of a true paradox, the key to understanding one position can only be properly appreciated by recourse to the counter-position. The same simply cannot be said in the case of any the synonyms we have explored, including dialectics. In the case of dialectics, the thesis-antithesis recurrence is one which is dictated by a broader pendulous logic which is ultimately directed towards synthesis, rather than the specifics of the positions and counter-positions presented.

However, it is important to stress that many of the paradoxes explored in this thesis have been examined by others using one or more of these close synonyms. Readers are also reminded that in some cases, there is disagreement between whether or not the tensions identified, including some of those covered in this book, are genuine paradoxes. So, for example, during the research for this project I had an intensive conversation with a Cambridge mathematician about Zeno's paradoxes (which we go on to explore in Chapter 5). While I remain persuaded that they do indeed qualify as paradoxes, his interpretation of the underlying mathematics was that they didn't. He did, however, concede that there was something 'mystifying'— to quote him directly—about the arithmetic. These reservations are duly acknowledged; in each case, then, and where appropriate, our task is to focus primarily on the characteristics of the tension under scrutiny which corresponds most closely to that which we regard as genuinely paradoxical.

Paradox: re-examined

Of the extant literature, Sorensen's (2003) work is arguably the most systematic in pursuance of a basic but eminently satisfying understanding of paradox. Sorensen (2003: xi, emphasis added) argues that paradoxes are '... the *atoms* of philosophy because they constitute the basic points of departure for disciplined speculation'. For Sorensen, then, philosophy is held together by its questions rather than by its answers. Invariably, it seems, the basic philosophical questions come from troubles within our ordinary conceptual scheme (ibid.). Indeed, in my view, philosophy only gains intellectual traction *because of* paradox. Beyond these, Sorensen makes some further pertinent and original observations about paradox, three of which are especially noteworthy. First, paradoxes are questions (in some cases, pseudoquestions) that suspend us between *too many* good answers (ibid.: xii); second, paradoxes mark fault lines in our common-sense world (ibid.); and, finally, paradoxes are ancient species of riddle which 'evolved from folklore and show vestiges of the verbal games that generated them' (ibid.: 3). I have consciously built upon these three observations, as will become clear later in this book.

But, of course, while a basic understanding is one thing, the analytical precision demanded for an arresting *definition* is quite another. It isn't entirely clear whether or not Sorensen explicitly advances a definition in his book (and given the nature of his subject matter for this he cannot be blamed). He does, however, consider the contributions of others. Notably he quotes Thomas Mann who imparts a damning definition: '[p]aradox is the poisonous flower of quietism, the iridescent surface of the rotting mind, the greatest depravity of all' (1955: 221–222, cited in Sorensen). Unsurprisingly, Sorensen doesn't have much time for Mann. To the extent that we *can* infer a sense of definition in Sorensen's work, it comes from an attempt to present the concept of argument as central to paradox. To this end, Sorensen's consideration of three extant definitions of paradox is instructive. These definitions are courtesy of the OED, Quine (1976), and Sainsbury (1995). The ancient Greek words *para* ('contrary to') + *doxa* ('opinion') underlie the OED's principal definition of paradox as 'A statement or tenet contrary to received opinion or expectation'. However, and quite rightly, Sorensen takes issue with this definition. He writes, 'the doomsdayer's "the end is nigh" is a tenet contrary to received opinion. But it is a paradox only if backed with a good argument'. Sorensen then goes on to invoke definitions advanced by both Quine (1976) and Sainsbury (1995) which, unlike the OED, explicitly acknowledge the salience of *argument*. For Quine (1976: 1) 'a paradox is … any conclusion that at first sounds absurd but that has an argument to sustain it'. Sainsbury's (1995) definition develops this further:

> [Paradox is] an apparently unacceptable conclusion derived by apparently acceptable reasoning from apparently acceptable premises. Appearances have to deceive, since the acceptable cannot lead by acceptable steps to the unacceptable. So, generally, we have a choice: either the conclusion is not really unacceptable, or else the starting point, or the reasoning, has some non-obvious flaw.
>
> *(Sainsbury, 1995: 1, cited in Sorensen, 2003: 104)*

Although certainly compelling, Sorensen does not subject Sainsbury's position to sufficient critique. Indeed, a significant part of the thesis presented in this book is that paradoxes are *not* unacceptable. On the contrary, I think they are desirable. And it is from here, I hope, that I can build on—but move beyond—the contributions of Quine, Sainsbury, and Sorensen in developing a fresh approach to our understanding of paradox.

A fresh approach to paradox

This book is guided by several objectives, each of which is outlined below.

To explore paradox as a transcendent aspect of life. This book examines paradox in relation to an unusually wide variety of disciplinary areas and applied topics. Listed alphabetically, these include (but are by no means limited to) art, architecture, anxiety, belief, bureaucracy, causality, change, choice, commitment, common sense, communication, completion, conflict, consciousness, [social] construction, consumerism, control, criminality, culture, Darwinian evolution, democracy, disability, distance, economics, emotion, enemies, ethics, experience, fashion, freedom, friendship, gender, geometry, happiness, history, hope, identity, ideology, individuality, infinity, intuition, mathematics, medicine, method, methodology, motion, music, morality, objectivity, observation, politics, pretence, pain, pleasure, prophecy, peace, philosophy, physics, progress, psychology, psychic distance, religion, repression, risk, routine, sacrifice, science, sociology, sociolinguistics, structure, success, suffering, symmetry, technology, time, truth, typology, utopia, war, and the will.

It would clearly be foolish to lay claim to scholarly authority in every one of these numerous domains. However, my native field—organization theory—is deliberately multidisciplinary and so provides an excellent vantage point from which to broker such a broad enquiry. Notably, a fundamental concern I have long harboured about the academy is how departmentalized we have become. Ancient history presents an array of polymaths but such a beast is virtually extinct today. Sadly, I am no polymath. However, I do stake a claim as a generalist; I am interested in transcendent themes across academic disciplines. And, in my view, the academy has become increasingly siloed over the centuries. As Tett (2009) has noted, rampant departmentalism has created a plethora of activities that are only understood by 'experts' who typically dwell in a silo as a result of the highly specialized areas in which they function. The problem, of course, is that although brilliant minds may occupy these silos, without a wider sense of context and an understanding of how their native belief systems interact, reproduce, and/or challenge those elsewhere, ideas remain entrenched and progress retarded.

Ultimately, the value of this project lies in the hitherto unrealized wide-angle picture afforded by this generalist position. In certain important but as yet overlooked ways the arts as well as both social and natural sciences are all subject to paradox. Furthermore, paradox not only emerges when we cross-examine the distinct foundations of disparate academic disciplines (which might be expected), but manifests itself *within* each discipline, despite the supposedly consistent internal logic that structures them: economics, sociology, psychology, physics, geography, and so on. And beyond those traditionally delineated subject areas, I further demonstrate that paradox characterizes the very research methodologies on which these disciplines rest. To this end, this book builds on provisional arguments first presented in a publication titled 'Methodology: From Paradigms to Paradox' (Vine, 2018b). Ultimately, readers are urged to recognize that 'progress' itself is subject to paradox. Critical thinking (as Boltanski and Chiapello demonstrated in their seminal 2005 thesis) has a tendency to lose its potency once it is adopted universally which is why critical thinking must forever remain incomplete—an ongoing enterprise. We might very well present this argument under a 'from crux to flux' banner in an attempt to encourage scholars to avoid any sense of moral or ideological closure, irrespective of how apparently desirable, just, or seductive they may initially appear. In all probability, and as we will see in Chapter 7, many of our 'good' intentions are morally misguided. In short, as a pedagogical device, paradox represents a form of intellectual atonement.

To invoke the experiential insights of organizational ethnography. Over the past two decades, I have gradually developed a hybrid professional identity as an ethnographer and organization theorist. This peculiar combination has enabled me to distinguish my approach to the study of paradox in a topical domain traditionally dominated by philosophers. Drawing on Bourdieu's work, Burkitt (1999: 87) suggests that 'understanding is a practical process – a way of being-in-the-world through embodied activity rather than cognitive reflection'. Equally, for Bronowski (1976: 115) '[w]e have to understand that the world can only be grasped by action, not by contemplation'. Indeed, it was during a conversation with my physicist father-in-law that it was suggested to me that just thinking about a problem is insufficient. Rather, he quipped, 'one needs to bash one's brains against it', after which we must deliberately put the problem down. At that point the subconscious brain might then provide a flash of illumination. Einstein, apparently, worked in this way. I can't claim that this has been my own approach. However, what I can say with more confidence is that my hands-on ethnographic experience—which owes as much to serendipity as it does to deliberation—has undoubtedly driven my intellectual curiosity and specific conceptual enquiries. In this sense, I firmly believe that approaching philosophical problems through the meta-medium of experience has its place (a comparable approach was used to great effect by Danish philosopher and theologian, Søren Kierkegaard). The ethnographic method (which, at its most rudimentary, involves the study of human behaviour by means of participant observation) is of course more akin to anthropology than to philosophy. But—crucially—anthropology has been described as 'philosophy with the people in' (Ingold, 1992: 696). Broadly speaking this represents my methodological platform. I impart autoethnographic reflections, too, and in so doing build on Bochner and Ellis's (2016: 67) depiction of autoethnography's liminality—'it's between-ness [and its ability to sit] in the middle of things .... between art and science, between rationality and emotionality'. Furthermore, and as they note, it is regrettable that 'explaining experience has taken priority over rendering it'. 'To some extent', they continue, 'autoethnography attempts to restore some balance, insisting that something crucially important has been omitted from research in the human sciences' (ibid.: 116).

Beyond these ethnographic credentials, I very much hope that my background as an organization theorist further facilitates a fresh perspective on this philosophy-dominated field. Aside from the advantages afforded by the multidisciplinary character of organization theory previously noted, it is perhaps of no small significance that 'organizations recursively emerge where structure and action jointly constitute and shape one another' (Styhre, 2007: 85). With this in mind the theorist of organization finds herself in a privileged position in respect of interpreting the ontological and interactive complexity associated with the *lived experience* of paradox particularly in respect of the tensions inherent to discussions of the agency-structure conundrum. This is a primary focus of Chapter 9.

To urge readers to reflect on their own habits, assumptions, and experiences of paradox. It is hoped that this book emboldens readers to reflect on their own lives. One very simple way in which this can be achieved is by examining our use of language. The Sapir-Whorf hypothesis (see Kay & Kempton, 1984), for example, demonstrates that the languages we create in turn shape our cognition of the world. Have you ever wondered how many idioms are themselves the outcome of paradoxical logic? To take a few from the English language as examples: 'the grass is always greener on the other side'; 'you don't know what you have until it's gone'; 'you need to take the rough with the smooth'; 'try to please all and you ending up pleasing none'; and, perhaps most revealing of all, 'careful what you wish for'. More generally, we are compelled to ask what it is we are to make of these sorts of tensions. The most pertinent and puzzling of all, why is it that each of us seems to blissfully ignore these contradictions in our everyday lives? Taking these sorts of phrases as cues further validates an ethnographic approach to paradox (discussed above) in preference to the more conventional philosophical or metaphysical approach. And given that anthropology prioritizes lived experience over abstract cogitation, this lends a perspective which (1) recognizes the pervasiveness of paradox across our intellectual attempts to make sense of life and (2) enables us to envisage a hypothetical life without paradox and in so doing recognize the shortcomings of such an existence. As befits their remit, philosophers have tended to prioritize the configuration, analysis, and potential resolution of abstract and semantic paradoxes. To this end there has been some truly fascinating work, but it has come at the expense of paradoxes that both characterize and influence the fabric of our lived experience. Take the paradox of happiness, for example. Is it possible to be perpetually happy? At first glance, the question may seem rather glib. But there is considerable value to its examination. Time and again, our experience suggests it is not possible to be perpetually happy. Happiness gains no traction without episodes of sadness. Indeed, happiness loses all sense of *meaning* without sadness. And consider a question closer to my own field of research: is it possible to be perpetually motivated and satisfied at work? The simple answer is no—not without periods of demotivation and dissatisfaction. Why, then, do business school students pore over job motivation theories? If we accept the prevalence and pervasiveness of paradox (and the overwhelming evidence presented in this book suggests that we should), job motivation theories are largely bunk. As unequivocal counsel, they are predestined to fail.

To challenge our historical reticence to engage analytically with paradox. Formal education is underwritten by a rarely challenged ontology (a concept we go on to unpack in Chapter 6) characterized by linear cause-and-effect. Our reticence to engage analytically with paradox is most likely due to the fact that we are—especially in the West—imbued from a very young age with a belief that the world around us conforms to linear cause-and-effect. Virtually without exception, our epistemological apparatus have hitherto favoured this approach to logic. It is this predisposition that makes encountering paradox all the more perplexing. My intention is to help move us beyond linear cause-and-effect. The apparently infinite complexities associated with happiness, motivation, and satisfaction are just three examples of the ways in which the bias towards linear cause-and-effect ontology continues to frustrate and disappoint. This book compels the academy to acknowledge this bias, a bias which exists across both mainstream and critical discourses. However, I am conscious that in departing from linear cause-and-effect norms, I run the risk of being labelled an 'intellectual vagabond' or even more derogatorily a 'New Age hippie'. And—let's face it—universities the world over harbour far too many charlatans. But the vital point is, I think, that academic rigour need not imply cause-and-effect rationality. If life could be 'unravelled', or reduced in some way to linear cause-and-effect, it would no longer be life. If a 'theory of everything' could be found, our sentient, cognitive, conscious existence would be utterly undermined. We are, therefore, probably better off postulating—paradoxically—a 'theory of nothing' or 'infinite complexity'.

To stress that my intention is not reductionist. I am not seeking to do for paradox what others have tried to do for class (i.e. Karl Marx), sex (i.e. Sigmund Freud), or power (i.e. Michel Foucault). 'No view of the whole, and in particular no view of the whole of human life, can claim to be final and universally valid. Each doctrine, however seemingly final, will be superseded sooner or later by another doctrine' (Strauss, cited in Bauman, 2017: 18). Knowledge is inescapably ephemeral. My objectives for this book, then, are subtly different; I conceptualize paradox not as a deterministic logic, but as an existential pattern. To this end, I reflect on Popper's (1962: 73, cited in Weick, 1977: 287–288) cautionary note:

> Without waiting, passively, for repetitions to impress or impose regularities on us, we actively try to impose regularities upon the world. We try to discover similarities in it, and interpret it in terms of laws invented by us. Without waiting for premises, we jump to conclusions.

I cannot stress enough that our thesis should not be interpreted as a means to impose regularities on the world; to do so would be a fundamental misinterpretation. It would be back-to-front. It would undermine it. Instead, I focus on emergent patterns. The choice of vocabulary (i.e. pattern rather than law, rule, or even regularity or repetition) is deliberate.

To demonstrate that paradox perpetuates an existential pattern. Paradox discerned as pattern can help us better understand the concept of 'being-in-the-world' as an organizing principle. Pattern is here regarded as a form of description or recognition and *not* as an explanatory tool. To see it as an explanatory tool would miss the point (and trigger a descent into the familiar—but flawed—world of causality), just as to see either evolution or relativity as explanatory tools misses the point; rather, they are *enablers of understanding*. Although the concept of pattern is integral to this thesis, I go to significant lengths to ensure I do not fall victim to the aforementioned Apophenian trap (or 'illusory pattern perception'). Notably, some significant advances in recent centuries are based on the observation of patterns. Darwin, for example, identified a pattern which ultimately enabled us to think in terms of evolution. Einstein, too, recognized a pattern that would otherwise go by the name of relativity. While I certainly do not wish to reify either evolution or relativity (to do so would be a grave mistake, one most scholars recognize as a form misplaced concreteness), I do recognize these concepts as important exemplars. More recently, in *The Human Swarm*, Moffett (2019: 232) has suggested that '[h]umans follow ritualised patterns more than we may imagine, going far beyond simply mirroring each other's speech and emotions'. He notes, for example, that the civilisations which evolved independently around the world—despite complete isolation from one another—bore extraordinary similarities. They all contained, for example, 'roads, canals, cities, palaces, schools, law courts, markets, irrigation works, kings, priests, temples, peasants, artisans, armies, astronomers, merchants, sports, theatre, art, music and books' (ibid.). Of course, while Moffett trained his attention on the transcendent implications behind the simultaneous invention and creation of physical objects, in this book, we focus instead on existential patterns that apparently transcend humankind.

To retrain attention away from a preoccupation with solving paradox. I am careful to point out that our endeavours should seek not to attempt to resolve paradox; rather paradox should be celebrated as a principal aspect of—and prerequisite for—human existence. I go on to argue that life without paradox would, most likely, be intolerable. This is because a lived experience without paradox (and hence one in which life could be reduced to predetermined linear calculus) would be stripped its very vitality. Attempts to solve, resolve, or dissolve paradox are therefore misguided. This is not to suggest that intellectual enquiry is bunk and that we should revel in ignorance. On the contrary, a recognition of the salience of paradox enables us to approach our understanding of life (and in so doing rekindle a sense of what might be described as *Aristotelian lifecraft*), with a much greater degree of prudence. If this book achieves just one thing, I hope that one thing is that readers are able to recognize that the concept of paradox helps define and delineate the dynamics of the outermost constraints of our *lifeworld*. It was mathematician and phenomenologist Edmund Husserl (1936) who introduced us to the term *lifeworld*, a word he used to describe the universe as 'given' and experienced collectively. It is hoped that the fresh approach afforded by these guiding principles will enable readers not only to challenge linear logic, but to recognize that paradox can be discerned by examining the existential constellations (or patterns) it perpetuates. I contend that these patterns are distinct from those associated with dualities, dialectics, and other comparable analytical devices. In a sense that is perversely familiar and yet perennially overlooked, I argue that our everyday experience of life is mediated through paradox. Indeed, I suggest that paradox is what makes 'being-in-the-world' exceptional. On the one hand, paradox renders life staggeringly complex, chaotic, and difficult to fathom. On the other, it makes for an arresting, spirited, and ultimately rewarding existence. I also very much hope that my readers will recognize the pedagogical value of paradox and in so doing acknowledge that endeavours to solve, resolve, or dissolve paradoxes are misguided; paradox should be celebrated. As Dostoevsky's narrator in *Notes from the Underground* declares of his predicament: '… an anguish would boil up inside me; a hysterical thirst for contradictions and contrasts …' (Dostoevsky [1864] 1972: 51). Similarly, it is no accident that Wittgenstein reflects on what he describes as 'the pleasant feeling of paradox'

(Wittgenstein, 1976: 16, cited in Sorensen, 2003: 345). Paradox keeps us on our intellectual and ideological toes and provides a means for us to better understand the notoriously thorny, circuitous, and wicked existential questions concerning agency, consciousness, and relativism.

Chapter synopses

In this chapter, I have outlined what I hope are the foundations for developing a more nuanced—and existentially gratifying—understanding of paradox. The subsequent thesis is broadly divided into two parts. In the first part of the book (Chapters 2–6) I present a systematic case for understanding paradox as a pervasive logic that undergirds our lives, irrespective of cultural inclination, discipline, or professed lifestyle. As part of this broader discussion, I explore the prevalence of paradox across an extremely diverse range of academic fields including, among others, architecture, business, economics, philosophy, and zoology. Of course, and as Dychtwald (1982: 108–109) notes, subject categorizations are arbitrary, and so I have no desire to reify—less still reinforce—them here. In this sense, the delineations between subject areas are presented for convenience. In Chapter 2, I focus on paradox in the arts. In Chapter 3, the various paradoxes that characterize—and often trouble—traditional social scientific endeavours are explored. Chapter 4 explores the mitigating effects of paradox in studies of work and organization. Chapter 5 examines the concept of paradox and the role it plays in the natural sciences. Finally, in Chapter 6, I evaluate the manner in which paradox underpins the transcendent concerns of ontology, epistemology, and belief across these disparate disciplines.

In the second part of the book the focus shifts. Here I develop my specific argument in respect of the pedagogical value of paradox. In so doing, we turn our attention to the *role* of paradox and in so doing acknowledge that it is indispensable. This part of the book thus represents a systematic defence of paradox by recourse to a recognition that paradox elicits three key 'logics'. Chapter 7 explores the relationship between paradox, ethics, and the will. Ultimately, it argues that paradox thwarts moral closure, our first logic. Chapter 8 takes a fresh approach to examining the way in which paradox binds together the ostensibly disparate concepts of pain and pleasure, melancholy and happiness. Ultimately, Chapter 8 reveals our second logic of paradox: it elicits an egalitarian inertia by helping to even out subjective experience between 'the haves' and the 'have nots'. In the penultimate chapter, Chapter 9, we explore a practical function for paradox in respect of consciousness, agency, and relativism. In so doing, we advance our third—and final—logic of paradox: it justifies the emergence of sentient, conscious, and agentic beings. Such an existential configuration is, we argue, necessary to navigate the complexities of a world characterized by paradox. I summarize and reflect on the overall thesis in the concluding chapter (Chapter 10) by advancing what I refer to as a rigorous epistemology of balance.

Reader guidance

Grappling with paradox is discombobulating. Inevitably, and despite my best efforts to present the material in an accessible manner, the reader will be expected to perform cognitive acrobatics at various points. To get the best from the thesis, the book should be read in short sections, and in accordance with the reader's capacity for analytical focus. In fiction, some authors periodically punctuate their narrative with a series of asterisks (or *dinkus*). These serve several purposes, one of which is to signal to readers appropriate points to take breathers. I have decided against including such markers, but urge you to take frequent short breaks as and when you deem it necessary, and to use these interims to reflect on and digest what you have read.

Naturally, this thesis draws on material I have presented elsewhere (specifically, Vine, 2016; Vine, 2018c, Vine et al., 2018, and Vine, 2021). However, in this current text I bind together these disparate remarks and from there advance what I hope is a comprehensive treatise on the metatheoretical potential of paradox.

Enjoy the book.

PART I

The Pervasiveness
of Paradox

2

PARADOX AND ART

More so than either the social or natural sciences, the concept of paradox is typically well-received in the arts. This is true thematically, methodologically, and by way of reflecting on artistic content more generally. Unlike the linear logic that mainstream science routinely relies upon (and reproduces), the arts invariably has more freedom. Paradox is controversial and compelling. For these reasons, those in the arts are likely to be at the very least accommodating of the concept. Indeed, if art *did* adhere rigidly to a linear logic, it would more than likely be lambasted. I can still remember the dulcet tones of my English teacher, Fr. Porter, during my first year at a Jesuit senior school in 1989. He asked the class, 'What is a story?', to which a dim-witted but eager classmate proudly replied: 'It's something with a beginning, middle, and end'. 'No!', Porter boomed, 'Storytelling is not fucking paint-by-numbers!'.

Given that a principal focus of our thesis is on the lived experience of paradox—rather than its representation—one could be forgiven for assuming that paradox in the arts has limited significance for our purposes. However, art does more than represent; it is part and parcel of lived experience. Paradox in the arts also takes on a crucial role as a pedagogical device. But beyond this practical consideration, and as our discussion of Marsden's (2002) work will demonstrate, it is probably the arts—and not the sciences—that provides the most compelling and existentially gratifying rendering of life; the creative insights yielded by the former more often than not trump those achieved through means of natural cognition. This chapter explores the exposition of paradox in the visual arts, literature, cinema, and music.

DOI: 10.4324/9781003203339-3

The visual arts

It is no accident that I launch this wide-angled treatise on paradox with an exploration of the visual arts. In many respects, the visual arts constitute the most accessible means of demonstrating paradox. Indeed, for some (e.g. Goldstein, 1996), visual paradoxes are expedient pedagogical devices for interpreting other—non-visual—paradoxes.

The research I undertook for this book in respect of paradox in the visual arts was gloriously indulgent. I visited galleries; talked with well-bred, if eccentric, fine arts students; got lost in dusty leather-bound tomes on art history in the British Library's Rare Books Reading Room; and took delight in the musings of the numerous art critics to have starred in televised documentaries over the years, including those of Andrew Graham-Dixon, Will Gompertz, Waldemar Januszczak, Robert Hughes, and Sister Wendy. In the event, it was not especially challenging to find explorations of paradox in the visual arts. Ultimately, my research distilled specific thematics within the visual arts that we can readily associate with paradox, the most prevalent of which are illusion, symmetry, colour, and beauty.

Illusion. In the field of cognitive psychology, Robert Solso (2001) notes that while illusions distort reality, they are generally shared by most people. The pertinent question here then is: are illusions, artistic or otherwise, 'real'? In our formative years, many of us encounter visual illusions as learning aids. These normally take the form of what have become known as 'ambiguous images' and typically include the *Duckrabbit* (Anonymous, 1892), *Rubin's Vase* (Rubin, 1915), and Hill's *My Wife and my Mother-in-Law* (Hill, 1915). I first encountered *Duckrabbit* (Figure 2.1) aged 6 or 7, while at primary school. I distinctly remember feeling a sense of unmitigated delight. At the time, I don't think I really appreciated the point, that is, that the image could

FIGURE 2.1 *Duckrabbit (Anon, 1915).*

FIGURE 2.2   *Rubin's Vase* (Rubin, 1915).

be seen as *either* a rabbit or a duck. Rather (and if memory serves me loyally) I saw the image as a peculiar hybrid animal. This, of course, is the time in many children's lives—including mine—during which dinosaurs present an awe-inspiring fascination, not least because they are extinct and hence remain forever the stuff of fantasy. I reckon I saw Duckrabbit in that context. In any event, children's minds are inherently more open to ambiguity and fantasy as they have not yet been subjected to years of imprinted linear logic. In the spirit of robust and efficacious scholarship, during the latter stages of the research for this book I showed the Duckrabbit image to my three-year-old daughter and asked her what animal she thought the image represented. 'It's a seagull!', she said without hesitating. Touché.

I encountered *Rubin's Vase* early on in secondary school (Figure 2.2), probably in a maths lesson, but I can't recall for sure. This time, the artist's purpose was clearer to me. I liked it but it didn't have the same effect on me as *Duckrabbit*. While I recognize that it remains a popular pedagogical device, it seems to lack sufficient complexity to elicit the desired insight.

I was in my final undergraduate year at the university when Professor Gibson Burrell presented us with Hill's infamous image, *My Wife and my Mother-in-Law* (Figure 2.3). At the time, I don't think its sexist connotations were considered especially significant. The image pissed me off not because it was sexist (although I was a proud feminist in those days primarily because I figured it would get me laid) but because I could only see the mother-in-law.

FIGURE 2.3 *My Wife and My Mother-in-Law* (Hill, 1915).

Burrell and others on my course assured me that the wife (or 'young' woman) was there. But I could only see the 'old' woman. Others in the group, meanwhile, said they could only see the young woman, not the old woman. This was shortly after the fad for magic eye autostereogram images. In order to stand any chance of actually seeing the three dimensional (i.e. the 'magic eye') image emerge from the page, the viewer was instructed to relax their focus such that their gaze becomes 'wall-eyed' (where each eye is directed at the image in parallel). I was instructed to take this approach to Hill's drawing. I did, and eventually I saw the young woman. If I'm honest, it was a bit underwhelming. Having said this, I incorporate the image—and the lively discussion it typically elicits—into my own classes today.

Why, then, have these 'ambiguous images' become so popular as pedagogical devices? Quite simply, they reveal to us the workings of perception and help draw attention to the fact that our eyes—or, more accurately, our brains—can play tricks on us. For students grappling with interpretative approaches to research, such images are also instructive for illustrating the manner in which the phenomenological method is pivotal to readings of existentialism (see, e.g. Mairet, 1989: 13). To this end, such images remind us that interpretation involves drawing upon existing knowledge or assumptions; they thus illustrate the manner in which our prejudices emerge.

Several artists have consciously incorporated illusive paradox into their wider body of work. Of these, the Dutch artist, M. C. Escher (1898–1972), is almost certainly the most celebrated. His work is routinely invoked in discussions of paradox, so much so that it borders on the banal. This should not, however, detract from its pertinence. Escher's ability to flirt with the tensions between the second and third geometric dimensions have had profound and far-reaching implications beyond the world of art, particularly in mathematics. Escher is thus one of a small number of artists to have developed a following among those more inclined to appreciate science—than art. This of course is interesting in and of itself. But here we focus on Escher's surrealist ability to use two-dimensional artistic media to distort three-dimensional constructions by way of illusion. Early on in his life, Escher lost interest in regular visual planes which bound most artists and instead became famous, albeit posthumously, for his so-called 'impossible constructions' including, for example, *Relativity* (1953) (Figure 2.4). These would later become his trademark. Indeed, his work here is prolific. Arguably, traditional canvass-based art is at a disadvantage when it comes to realist representation. However, Escher brings to the fore one of its specific advantages, that is, its ability to render physical representations which would be otherwise be impossible in three-dimensional art such as pottery or sculpture.

Escher produced unpretentious art that any old Tom, Dick, or Harry can appreciate. It provokes in an immediate sense. Much like the 'ambiguous images' discussed earlier, Escher's art has an unequivocal pedagogical purpose; it illustrates in a highly accessible manner what is meant by paradox. Much like the 'ambiguous images' discussed earlier Escher's art is an invaluable pedagogical tool for advancing an interest in paradox. However, some have suggested that the disciplined study of Escher's art will help reassert conventional logic.

> [I]in the case of the visual paradoxes, knowledge of various means of representing distance enables us to explain how the paradoxical effect is achieved. A novel approach to solving [non-visual] paradoxes consists in coming to understand how the impossibility of their conclusion arises by means analogous to those by which visually impossible objects are produced.
> *(Goldstein, 1996: 299)*

This is an arresting argument. However, and although it is certainly clear that paradoxes presented in the visual arts are extraordinarily effective pedagogical devices, my concerns with Goldstein's specific approach are twofold. First, he is determined to use visual paradoxes as a didactic means

FIGURE 2.4 *Relativity* (Escher, 1953).

of enhancing our approach to *finding solutions* to non-visual paradoxes. As stressed in the opening chapter of this book, our overriding concern ought to be to find value and purpose in the paradoxes themselves, rather than in a misguided attempt to solve them. Second, his wider thesis remains trained on what he refers to as logico-semantic paradoxes, such as the Liar paradox, which as noted earlier are of limited relevance to the lived experience of paradox. However, Goldstein does impart another observation that is of extraordinary pertinence. He notes the following in respect of Escher's *Belvedere* (see Figure 2.5): 'World knowledge of pillars ... plays a prominent role in our finding Escher's *Belvedere* perplexing, and to recognize this is to account for that perplexity, and therefore solve the picture' (Goldstein, 1996: 304). He continues:

> By contrast, the impossible gallows in Bruegel's *The Magpie on the Gallows* (1568) (see Figure 2.6) is not so visually unsettling because we

FIGURE 2.5 *Belvedere* (Escher, 1958).

can easily interpret the gallows as rather rickety, the verticals badly bent and twisted, as is quite possible with old timber.

Goldstein thus draws attention to why it is that the impossible objects of antiquity (such as Bruegel's) are less disorienting than those presented by Escher. This simultaneously reminds us that part of the reason why we find Escher's impossible objects so unsettling—and concurrently compelling—is

FIGURE 2.6 *The Magpie on the Gallows* (Bruegel, 1568).

because they invoke and challenge our epistemological assumptions (in this case that pillars must be made of stone and hence are nonmalleable).

No discussion of paradox and the arts would be complete without at least a cursory glance at the work—and cultural influence—of René Magritte. It is of course his infamous *The Treachery of Images (This is Not a Pipe)* (see Figure 2.7) that Magritte is most famous for.

Govan (2006: 6) describes this piece of art as an endlessly evocative painting, which succinctly portrays the paradoxes of visual and verbal representation. 'Deceptively simple', he continues, 'it presents the image of a pipe and then below it a text that undermines the assumptions behind such representation' (ibid.: 17). A painted pipe is not a real pipe but a depiction thereof.

> Ah, the famous pipe. I've been criticized enough for it! And yet, can it be stuffed with tobacco, my pipe? No, it can't be, it's just a representation. So if I had written, 'This is a pipe' below the picture, I would have been lying.
>
> *(Magritte, as cited in Govan, 2006: 17)*

FIGURE 2.7   *The Treachery of Images (This Is Not a Pipe)* (Magritte, 1929).

Symmetry. Unlike illusion which hints at an underlying cerebral complexity, symmetry represents a simpler—but perhaps more elegant—paradox. Symmetry is, concurrently, the same and the opposite. A generation after Escher, and as installation art took hold both within and beyond galleries the world over, Whiteread's *House* (1993) (see Figure 2.8) courted the inevitable, but most likely calculated, controversy.

For this work, the artist arranged to have a suburban terraced house filled with liquid concrete.

> The structure of the house—its walls, roof, doors and windows—was then removed, producing through this upheaval an inverted cast of the spaces of the domestic home ... Profoundly unsettling by making the innards of the privatised family space so overtly public, *House* generated reactions of love and hate in those who saw it.
>
> *(Dale & Burrell, 2011: 115)*

After the external structure was removed, a mould of the 'empty' space inside was thus left behind for the public to gawp at. Aside from the tacit obligation for an artist to shit on expectation and challenge established belief systems, pieces such as *House* invert not planes (as Escher did), but physical spaces in a manner analogous to the celluloid negative. But is this in any way a paradox? No, at least not in the sense that Escher's is. However, it does demonstrate that the usable spaces of a dwelling are difficult to *represent* (which is of course the overriding objective of most art); the point is that the physical exteriors of dwellings are much more usually represented in art, and yet it is the inner physical spaces that invoke social significance (think in terms, as Dale and Burrell do, of how *space* becomes *place*. Even

FIGURE 2.8 *House* (Whiteread, 1993).

film struggles to represent this as the transition between (utilitarian) place and (encultured) space takes years, decades even; such a feat is inevitably difficult to capture in a 90-minute flick, or even in a box set series). Of course, Whiteread doesn't achieve this either, but in my mind what she does do is bring to the fore this difficulty for debate and dissection as part of public discourse.

Colour. Colour lies at the heart of the artistic medium and here too we can discern a paradox. This is found most obviously in respect of complementary colours. Complementary colours are pairs which provide a striking contrast to one another while simultaneously enhancing one another. Complementary colours often serve very practical applications. For example, buoyancy aids used at sea are not yellow or red, but orange. Why? Because orange elicits the most striking contrast to the blue sea. Artists have known about this tension associated with colour for quite some time. They typically use subtly distinct hues of the same colour to provide a sense of depth and texture. However, too distinct hues adjacent to one another look jarring, as do different colours which do not yield a harmonious bond. But artists also use complete opposites to extraordinary effect. The most famous of these is probably Vincent Van Gogh. Having advanced beyond the gloomy—but nonetheless compelling—scenes of his early career (e.g. *The Potato Eaters* (1885); coincidentally one of my favourite pieces of art), his most celebrated works are those which use complementary colours to great effect: red and green in *The Night Café* (1888); purple and yellow in *Irises* (1890); and, most famously of all, orange and blue in *Self-portrait* (1889) in which he deliberately selected a blue background to contrast with—and enhance—his infamous ginger locks.

But how exactly do we conceptualize this as paradox? Well, suppose for a moment that you are tasked with interior decoration. You decide to configure your scheme around a favourite object, in this case a bottle green lampshade. Aesthetically, you might well consider multiple hues of green. You're unlikely to go for, say, pinks or purples because these will probably clash with the bottle green colour. However, a dark red will likely sit in harmony with your bottle green lampshade; unlike the pinks or purples which would elicit an off-key contrast, the red will generate a harmonious contrast. We have here, then, our first example of the peculiar dynamics associated with extremities: A light touch (i.e. other shades of green) will work well, but so too does the heaviest touch (a red). It is the 'in between' colours that will most likely present a problem. The peculiar dynamics associated with extremities is something we see crop up time after time across fields in respect of paradox, as the latter chapters in this book go on to illustrate.

Beauty. As the ghastly cliché goes, beauty is in the eye of the beholder. This is probably true, at least to some extent. But our fixation on this platitude obscures a more interesting observation, that is, the suggestion that artistic beauty and ugliness find themselves in paradoxical tension. This is certainly the case for many of the more discerning—or portentous(!)—appreciators of art. So much so, in fact, that the Victorians deliberately built artificial ruins and follies in their back gardens. There is, it seems, a beauty associated with decay. The sociolinguist and novelist, Umberto Eco, has explored this relationship in his book, *History of Beauty*, which is notably part of a twinset volume on ugliness and beauty:

> The aesthetics of ruins that developed in the second half of the eighteenth century is an expression of the ambivalence of Neoclassical beauty. That

the ruins of history could be perceived as beautiful was a novelty the reasons for which lay in an impatience with traditional objects and in a consequent search for new themes, over and above canonical styles. It is not far-fetched to compare the rational and at once melancholy way in which Denis Diderot or Johann Joachim Winckelmann contemplated the ruins of an ancient building with the way in which [Jacques-Louis] David saw the murdered body of Marat, who no painter in the previous generation would have portrayed in the bathtub. In David's painting the need to respect historic truth right down to the details does not signify a gelid reproduction of nature, but a blend of contradictory sentiments: the stoic virtue of the murdered revolutionary makes the Beauty of his limbs the vehicle for a reaffirmation of faith in the values of Reason and the revolution.

(Eco, 2004: 249)

Such a tension in respect of beauty and ugliness, Eco suggests, goes far deeper than architecture, and extends back to antiquity. He argues that even the infamous ancient Greek reading of beauty, for example, 'emerges as being far more complex and problematic than the simplifications of the Classical traditions would suggest' (ibid.: 55). Lofty discussions of the existential significance of architectural ruins aside, a more familiar example of the paradox associated with beauty is that of the beauty spot or beauty mark. Ostensibly melanomic imperfections, beauty spots have become trade marks for both sex symbols (Dolly Parton) and super models (Cindy Crawford). So pervasive is the idea of the beauty spot that artificial beauty spots—or 'mouches'—became prevalent in 16th-century Europe, an embellishing practice that continues today, sometimes characterizing entire cultures. The Bindi, for example, is an important religious motif in Hinduism, Sikhism, Buddhism, and Jainism (whereupon it is regarded a portal to a wider universe). However, such is its popularity, the Bindi is frequently sported simply as decoration, and—controversially—not always by religious adherents (see, e.g. Kaufman, 2013).

Literature

In this subsection, we explore the various ways in which paradox is discerned vis-à-vis fiction. We begin first with brief commentary on the paradox inherent to the mechanics of language. We then explore key paradoxical motifs in literature. Inevitably, I have had to be extremely selective in sampling relevant literature. To this end, I make no claim that my findings are exhaustive. On the basis of work undertaken, however, I have identified five key paradoxical literary motifs. These include 'the bittersweet story', 'self-fulfilling prophecy', 'existential predicament', 'Catch-22', and 'utopian circularity'. Existential predicament is by far the most interesting of these motifs and for this reason dominates our attention.

The mechanics of language. Before tackling paradoxical motifs in the world of literature, it is apposite to comment briefly on the manner in which the architecture of our linguistic systems itself reveals a sense of paradox. The contradictory wisdom invoked in idioms (several of which we discussed in the opening chapter), for example, is by no means limited to the English language. Beyond this, consider what are known as contronyms. These are words with two contradictory meanings. One of the most prevalent—certainly for my generation—is the word *bad*. In the wake of Michael Jackson's album of the same name, and much to the bewilderment of teachers and parents in the 1980s, the word bad was adopted by youngsters to describe something that was, well, good. And—like the paradoxical nature of many idioms— contronyms are by no means unique to English. On the contrary, they are cited as a principle means of 'enriching the lexicon' of many languages (see, e.g. Zuckermann, 2003). Perhaps even more interesting, the very fact that we coexist in a world with multiple languages might itself be paradoxical. Evolutionary linguist Mark Pagel invokes the biblical story of the Tower of Babel in which God gifts different groups of people different languages to prevent them from uniting to build a tower tall enough to reach heaven. The irony of this story, the linguist points out, is that 'language exists to stop us communicating' (Pagel, cited in Moffett, 2019: 98–99). Finally, consider the paradoxical potential of the constraints imposed on us by language. In the introductory chapter, we commented briefly on the Sapir-Whorf hypothesis, that is, the suggestion that the language we speak inevitably delimits the outermost parameters of our cognitive capacity. In lay terms, it is extremely difficult to think outside the constraints (i.e. the vocabulary and grammar) of the language we speak. However, during the proofreading stages of this manuscript, I had an extremely insightful conversation with the poet Neil Gregory. He was keen to stress the extraordinary degree to which a constraint in creative writing—for example, a rhyming scheme in poetry— actually rouses artistic creativity. As Gregory (2013: 22) notes of his own evolving approach to poetry, 'compared with some of my previous work— which has often been too driven by thought—it was liberating to be guided so firmly by language'.

The bittersweet story. For Gastin (2017) it is a bittersweet conclusion that distinguishes the very best stories. In some respects, bittersweetness is oxymoronic, that is, a contradiction in terms. In others, one might present bittersweetness as a more realistic or achievable end—a compromise, if you like, more in tune with our workaday experiences of life. However, and conscious of our guiding discussion of paradox in the opening chapter of this book, if we are to fruitfully conceptualize bittersweetness in terms of paradox it must amount to more than mere compromise. So is there any way in which bittersweetness *enhances*? One approach is to unbutton the concatenation and examine each of the component terms separately. For many of us bitterness is disagreeable. However, and as Moncel (2019) notes, while many of us are innately opposed to bitter flavours, a liking for them can be—and is—acquired. This is interesting: our default response to a bitterness is disagreement, but in time we can learn to appreciate it. Conversely, sweetness is by default desirable and yet, in time, we can—and do—become sick of sweet things, be they foodstuffs, twee villages, or vacuous narratives. Perhaps, then, the value of bittersweetness is less about compromise and more the degree to which it combines each extreme (bitterness and sweetness) in a manner that enables each to enhance the other. In this way, it becomes a genuine paradox. Arguably, bittersweetness is an essential trope for the novelist who wishes to capture the human condition. It is, perhaps, for this reason that bittersweet stories remain so popular. For my money, Vonnegut ([1969] 2000: 88) puts it best when, in Slaughterhouse 5, he writes: 'Everything was beautiful and nothing hurt', a satirical dig at those who are naïve of the paradox inherent to pleasure (see Chapter 8). It is perhaps not surprising, then, that Susan Cain's (2022) populist text, *Bittersweetness: How Sorrow and Longingness Make Us Whole*, has already become a *New York Times* bestseller.

Self-fulfilling prophecy. The concept of self-fulfilling prophecy has underpinned some extraordinary research across both social and natural sciences over the last century. Numerous studies have demonstrated, quite simply, that fear of failure produces failure. For example, sociologist Robert K. Merton demonstrates how fear of economic failure precipitates precisely this. Rumours about a failing bank, Merton (1949) says, will prompt savers to withdraw cash hence leading to its downfall. More recently, in the field of medical science, a study of the risk of falling among elderly people concluded that high levels of perceived fall risk can lead to future falls, independently of the actual risk (Delbaere et al., 2010). Meanwhile, albeit approached with a focus on success rather than failure, a psychological experiment conducted by Rosenthal and Jacobson (2003) in American elementary schools demonstrated that if teachers were led to expect enhanced performance from children, then those children's performance was indeed enhanced. Similarly, if teachers were led to expect lower performance from children, then the children's performance would decline. This is sometimes described as the Pygmalion Effect, named after the Greek myth of Pygmalion, a sculptor who became so besotted with the perfectly beautiful statue he had created that the statue came to life. But perhaps most arresting of all is an evaluation of military conflict by recourse to self-fulfilling prophecy. The example of the 2002 Iraq conflict is instructive. The belief in the West that Iraq was a terrorist threat was erroneous, but such was the conviction of this belief that it contributed to Iraq *becoming* a terrorist threat (see, e.g. Hinnebusch, 2007). Finally, in biochemistry, the placebo (Chaplin, 2006) and nocebo (Kennedy, 1961) effects are, of course, derivate forms of self-fulfilling prophecy.

Whereas the empirical examples of self-fulfilling prophecy are all drawn from the twentieth and twenty-first centuries, its literary roots are significantly deeper. The former, it seems, has much to learn from the latter. Self-fulfilling prophecy has been a pervasive theme in literature—and prior to literature, mythology—for millennia. The ancient Greeks gifted us the tale of *Oedipus* (who unwittingly fulfils a prophecy that he would end up killing his father and marrying his mother), while the Romans left us the story of *Romulus and Remis* (twins who became powerful precisely because they were perceived as a threat and hence abandoned as infants). Beyond the West, *Arabian Nights* (in which self-fulfilling dreams constitute a principal theme) is a rich source of paradox, and in classical Sanskrit literature we have been entrusted with the legends associated with Krishna; for some, 'The God of Paradox' (see, e.g. Goswami, 2017). From its emergence in antiquity, self-fulfilling prophecy then became a prevalent trope in medieval literature, particularly in children's stories. One of my three-year-old daughter's favourite stories is *The Fish and the Ring*, for which self-fulfilling prophecy constitutes a major plot device. In the story, a father's actions to prevent his noble son from marrying a peasant woman yields the very wedding he proscribes. Many of the infamous folk tales curated by the Brothers Grimm apply similar tropes. Finally, self-fulfilling prophecy represents a principal theme in Shakespeare's infamous tragedy, *Macbeth*. For disinterested 12-year-old minds tasked with tackling the bard in English classes, the ethereal scene in which the three witches convey their prophecy must surely represent one of the more memorable aspects of Shakespeare's dense canon.

Existential predicament. Dostoevsky's ([1864] 1972) *Notes from the Underground* and Camus's ([1942] (2000)) *The Outsider* give us a good flavour of how paradox has been used by the most celebrated of writers. I'm no literary theorist and certainly won't pretend to be an authority on Dostoevsky, Camus, or any of the novelists I explore in this chapter. In each case, the interpretation I advance is both raw and honest. Nonetheless, it is one geared towards broader scholarly traction. In any event, an ability to discern a sense of paradox is hardly challenging in the case of Dostoevsky (he even proclaims an explicit interest in the concept as part of the postscript in *Notes from the Underground*). The novel was my first encounter with the Russian bard. I was pleasantly surprised. I enjoyed it. In fact, I loved it. But it is difficult to explain *why* it brought me such delight. Perhaps I encountered it at the right stage of my life? Did I get lucky in respect of a biographical sweet spot? The novel's protagonist is more or less the same age I am now, and has harboured comparable pretensions and existential frustrations. He is also full of shit, something the younger—and beta(?)—version of myself can certainly relate to. From the outset, I was engaged. The opening sentence brought to mind Woody Allen, and I feel certain Allen must have read Dostoevsky in his formative years.

> I am sick man ... I am an angry man. I am an unattractive man. I think there is something wrong with my liver.
>
> *(Dostoevsky, [1864] 1972: 15)*

I roared with laughter much to my wife's annoyance, who was lying in bed, trying to sleep, next to me. What an opening! And from here, the unnamed narrator's sense of existential anxiety only becomes more pronounced:

> I swear to you that to think too much is a disease, a real, actual disease. [...] Can a thinking man have any self-respect whatever?
>
> *(17, 25)*

But it was a comment the narrator passes in respect of pleasure that really piqued my interest:

> I should certainly have known how to find pleasure in it, the pleasure, of course, of despair.
>
> *(19)*

This was just the kind of thing I was after. *The pleasure of despair*. It brought to mind the Manic Street Preachers, the go-to band for pretentious indie kids such as myself in the early- to mid-1990s. *I'm happy being sad!*, they crooned. A little further on, Dostoevsky provides for us an experiential example.

> Ha, ha, ha! After that, you will be looking for pleasure even in toothache!, you will exclaim, laughing. [...] 'Why not? There is pleasure even in toothache', I shall reply.
>
> *(24)*

This I could certainly relate to. In fact, it provoked another vivid recall, earlier this time. I spent many a night as a young child dislodging my loose baby teeth and pushing them one way then the other, until I felt a peculiarly pleasant type of pain. A proto form of masochism, perhaps? There *was* pain in pleasure!

> What if it sometimes so happens that a man's advantage not only may but must consist in desiring in certain cases not what is good but what is bad for him?
>
> *(29)*

This has the paradoxical philosophy of Nietzsche written all over it, and is something we unpack in more detail in Chapter 8. And a little later in the narrative, a terse quip directed my faculties to the misguidedness of middle class 'helicopter parents' so determined to fill Little Johnny's day with ostensibly creative and educational chores. The shrewder among us, including Dostoevsky, might remonstrate:

> Of course, boredom leads to every possible kind of ingenuity.
>
> *(33)*

What chance does the hyper-stimulated Little Johnny really have if he is unwittingly denied a fundamental determinant of ingenuity? Dostoevsky then ventures into my own field, organization theory. First, a proto form of Schumpeterian creative destruction, and then the lore associated with the pleasure of process above and beyond the deflation associated with completion.

> Man loves construction and the laying out of roads, that is indisputable. But how is it that he is so passionately disposed to destruction and chaos? [...] To say the least, something uncomfortable is to be noticed in man on the achievement of similar goals. He likes progress towards the goal, but he does not altogether care for the achievement of it, and that, of course, is ridiculous.
>
> *(39–40)*

And, finally, Dostoevsky touches upon the love/hate relationship, the undergirding of the human condition:

> How I hated her and how strongly I was attracted to her at that moment! One feeling reinforced the other.
>
> *(118)*

This, of course, evokes in the reader the dizzying confusion elicited in the early stages of our sexual awakening, during which we try desperately to make sense of—and disentangle—love from lust, and lust from romance.

Although Dostoevsky established the existentialist genre, Camus's *The Outsider* remains the book of choice for pretenders. As an undergraduate at Warwick University in the late-1990s and early-2000s, I would regularly people-watch in the Student's Union bar. You could bet your bottom dollar that chump in a trench coat sat at the bar struggling to roll his Golden Virginia had a well-leafed paperback copy of *The Outsider* stowed in an inside pocket. Pretence aside, the novel is a rich source of the paradoxical. This is, most probably, because the story implicitly explores the notoriously complex relationship between agency and structure, which is itself intrinsically paradoxical (and something we go on to explore in Chapters 5, 6, and 9). But there is plenty beyond the broader concerns of agency/structure; indeed, a sense of the paradoxical is marbled throughout *The Outsider.* The character of Salamano is a case in point. Salamano is neighbour to the protagonist (and narrator), Meursault. Salamano's relationship with his dog, for example, is intriguing. Although he regularly yells at and beats his dog, he breaks down sobbing when he loses him.

> Then [Salamano] said 'Goodnight'. He closed the door and I heard him pacing up and down. Then his bed creaked. And from the peculiar little noise coming through the partition wall, I realized that he was crying. For some reason I thought of mother.
>
> *(42)*

Salamano is thoroughly unpleasant to his dog yet expresses sadness at his loss. Meanwhile, Meursault expresses no emotion at the loss of his own mother, but is certainly not mean to her. The contrast with Salamano is striking, and represents a sort of emotional paradox. In so doing, Camus chastises his readers for empathizing with the former (Salamano), but not the latter (Meursault). In many cultures, of course, a failure to show emotion implies moral failure. A little later in the narrative, Camus reveals to his readers a sense of moral relativity when Meursault seeks to reassure Salamano.

> I replied that you could never change your life, that in any case one life was as good as another and that I wasn't at all dissatisfied with mine here.
>
> *(44)*

This resonates with a broader argument I advance later in this book—the argument that paradox helps to *even out experience.* And further on still, at the point in the story when Meursault is imprisoned, Camus hints at what sounds very much like a proto form of hedonic adaptation (explored later in this book as part of the pleasure paradox):

> I suddenly realized how closed in I was by my prison walls. But that only lasted a few months. After that, I thought like a prisoner. I'd look forward to my daily walk in the courtyard or to my lawyer's visits. And I managed quite well the rest of the time. I often thought in those days that even if I'd been made to live in a hollow tree trunk, with nothing to do but look up at the bit of sky overhead, I'd gradually have got used to it. I'd have looked forward to seeing birds fly past or clouds run together just as here I looked

forward to seeing my lawyer's curious ties and just as, in another world, I used to wait for Saturdays to embrace Marie's body.

(75)

This all-too-human observation flies in the face of our typical imaginings of what prison life is like. And yet it *makes sense.* Hedonic adaptation is something we explore in more detail in Chapter 8. And, then, towards the end of the story, Meursault's lawyer notes the following.

Here we have the epitome of this trial. Everything is true and yet nothing is true!

(88)

At this point in the narrative, Meursault's lawyer is beginning to understand the ontological tensions that plague Camus's sensorium. The point, of course, is that the cold hard facts rarely ever convey *the truth of the matter.* And then—finally—in the postscript in which Camus—as philosopher—speaks reflexively about the novel, he says the following:

the hero of the book is condemned because he doesn't play the game. ....
to get a more accurate picture of his character ... you must ask yourself
in what way Meursault doesn't play the game. The answer is simple: he
refuses to lie.

(118)

Catch-22. Perhaps most famous of all literary paradoxes is that advanced in the book of the same name, *Catch-22,* by Joseph Heller. So influential was the novel that the term catch-22 has become a prevalent part of English language parlance, more so probably than paradox. A catch-22 has come to describe a set of circumstances in which an individual cannot escape because of contradictory rules or limitations. It is, however, of limited analytical value for the purposes of our thesis, not least because we get the sense that Heller's motivation for Catch-22 was not so much as a treatise on the human condition but as a no-holds barred damning of bureaucracy. In the novel, the term is introduced by Doc Daneeka, an army psychiatrist who invokes 'Catch-22' to explain why any pilot requesting mental evaluation for insanity—hoping to be found not sane enough to fly and thereby escape dangerous missions—demonstrates his own sanity in creating the request and thus cannot be declared insane:

'You mean there's a catch?' 'Sure there's a catch', Doc Daneeka replied.
'Catch-22. Anyone who wants to get out of combat duty isn't really crazy'.
There was only one catch and that was Catch-22, which specified that a

concern for one's own safety in the face of dangers that were real and immediate was the process of a rational mind. Orr was crazy and could be grounded. All he had to do was ask; and as soon as he did, he would no longer be crazy and would have to fly more missions. Orr would be crazy to fly more missions and sane if he didn't, but if he was sane, he had to fly them. If he flew them, he was crazy and didn't have to; but if he didn't want to, he was sane and had to. Yossarian was moved very deeply by the absolute simplicity of this clause of Catch-22 and let out a respectful whistle.

(56)

While this is far from the only paradox that readers encounter in Heller's novel, the others all stem from this same incident and are all related to bureaucratic obstinacy. Although the book certainly represents an important critique of war, it doesn't really do it for me in the same way the novels of Dostoevsky or Camus do. The reader comes away from Heller's book with a sense that the author uses paradox as a convenient device to bash bureaucracy and in so doing he reveals a sense of certainty (i.e. that bureaucracy is problematic and hence must be eliminated) which, in my mind at least, undermines the whole point of paradox. It is as though Heller is saying: some aspects of life are plagued by Catch-22 forces but others are not. Dostoevsky and Camus do not seem to make this same mistake.

Utopian circularity. Utopian and dystopian tropes reveal paradoxical tendencies. When we speak of dystopia, we are simultaneously—and paradoxically—speaking of utopia. This is because it is typically from utopian intentions that dystopian ends manifest. On the face of it, then, dystopia represents an opposite to utopia. However, to consider dystopia as an entity distinct from utopia (let alone its opposite) is a misnomer. Dystopia and utopia are inextricably linked. A lay interpretation of this might, for example, note that one person's utopia is another's dystopia, or where utopia becomes saturated by ideological fanatics, it degenerates into dystopia. A more nuanced approach will, however, recognize this tendency across *all* utopian aspirations. Utopia and dystopia ought not to be characteristic of opposing poles on a straight continuum; rather they ought to be considered as highly volatile counterpoints on opposite ends of a shape reminiscent of a horseshoe. In this way, their conceptual rendering is comparable to the way in which the political spectrum is often presented when ideological nuance is taken into consideration (see Chapter 3).

So where is the evidence for this? While it is certainly the case that some early attempts at imagining utopia painted naïve worlds characterized by an overarching equality; in later contributions it is precisely these constructs which have—in turn—become dystopias. In the vast majority of cases, the dystopian worlds articulated in literature (and film) were originally designed as utopias. More's *Utopia* ([1516] 1998) is genre-setting and thus represents an important frame of reference. The text is composed of two parts, the first of which transitions from fact to fiction through the conversation between More himself, a voyager called Raphael Hythloday, and a civil servant called Peter Giles. Book II consists of Hythloday's travels and experience on the island of Utopia, and here the authoritarian nature of the utopia becomes clearer. 'To keep cities from becoming too sparse or too crowded, they have decreed that there shall be six thousand households in each, with each household containing between ten and sixteen adults' (ibid.: 55). More's island is further characterized by patriarchy (44), homosocial identity (50), and ubiquitous surveillance (60). There is, of course, disagreement as to whether More intended his fictional society as desirable. Most critics suggest, in part at least, that he did. Such a society was reasonably ambitious in More's time, a period characterized by monarchical rule and despotism. 'More's own society was rigidly hierarchical and highly regulated, so Utopia may not have seemed as restrictive to him as it does to us' (Logan & Adams, [1516] 1998: x).

Notably, the utopian premises of More's society are routinely invoked as the dystopian subject matter of early-20th century authors. Of these latter authors, most combine unrestrained technological advance with bureaucratic dominance. Huxley's *Brave New World* ([1931] 1969), for example, presents a clear challenge to the social utopia presented by More. The world Huxley describes shares similar 'virtues' to More's utopia: there is no war, no official torture, no terrorism, no hunger, no crime, and no conflict. Bureaucratic techno-authoritarianism reigns, however. As Huxley ([1959] 2004: 4) himself comments, Brave New World is 'the nightmare of total organization'. Indeed, the plot unfolds in a world in which the industrialist, Henry Ford, is considered god-like. The religious connotations inherent in the peoples' profession, 'Our Ford' and their timely making of 'the sign of the T', are especially noteworthy.

In the much celebrated novel *Nineteen Eighty-Four* ([1949] 1999), George Orwell explores the totalitarian ramifications of surveillance. Under the jurisprudence of the ubiquitous Big Brother, this surveillance is achieved through pervasive propaganda, the thought police, and even the development—or rather the diminishment—of the spoken language as a mechanism of social control: 'The purpose of Newspeak was not only to provide a medium of expression for the world view and mental habits proper to the devotees of Ingsoc, but to make all other modes of thought impossible' (Orwell, [1949] 1999: 236). For both Huxley and Orwell, authoritarianism was ripe for satire. For both, strict regimentation and surveillance emerge as definitive dystopian motifs. Notably, both writers lived during a period in which the social experiment of state socialism—with its huge bureaucracies—was beginning to unfold; this of course presented a formidable target for literary critique, something that is particularly evident in the work of Orwell.

Player Piano by Kurt Vonnegut ([1952] 2006), meanwhile, foresees technological catastrophe following the unconstrained advances in automation and computerisation. Each member of society carries an identity smart card on which comprehensive personal records are recorded. 'Computers regularly sift through these details, and anyone who is found doing a job that can now be done by machine joins the unemployed' (Carey, 1999: 442). As humanity slowly becomes subordinated to technology, a resistance group emerges and in its credo declares that

> [T]here must be a virtue in inefficiency, for man is inefficient, and Man is a creation of God ... You perhaps disagree with the antique and vain notion of Man's being a creation of God. But I find it a far more defensible belief than the one implicit in intemperate faith in lawless technological progress—namely, that man is on earth to create more durable and efficient images of himself, and hence, to eliminate any justification at all for his own continued existence.
>
> *(Vonnegut, [1952] 2006: 302)*

Further implications of the controlled supplanting of humanity with technology are found in Forster's *The Machine Stops* ([1909] 2011). In Forster's fiction, the delineated future is one in which a nebulous 'Machine' controls every aspect of human life as an early anticipation of the potential for artificial intelligence. Accordingly, human life has itself become mechanical and dehumanized. Invariably, the 'Machine' is representative of both bureaucracy and industrial alienation more generally.

And—interestingly it is often those with (in)direct experiences of state socialist experiments that become their fiercest critics. This is certainly the case for Russian-born and -educated Ayn Rand, for example, whose vast—and frankly unreadable—*Atlas Shrugged*, published in 1957, paints a damning picture of government intervention while simultaneously championing the apparently irrefutable virtues of free-market libertarianism. To some degree at least this foreshadows our discussions of political conviction in Chapter 3.

In any event, the fact that utopia has nowhere been realized is testament to the prevalence—and pervasiveness—of paradox: 'As Machievelli noted, no Utopia can be achieved on Earth, not because of the frailties and imperfections of mankind, but because every conceivable ideal society is meant to satisfy mutually incompatible, that is, paradoxical goals' (Stent, 2002: 232).

Cinema

Whereas in the late 19th and early 20th centuries, our encounters of paradox were driven primarily by the world of literature, in the latter parts of the 20th and early 21st century, film increasingly provides for us this encounter. While relatively few of us have the patience and determination to grapple with a Dostoevsky novel, many more of us have revelled in the delights of, say, Kelly's (2001) *Donnie Darko*. Like its literary counterpart, then, existential cinema frequently evokes paradox, if not in name then certainly by way of thematic. Indeed, to the extent that cinema is a vehicle for conveying a fictive narrative, it is not dissimilar to literature. It seems, therefore, that cinema represents a means of democratizing paradox and for this very reason, is something we circle back to in the conclusion whereupon we champion paradox as a distinct pedagogical device. In preparing the content for this subsection, I have been careful to avoid repetition of the themes explored in the preceding subsection, and hence restrict those here which are peculiar to the celluloid form. These include, in particular, the nonlinear narrative which—it seems—can be conveyed more effectively on the screen.

No exploration of celluloid paradox would be complete without a discussion of David Lynch's cinematographic canon. Of course, for most of us, we are familiar with Lynch's work courtesy of his infamous television series *Twin Peaks* from the early 1990s. It is, in short, brilliant. It aired at a time when TV series were about bravado, curly bangs, and big tits; think *The A-Team*, *Dallas*, and *Dynasty*. *Twin Peaks* was worlds away. It was surrealist, and—for that very reason—compelling. However, it didn't—consciously, at least—explore paradox. Lynch's later filmic work, however, did. Films such as *Wild at Heart* (1990) (which became a preoccupation for Lynch, so much so that other directors were found to help conclude the Twin Peaks saga, which explains—for some—why the TV series lost its appeal), *Lost Highway* (1997), *Mulholland Drive* (2001), and *Inland Empire* (2006) all engage—consciously or otherwise—with the ideas central to paradox. While these films retained a sense of the surrealism and magic realism that was found in *Twin Peaks*, they introduced the discombobulating sense of the nonlinear (and sometimes circular) narrative. And—once again—they are compelling for precisely this reason. If nothing else, these films bellow to us: linearity is dull! The nonlinear narrative was also used to great effect by Quentin Tarantino, particularly in *Pulp Fiction* (1994). The hugely controversial French film *Irreversible* (2003), directed by Gaspar Noé, took nonlinearity to the next level; the film was presented in reverse order and elicited reactions of celebration and disapproval in more or less equal measure. Beyond Lynch, Tarantino, and Noé, films by David Cronenberg (*Crash*, 1996; *eXistenZ*, 1999), Richard Kelly (*Donnie Darko*, 2001), Doug Liman (*Edge of Tomorrow*, 2014), and Tony Elliott (*Arq*, 2016) are similarly compelling examples of this nonlinear genre. But for a truly harrowing experience look no further than Christopher Smith's *Triangle* (2009), an extraordinarily haunting voyage to the depths of existential despair.

More generally, paradox has become a relatively popular theme in (so-called 'intelligent') science fiction, too. Niander Wallace's quip in Denis Villeneuve's *Blade Runner 2049* (2017) is a case in point: 'Pain reminds you the joy you felt was real'. Pfister's *Transcendence* (2014) was poorly reviewed (and justifiably so), but this science fiction romp does touch upon the tensions inherent to discussions of free will and cognitive dissonance. For Paul Bettany's character, scientist Max Waters:

> I spent my life trying to reduce the brain to a series of electrical impulses. I failed. Human emotion; it can contain illogical conflict. [It] [c]an love someone, and yet hate the things that they've done. A machine can't reconcile that.

Unlike machines, human beings can mediate paradox; this observation foreshadows one of the principal arguments delineated later in the book under the guise of consciousness and agency (see Chapter 9).

Music

Whereas literature, art, and film all seek to *represent* a reality—fictional or otherwise—music does not do this. German philosopher, Arthur Schopenhauer, for example, singles music out for special consideration in his philosophical system because, unlike the other arts, it is he says 'a direct objectification of the will' (see Marsden 2002: 65). The composer and polemicist Richard Wagner made a similar observation. Put simply, music is its own entity. For this very reason, I felt that our consideration of music should not be restricted to a discussion of the arts. I have therefore reserved much of its potential for the concluding chapter of this book whereupon I take inspiration from the mechanics of music (i.e. considerations of tempo, beat, rhythm, and melody) to provide a metaphorical frame through which we can refract the existential pattern of paradox, and—more prosaically—to enhance our understanding of *lifecraft* vis-à-vis paradox.

However, the grandiose contributions of Schopenhauer and Wagner aside, it is also worth stressing that popular lyricists have sometimes played with the idea of paradox. One of the earliest instances comes courtesy of 'The Paradox Song' in Gilbert and Sullivan's opera *The Pirates of Penzance*:

> *A paradox,*
> *That most ingenious paradox!*
> *We've quips and quibbles heard in flocks,*
> *But none to beat that paradox!*

The purported paradox in this case concerns Frederic's age, bearing in mind he was born on the 29 February (and hence could be both 5 and 21 simultaneously). Sadly, it seems, Gilbert and Sullivan didn't really understand the notion of paradox. It's a jolly ditty, nonetheless. The song *Don't Let's Start* by They Might be Giants is significantly more arresting: 'No one in the world ever gets what they want and that is beautiful'. Similarly, and while her understanding of irony is infamously wide of the mark, Alanis Morrisette was perhaps more insightful than she is often given credit for in her lyric, 'Life has a funny way of helping you out' (Alanis Morrisette, *Ironic*). This is of course relevant in terms of the moderating effects of paradox, and her pertinent utterance foreshadows some of the deeper existential discussions of ontological paradox in the later chapters, particularly Chapters 5 and 8.

Postlude

Space has inevitably necessitated selectivity. Nonetheless, what we can glean from the coverage presented in this chapter is that paradox transcends the artistic medium: from the fine arts, through classical literature, and into contemporary cinema and music. Unlike the social or natural sciences for which there is pressure to adhere to a linear logic, the arts faces no such prohibition. This, of course, underpins the extraordinary value of the arts. We conclude this chapter, however, by proposing a controversial paradox: it is art, more so than science, which affords the more lucid—and perhaps even the more accurate—insight into the dynamics of our world. This lends valuable conceptual context for later chapters on both the natural sciences (Chapter 5), in which we expand upon the arts vis-à-vis science paradox, and ontology (Chapter 6), in which we explore a paradox between subjectivity and objectivity. In the interim, however, we turn now to examine societal paradoxes.

3

PARADOX AND SOCIETY

Although I tentatively position myself as a transdisciplinarian in this book, it was in the social sciences that I cut my scholarly teeth. This chapter explores the myriad ways in which paradox underpins—and purportedly constrains—key discussions and research trajectories in the study of society. For the purposes of managing the reader experience, I have structured the chapter around four distinct social scientific disciplines: politics, economics, psychology, and sociology. However, such categorization inevitably involved arbitrary sleight of hand. As we will see in the concluding pages of this book, it is the transcendent manner in which the documented paradoxes manifest themselves *across* different spheres of life (including across crudely delineated academic disciplines) that is most remarkable.

Homo politicus

I grew up in North London in the 1980s. When I was seven or eight years old, I developed a peculiar fascination with both punks and skinheads. My late mother concluded that my interest with punks was most likely explained by their brightly coloured mohawk hairstyles—but she was puzzled by my interest in skinheads. I think it concerned her. In any event, she felt compelled to regularly remind me that a shaved head generally implied that the individual in question was a racist. This association stuck with me. However, a few years on, I realized that at least some skinheads aligned themselves with Ska, a musical style which took in cues from Jamaican Rudeboy sounds. A white skinhead identity could therefore imply not a hatred of another's ethnicity or culture, but a profound respect for it. This violated the compartmentalization my mother had imparted. On one level, this anecdote represents little more

DOI: 10.4324/9781003203339-4

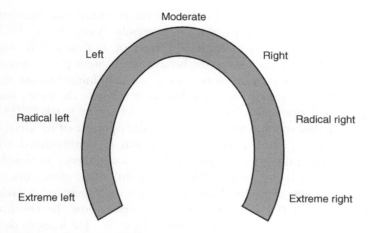

Moderate

Left   Right

Radical left   Radical right

Extreme left   Extreme right

FIGURE 3.1   The Political Horseshoe.

than the coming-of-age recognition that the world is more complex than the representations thereof our parents impart. On another, it is symbolic of the tension (or paradox) that goes to the very heart of identity politics.

We can discern numerous paradoxes related to politics. As we will see, paradox characterizes particular political positions and even democracy itself. But let us begin with what I refer to as *the paradox of ideology*. Conventional discussions of politics tend to reflect what has become known as the political spectrum, typically presented as a horizontal continuum from left to right. But ask yourself this: how different are the political Left and Right? A more nuanced approach to ideological difference tends to invoke not a linear spectrum but a horseshoe-shape (see Figure 3.1).

So why the horseshoe instead of the horizontal line? Well, in some respects, the further to the left an ideology is positioned, the more it tends to resemble those ideologies of the extreme right (and vice versa). In practice, Communists and Fascists have more in common than either side would care to admit. This was something that Italian political theorist Bruno Rizzi observed as early as 1939. And as history is only too keen to remind us, both Communists *and* Fascists have presided over large-scale humanitarian catastrophes: consciously in the case of Fascists; inevitably in the case of Communists. These ideological extremes both have totalitarian tendencies. Similarly, and by way of contemporary example, commentators have detected a symbiotic relationship between Islamic extremism and Far Right extremism (see, e.g. BBC, 2015a).

The paradox of ideology manifests itself in respect of electoral behaviour more generally. In a recent paper reflecting on the electoral surprises of 2016— i.e. Brexit and Trump's election as US President—I drew attention to the fact that we can observe a paradox of politics in the perennial misalignment between the public mood and psephological trends (Vine, 2020: 476). Psephology, the statistical study of electoral behaviour, is a niche field, but yields intriguing data in respect of human behaviour. As Stent (1978) notes, the left and right characterization of politics is self-sustaining because the existence of a left-wing society creates a backlash towards the right, and then back again (and vice versa). This sentiment is echoed by Bartle (2015), who reports that public opinion tends to be the polar opposite of the elected government. The two political positions should thus be distinguished not ideologically but temporally. In accordance with early social theory (especially that associated with Italian polymath Vilfredo Pareto), Stent subscribes to a cyclical understanding of political conviction, a sort of neo social cycle theory. With a focus of British politics, Bartle describes how the political centre invariably moves against the government of the day. He suggests that from 1964, the average left-right position generally tracked rightwards until 1980, the year after Margaret Thatcher came to power. Public attitudes then gradually moved left during the 1980s and remained there for the duration of the Major premiership. The mood shifted rightwards from 1997 under New Labour and left under the Coalition. In this way, he argues, those governments that achieve their parties' preferred policies unwittingly initiate their own downfall. Voting behaviour is notoriously difficult to predict. Why? Because it does not conform to straightforward cause-and-effect linear thinking; it is representative of a nonlinear system. Indeed, for Bartle, despite efficacious intentions, when interpreted retrospectively, we all-too-often vote *against* our own interests. And this is by no means peculiar to British politics. The pattern is pervasive, perhaps nowhere more so than in American politics and—in particular—in respect of Trump's presidency. Ultimately, politics eludes rationality. As Graeber (2016: 38) reminds us: 'anyone who claims to base their politics on rationality—and this is true on the left as well as on the right—is claiming that anyone who disagrees with them might as well be insane'. In any event, and as Bochner and Ellis (2016: 227) note, '[a]cting against is just another form of submission and dependence'. This is sometimes referred to as 'Newton's Law of Politics' (see, e.g. Hamilton, 2004); i.e. any ideological advance in one direction attracts a comparable counter advance in the opposite direction.

And there is yet another way to consider the paradox of ideology. Whereas conventional wisdom configures democracy and totalitarianism as polar opposites, to some political theorists democracy has a tendency to elicit extreme populist government, and can therefore provide unscrupulous demagogues with an ideal opportunity to seize power. Ivo Mosley—grandson and critic of notorious Oswald—argued that totalitarian regimes may well be the logical outcome of unfettered mass democracy (see Mosley, 2003). In adopting an ideological position, it seems, we automatically and unwittingly lend support to the opposite ideological position. And, finally, there is a sense of ideological paradox over time which takes the form of dialectical shift between permissive and conservative political attitudes *between generations*. This has become known as the Third Generation Effect or Hansen's Law. US Historian, Marcus Lee Hansen, quipped 'What the son wishes to forget the grandson wishes to remember' (see, e.g. Schlesinger, 1991: 41). In a bid to transition from dependence to independence and demarcate our own sense of identity, we inevitably rebel against our parents. In this way, there is good chance we end up sharing at least some of the attitudinal dispositions of our grandparents, who of course our parents will have rebelled against.

So does all this imply, perhaps, that we need to consciously move beyond ideological conviction? Some of the shrewdest members of our society appear to have done precisely this. The celebrated filmmaker, David Lynch (who we met in Chapter 2), for example, is reported to have both admired Republican Ronald Reagan and minimal government, on the one hand, and yet to style himself as a Democrat, on the other. Similarly, French singer-songwriter Françoise Madeleine Hardy is said to adopt a refined position vis-à-vis politics. On the face of it, Hardy presents as a card-carrying member of the liberal arts scene. Dig a little deeper, however, and her politics departs significantly from the standard leftist stuff; indeed, she seems to have injected more nuance into her ideological deliberation. Of course, approaches such as those espoused in 'syncretic' or 'third way' politics (e.g. Giddens, 1994, 1998; Bastow & Martin, 2003) lay claim to a reconciliation of left and right perspectives as a means of paving the way for a radical centrism (e.g. Olson, 2005). However, I wish to argue that a recognition of the paradoxes inherent to the left-right political spectrum— rather than their resolution—affords the keener insight. In fact, it may be that we can combine syncretism of the type discussed in Eco's 1988 *Foucault's Pendulum*, for instance, with paradox. In this way, paradox helps bind together disparate ideas. For example, left-leaning critics routinely point both to the job displacement effects of new technologies *and* to the fact that we appear to be working ever longer hours, despite technological innovation. Equally, those on the populist right who express concern about immigrants displacing indigenous jobs very quickly fall victim to what has become known as 'the lump of labour fallacy', that is, the assumption that there remains a fixed amount of work to be done. The broader point, of course, is that political-economic anxieties transcend political position. Indeed, for the late futurist Alvin Toffler (1970: 410), '... econocentric premises are buried so deeply and held so widely in both the capitalist and communist nations, that they distort the very information systems essential for the management of change'. And it is this quandary that preoccupied the distinguished psychologist Paul L. Wachtel in his 1989 book, *The Poverty of Affluence*, in which he explored the psychology of greed and materialism. He writes:

> There do seem to be a number of features of contemporary capitalism that are [problematic] ... for example, the preponderant emphasis on the profit motive; the deliberate generation of needs; the apparent requirement of growth to keep the system running at all well; the encouragement of greed and the rationalizations about self-reliance that discourage mutual aid. These characteristics are hard to reconcile with the kind of life I would like to see. But socialism alone—that is, a change in who owns the means of production without a concomitant change in values and consciousness—is clearly not a panacea. [Experience from] the Soviet Union and in Eastern Europe demonstrate rather unambiguously that ending private ownership alone does not in itself change values and consciousness. Without the latter kind of change, the growth and consumer way of life persist, perhaps less efficiently and effectively, but not for want of wanting. As [sociologist] Philip Rieff has put it, 'Both American and Soviet cultures are essentially variants of the same belief in wealth as the functional equivalent of a high civilization .... The answer to all questions of "what for" is "more"'.
>
> *(Wachtel, 1989: 146)*

We can lend further context to the paradox of ideology in terms of the distinction between freedom and equality. For Rappaport (1981) these are two equally positive values but when viewed one at a time lead us to maximize one and ignore the other. 'Because they are intimately intertwined they constitute an antinomy and present us with phenomena that are true paradoxes' (ibid.: 3). He thus insists that the very nature of political life is paradoxical.

The concepts of commitment and belief are characterized by a type of paradox comparable to that already observed in respect of ideological conviction. Reflecting on research originally undertaken by Kiesley et al. (1971), Salancik (1977) describes in detail an extraordinarily revealing social experiment. Some residents of New Haven in Connecticut were randomly divided into two groups; one group was given an opportunity to sign a petition while the other was not. A day later, half of each group was delivered with a broadside attacking the position taken in the petition. On the third day, attitudes were measured and the individuals were asked to volunteer to do work for organizations supporting the petitioned position. The attitudes of residents committed by signing a petition were significantly more favourable than those of residents not given an opportunity to sign the petition. Moreover, the petition signers who were sent the attack volunteered three and a half times as often as all other residents (42% vs. 12%). 'What is so amazing about this study is that with so little effort (an innocuous petition one day, a counter-argument slipped under the door the next) one can turn quiet New Haveners into ready activists' (Salancik, 1977: 37–38). Reflecting on the significance of the broadside, Salancik argues that the attack acts to remind individuals of their prior behaviour and the implications of that behaviour in light of current circumstances, presenting them with a challenging test of their newly committed position.

> When the attack comes, the new information is assimilated into the previous position and the person becomes even more bound to the position because [s]he actively rejects some aspect of the alternative. Thus, when presented with a third opportunity to act, [s]he behaves in a manner consistent with his previous behaviour. A number of [other] studies suggest the critical variable is not attack per se which is involved, but the implications of a committed behaviour for future behaviours.
>
> *(ibid.: 38)*

Further on, Salancik reminds his readers that Selznick (1949) and Pfeffer (1972, 1973) had each reached comparable conclusions in their studies of organizations. They both note, for example, how boards of directors are used by organizations to coopt the support of the organization's critical interest groups.

> Outsiders are invited into the organization, given a sense of participating, and over time find themselves supporting the organization and defending it to other outsiders .... The most ironic aspect of participation is that the more the appearance of freedom is given, the more coopted one becomes.
>
> *(Salancik, 1977: 45)*

Political conviction is, it seems, little more than a redux casting of chance. There is no 'essence' to it; perhaps this helps us understand why it is that paradoxes arise so easily. There is also a very important implication here for discussions about free will, the analytical focus of Chapter 7.

Beyond the manifestation of paradox *between* ideological positions, we can discern paradox *within* specific ideological designations, too. Indeed, paradoxes are detectable within the doctrines of conservatism, liberalism, and socialism. Of conservativism, Weil ([1962] 2020: 19) notes that conservatives too often 'fail to realise that, since conditions are always changing, the refusal to modify the system is itself a modification which may be productive of disorders'. In order to 'conserve', then, we must—paradoxically—change. Liberalism, meanwhile, is routinely touted as a distinct ideological position, in which the rights of the individual are championed. However, the self-determination that characterizes its economic manifestation—i.e. libertarianism—is ostensibly at odds with the inclusiveness that characterizes the sociocultural manifestation of liberalism. Finally, in the case of socialism, Graeber (2016: 20–21) presents what might be labelled a *paradox of working-class politics* when he reflects on the relatively recent re-casting of what it means to be left wing in America or Britain:

> Ultimately, the more [progressive] members of [the] professional-managerial elite became the social base for what came to pass as 'left-wing' political parties, as actual working-class organizations like trade unions were cast into the wilderness. (Hence, the US Democratic Party, or New Labour in Great Britain, whose leaders engage[d] in regular ritual acts of public abjuration of the very unions that have historically formed their strongest base of support). These were of course people who already tended to work in ... schools, hospitals, or corporate law firms. The actual working class, who bore a traditional loathing for such characters, either dropped out of politics entirely, or were increasingly reduced to casting protest votes for the radical Right.

It seemed, therefore, that the traditional left-wing working classes in America and Britain would now sooner pair with the radical right than share ideological head space with the cappuccino-sipping cosmopolitans. This played out most noticeably in the mid-2010s with the election of Donald Trump in the US and the successful Brexit campaign in the UK. In each case, the traditional working classes sided with radical right-wing sentiment. In turn, this observation ushers in a derivative but distinct paradox which we might call *the paradox of populist uprisings*. Walver imparts to us the following caution:

> If states ever become large neighbourhoods, it is likely that neighbourhoods will become little states. Their members will organize to defend their local politics and culture against strangers. Historically, neighbourhoods have turned into closed and parochial communities ... whenever the state was open.
>
> *(Michael Walver, cited in Bauman, 2017: 49)*

Brexit and Trumpism, as I have argued elsewhere (see Vine, 2020) were the result of deeply paradoxical machinations. They had very little to do with economics—or even politics. Rather, they were the upshot of a deeply felt but largely benign threat to identity. As Bauman (2017) notes, a neighbourhood filled by strangers is a visible, tangible sign of certainties evaporating, and the prospects of life—as well as the fate of pursuit of them—drifting out of control. For Lakoff (2004), too, 'People do not necessarily vote in their self-interest. They vote their identity. They vote their values. They vote for who they identify with'. Bauman reproduces a pertinent passage from Huntington's

The Clash of Civilisations and the Remaking of World Order, which was in turn taken originally from Michael Dibdin's novel, *Dead Lagoon*:

> There can be no true friends without true enemies. Unless we hate what we are not, we cannot love what we are. These are the old truths we are painfully rediscovering after a century and more of sentimental cant. Those who deny them deny their family, their heritage, their culture, their birthright, their very selves! They will not lightly be forgiven.
>
> *(Dibdin, 1994: 327)*

As dark and foreboding as this advice sounds, the really worrying thing is that an advanced understanding of identity dynamics supports it. Is conflict a necessary part of the human condition? Unless we are willing to turn hatred onto ourselves, the answer it seems is—inevitably—yes.

Homo economicus

The field of economics presents myriad paradoxes, some of which readers may already be familiar with. These include the *paradox of rationality* (the empirical observation in game theory that players who make naive or irrational decisions tend to receive better payoffs than those who make ostensibly rational choices), and the *paradox of thrift* (our tendency during a recession is to save, and yet this very action serves only to intensify the economic downturn). The paradox of thrift is of course a compelling example of the 'fallacy of composition'—the idea that what is true of the parts must be true of the whole. Some readers may also be familiar with the elegiac tensions at the very crux of capitalism: Schumpeter's concept of *creative destruction* is perhaps the best known, but Ewen's less well-known paradox is more incendiary: '[s]atisfied customers are not as profitable as discontented ones' (Ewen, 1976: 39). This subsection considers some of the most pervasive paradoxes of economics. These include paradoxes vis-à-vis *specialization, resources, choice, price, competition, prosperity*, and—most pertinently—*economic ideology* itself.

Specialization. Specialization is a precursor to civilization. To all intents and purposes specialization enabled both agricultural and industrial revolutions. It represents the basis of economics; it is after all through specialization that the very foundations of exchange are built. A baker is unlikely to have the skillset to build a sturdy doorframe, while the joiner's attempt at sourdough may end up re-purposed as a door stop. But the effects of specialization are more far-reaching than the straightforward facilitation of exchange. Specialization underlies that most dubious of concepts, technological advance; and it is of course specialists that are venerated in our society. Considered the pinnacle of formal education the world over, expectations for earning a PhD continue to marshal the student towards *knowing more and more about less and less*. This was something my own doctoral supervisors routinely reminded me as I got distracted by yet another captivating piece of research that fell outside the remit of my project. On the other hand, it is the generalists who have a far superior handle on context, and the broader ramifications of action beyond their native field. With this in mind, the engineer who reads psychology or cultural theory may well produce more effective—and more efficacious—machines. Here, then, we posit *a paradox of specialization*.

Related to specialization is what I refer to as *the paradox of the division of labour*. When you're next on British shores, pick up a £20 note (admittedly a rarity in this electronic age) and flip it over. The bold but controversial epitaph accompanying the image of Adam Smith reads: 'The division of labour in pin manufacturing (and the great increase in the quantity of work that results)'. Smith demonstrated how the division of labour enhanced productivity within factories in at least three ways. First, it facilitated increased dexterity on the part of the worker; second, it enabled the mechanization of routine tasks (recent advances in 3D printing notwithstanding, the prospect of designing a single machine to build a chair from scratch is nigh on impossible; it is significantly easier to design a *series of machines* each of which is dedicated to a component part of that chair); and, ultimately, it saved time. Indeed, dating back to at least Smith—and probably earlier—the division of labour has been celebrated as an effective means of *getting things done*. Perhaps the earliest (albeit *proto*) form of the division of labour was between men and women. Men hunted, we are taught, while women cared. It is, however, this early example of the division of labour that reveals its limitations—specifically its propensity to pair demographic divisions with task divisions, in this case between expectations of 'men's work' vis-à-vis 'women's work'. Another—very different—application is what is sometimes referred to as the *international division of labour*; most white-collar roles are in the West while most blue-collar roles are in the East. But beyond these demographic concerns, Smith himself noted a more fundamental problem; the division of labour has degrading effects:

> The man [sic] whose whole life is spent in performing a few simple operations, of which the effects too are, perhaps, always the same, or very nearly the same, has no occasion to exert his understanding, or to exercise his invention in finding out expedients for removing difficulties that never occur. He naturally loses, therefore, the habit of such exertion, and generally becomes as stupid and ignorant as it is a human creature to become.
>
> *(Smith, [1776] 1900: 613)*

While the division of labour represents a cornerstone of modern economics, at its crux lies a fundamental social and moral limitation. And as biologist Mark Moffett (2019: 105–106) notes of the insect world: 'Among ants, brain size actually declines in species that have large societies. Workers in a small colony are mentally challenged, as much as ants ever are, because they are jacks-of-all-trades'. On the one hand, then, a division of labour enables huge leaps in productivity. On the other, it deadens the mind.

Of course, what we have said so far in respect of a division of labour doesn't really amount to a paradox; rather, the 'mind-deadening' is a drawback or side effect. However, the division of labour is integral to *cooperation* (either in the sense that workers—as eponymous 'cogs'—must mesh together effectively to yield a collective output, or—more broadly—in the sense that division of labour necessitates interaction through trade); and this might more readily be conceptualised as a paradox. As Šubrt (2019: 77) has astutely observed, cooperation is, paradoxically, premised on division: 'According to the ideas of consensus theory, collectively shared beliefs (or value systems) and co-operation is based on the division of labour'.

Resources. Charles Handy is best known for his near celebrity status as management theorist, but has commented extensively on what are at heart—paradoxes of economics. In his popular 1994 book, *The Empty Raincoat* (revealingly published in the US as *The Age of Paradox*), Handy's discussions yield several pertinent economic contradictions. These include what I have rearticulated as the paradox of time-as-resource, the paradox of growth, and the paradox of wealth.

Of *the paradox of time-as-resource*, Handy (1994: 31) writes:

> In this turbulent world we never seem to have enough time, yet there has never been so much time available to us. We live longer, we use less time to make and do things as we get more efficient, and should therefore have more time to spend.

He continues: 'Yet we have made this strange commodity into a competitive weapon, paying over the odds for speed. If we were wise would we not take the price-tag off time, and give ourselves time to stand and stare?' (ibid.: 32). It is to such a bind, of course, that so much New Age philosophy is geared, urging us to slow down and take stock. But ironically, we appear to have unwittingly commodified—and rendered as temporal resource—even this wisdom (see, e.g. Carrette & King, 2004). Configured as an economic resource, then, time is plagued by paradox. In a similar vein, we can posit a *paradox of growth*:

> Economic growth depends, ultimately, on more and more people wanting more and more of more and more things. Looking at the world as a whole,

then, there should be no shortage of growth potential. If, however, we look only at the rich societies, we see them producing fewer babies every year and living longer. Fewer babies mean fewer customers ... Older people, even when they have the money, are in a slimming down, passing-on stage, not a stocking up one. We could be running out of customers at home .... Growth, then, which—it seems—is necessary for society, is increasingly dependent on a climate of envy in that society, increasing its divisions. Paradox again. There are, however, some signs that the 'Gucci factor', the high-fashion luxury trade which is based on envy, may have peaked in the Eighties, along with the firm of that name. It is, said the Financial Times, 'the demise of de luxe'. Consumers have become more discerning, less interested in conspicuous consumption, asking more often 'Will it work well?' or 'Will it last'? We have, paradoxically, to wonder whether this is good news or bad. It is bad for growth, good for common sense.

(ibid.: 36, 37)

As Wachtel (1989: 9) presciently noted in the 1980s, '... the pursuit of economic growth may actually make things worse'. He suggests that

something about our commitment to growth seems to be akin to the phenomena observed in individual neuroses. For me the heart of the notion of neurosis is the occurrence of vicious circles in people's behaviour in which their sense of security is undermined by the effort they make to bolster it.

(ibid.: 60)

Most chilling of all, however, is Wachtel's assessment of 'false profits': A rising standard of living for all (even if unequally distributed) was seen as everyone's birthright. The idea of more become a mainspring of the Western psyche (ibid.: 68). He suggests that we have become so used to counting and to giving meaning to our activities in quantitative terms that it all too often comes as a surprise to us to find that not all cultures share this trait. Wachtel invokes the concept of gross national product (GNP) as a case in point.

Originally the GNP was developed by economists as a technical tool to gauge the performance of the economy ... It was not long, however, before the GNP began to be regarded not just as a tool for economic policy-making but as a measure of economic welfare, of how 'well off' we were.

(ibid.: 87)

Perhaps the most arresting way in which to illustrate the paradox of growth is courtesy of the infamous idea of 'creative destruction'. While associated primarily with Schumpeter, it is to Nietzsche that we must attribute the conceptual context. Nietzsche argued that erecting ideals is fundamentally problematic since their creation involves destruction:

> Have you ever asked yourselves sufficiently how much the erection of every ideal on earth has cost? ... If a temple is to be erected a temple must be destroyed: that is the law—let anyone who can show me a case in which it is not fulfilled!
>
> *(Nietzsche 1887, II, s24; 1989: 95)*

Is it any wonder that in recent years we have gradually seen evidence of a critical backlash against fixation on economic growth? Notably there have been several academic conferences dedicated to exploring what is tentatively described as 'The post-growth economy'. For some, a contradiction in terms. For others, an ecological axiom.

Having explored the tensions around time and growth, later in his book Handy trains his attention to what I have labelled *the paradox of wealth* (and we'll forgive him this once for his gender assumptions, and focus instead on the broader argument he advances):

> [S]tatistics only measure the visible transfers of money. So, for instance, and most notoriously, they don't measure the unpaid work in the home. If, however, the wife dies and her husband hires somebody to do the work which she did for nothing, the apparent prosperity of the country would rise by the $18,000 which the Legal and General Insurance Company say it would cost in the 1990s. Voluntary and charitable work—gift work—is not included because no money changes hand, nor the caring of the elderly if it is done for love or compassion in one's own home. Put your parents in a home for the elderly, however, and society, by these accounts, is immediately richer. More insidiously, if the cars and the highways are so bad that accidents proliferate, then hospital, car-repair and insurance bills increase, and so does the supposed wealth of the country as these transactions find their way into the national accounts. You can spend money with the polluting of the clean air of the countryside with a factory, muck up its rivers and destroy the peace and stillness of the place, and it will all be counted as an increase in wealth because nothing is deducted for the damage. If the firm were fined, or charged, for what they had done, it would, apparently make us even richer. We are encouraged to be a disposable society by the way we count. The more you throw things away and buy new things instead of having them repaired, the richer the society becomes.
>
> *(Handy, 1994: 220–221)*

The scenario Handy describes here is comparable to that which French economist Claude-Frédéric Bastiat refers to as the 'glazier's fallacy' (see

Bastiat, [1850] 2010). The glazier's fallacy is a parable in which we are invited to ponder the following question: *When a child accidentally smashes a window, necessitating its repair, does this constitute a benefit to society by virtue of the economic activity created in replacing the window pane?* And— if it does—does this mean we ought to encourage our progeny to go around smashing windows?

To the three paradoxes of resources Handy presents, we can add a fourth: *the paradox of plenty*, sometimes referred to as the 'resource curse' (see, e.g. Smith & Waldner, 2021). This paradox describes the tendency for countries with plentiful natural resources (e.g. Nigeria) to be comparatively poor, whereas those that have limited natural resources (e.g. Japan) are comparatively wealthy. We revisit this idea in the concluding chapter of this book as part of a discussion of the mediating effects of paradox.

Choice. While paradoxes gleaned from Handy all hinge on resources (time, growth, and wealth), Schwartz (2004) suggests that paradox also affects the process, practice, and psychology of *choice* in matters of economics. Why do some of us sometimes prefer to watch a scheduled film on television when there are thousands at our fingertips courtesy of Netflix? Well, the former is significantly less onerous in terms of choice; this is an example of what has become known as *overchoice*, or, in our preferred vocabulary, *the paradox of choice*. Overchoice is something with which we are each intuitively familiar, but it also bears out formal research. In what is now a rather dated piece of research, Schwartz (2004) reports that Americans spend more time shopping than the members of any other society. Americans go to shopping malls about once a week, more often than they go to houses of worship, and Americans now have more shopping malls than high schools. However, when respondents of a survey were asked to rank the pleasure they get from various activities, Schwartz reports, grocery shopping ranks next to last, and other shopping fifth from the bottom. Apparently, people are shopping more but enjoying it less. At the crux of this tension is the rapidly expanding horizon of choice. From a purely rational perspective added options are surely a good thing. Those of us who care will benefit, and those of us who don't care can always ignore the added options. Right?

> This view seems logically compelling; but empirically, it isn't true. A recent series of studies, titled 'When Choice Is Demotivating', provides the evidence. One study was set in a gourmet food store in an upscale community where, on weekends, the owners set up sample tables of new items. When researchers set up a display featuring a line of exotic, high-quality jams, customers who came by could taste samples, and they were given a coupon for a dollar off if they bought a jar. In one condition of the study, 6 varieties of the jam were available for tasting. In another, 24

varieties were available. In either case, the entire set of 24 varieties was available for purchase. The large array of jams attracted more people to the table than the small array, though in both cases people tasted about the same number of jams on average. When it came to buying, however, a huge difference became evident. Thirty percent of the people exposed to the small array of jams actually bought a jar; only 3 percent of those exposed to the large array of jams did so.

(Schwartz, 2004: 18)

Published in 2004, Schwartz's discussion precedes—only just—the global phenomenon of online shopping. However, the paradox associated with choice Schwartz identifies is even more arresting in the world of internet commerce where choice is, more or less, without limits. Indeed, for Manolică et al. (2021) overchoice is in certain cases causing what they describe as 'decision paralysis'.

Price. There are at least three paradoxes of price that demand our attention, each of which has long fascinated me: (1) Giffen goods, (2) Veblen goods, and (3) investment escalation. Giffen and Veblen goods are commodities for which, paradoxically, demand increases as price increases. But each does so for a different reason. In the case of Giffen goods, demand increases following a price rise because substitute goods remain comparatively more expensive. The example often cited is the market for bread. Bread is considered a relatively inexpensive commodity. However, for this very reason, among those with limited income an increase in the price of bread means that— paradoxically—they demand more of it. This is because they can no longer afford to supplement their diet with ostensibly more desirable alternatives to bread, such as fish and meat.

One might, of course, conclude that this paradoxical trend is peculiar to those with limited economic resources. However, we observe something very similar among those with more substantial economic resources. This was something the American economist Thorstein Veblen noticed at the turn of the twentieth century. He recognized that very expensive, luxury items, such as designer handbags or hand-built cars will actually experience an increase in demand as the price increases. This happens for two reasons: first, quality is sometimes difficult for prospective customers to discern and so consumers use price as a convenient proxy for quality—and a higher price denotes higher quality. Second, part of the appeal for haute couture is exclusivity. Buyers in this market make the assumption (unwittingly, in turns out) that the higher the price, the more exclusive the item: the Veblen effect means precisely the opposite is true. Interestingly, this effect can transcend haute couture. For the wine drinkers among you, a simple reflection on your own buying behaviour will more than likely illustrate this effect. When you peruse the wine shelves in your local supermarket, you will possibly have a grape variety or region in mind but beyond that your decision is determined almost entirely by price. This is because you have very little to go on in terms of taste and quality. You could of course crack open a bottle in the store and take a swig. But you're unlikely to do this, not least because it will attract the mire of a burley security guard. You don't get to try before you buy (and even if you did, part of the pleasure of wine consumption is the manner in which the flavour complements your meal or the ambience of the occasion; and this is something you are unable to recreate in a supermarket). Inevitably, then, you select on the basis of price. A savvy wine merchant will know this and so—potentially at least—bottle crap wine and slap a high price on it, safe in the knowledge that it will sell like proverbial hot cakes. In any event, you will almost certainly find yourself ignoring low-priced bottles. Each year, I have huge fun with my MBA students exploring the ramifications of the Veblen effect. Suffice to say, they are delighted at the end of the class when they go home and declare to their bosses: 'if we want to boost our sales, we need to raise our prices'!

Giffen and Veblen goods aside, Salancik, (1977: 37) provides an instructive account that explores another manifestation of the price paradox: investment escalation. Investment is (or at least can be) exciting and for this very reason investors often behave in ways contrary to rational calculation.

> The escalation phenomena are similar to other phenomena described by Schelling (1960) as 'entrapment', in which investments once begun are escalated beyond the bounds justified by the value of the object. Tom Stoppard, the playwright, noted that Rosencrantz and Guildenstern had simply 'travelled too far, and … momentum has taken over'. Shubik (1971) has created an auction in which the momentum builds so nicely that normal individuals can be found bidding more than a dollar for a dollar just to make sure they get the dollar.

Once again, consider your own behaviour. For those of you who have participated in an auction—either physically or via an online platform—as the bidding period comes to a close the sense of excitement and prospect of ownership often means we pay over the odds. This phenomenon is lent some light-hearted treatment by the writers of television sitcom, The Big Bang Theory, in this case from *The Nerdvana Annihilation* episode:

Leonard: Some guy is auctioning off a miniature time machine prop from the original film and no-one is bidding on it.
[…]
Howard: Oh, that's cool.

Leonard: Uh-huh.
Raj: It's only $800?
Leonard: Yeah. And that's my bid.
Sheldon: You bid $800!
Leonard: It was a spur of the moment thing, I figured it would go for thousands and I just wanted to be a part of it!

Price aside, there is paradox related to money itself. Historian Yuval Noah Harari (2014: 207) explains that for thousands of years, philosophers, thinkers, and prophets have besmirched money and called it the root of all evil and yet—he says—money is also the apogee of human tolerance. 'Money', he continues,

> is more open-minded than language, state laws, cultural codes, religious beliefs and social habits. Money is the only trust system created by humans that can bridge almost any cultural gap, and that does not discriminate on the basis of religion, gender, race, age or sexual orientation. Thanks to money, even people who don't know each other and don't trust each other can nevertheless cooperate effectively.

Related to—but distinct from—paradoxes of price and money is what might broadly be referred to as the *paradox of consumption trends*. Towards the end of the twentieth century, certain sections of the middle classes—not just in the West but elsewhere too—began to view mass-produced goods as undesirable and inauthentic, and so they began to pay more for bespoke, tailored, customized items. This, in turn, had the effect of rekindling more traditional methods of production. An irony here is that as 3D printing democratizes bespoke items, there is a very good chance bespoke items will become undesirable themselves, and there may well be a resurgence in demand for items manufactured in accordance with 'traditional' production line processes. One way in which this is already happening is in respect of classic cars. Cars that are 'original' and that have not been personalized by their owners or modified beyond their original factory specification typically command higher values.

The more consumers seek out 'the authentic', the more the market responds and supplies 'the authentic', but in so doing 'the authentic' becomes just another capillary of monetized logic and hence loses its sense of authenticity in the process. More generally, and according to Kvale (2006: 494):

> Our purchases are directed less by the value of concrete use of the products than by the experiences, dreams and lifestyles associated with the products through sophisticated marketing techniques. The meaning of life is found

in consumption, an empty self is filled, shaped, and reshaped, by the purchase of products with the appropriate logo. An insecure self, emptied by loss of tradition and social bonds, is now saturated by the consumption of experiences in continual identity shopping.

Kvale reveals an ideological—probably Marxist—prejudice here in writing 'emptied by loss of tradition and social bonds'. This is a value judgement; personally, I would sooner side with an existentialist interpretation. Nonetheless, the broader point is pertinent. Kvale hints at what we might legitimately describe as another paradox of consumption. It's probably part of the reason why we perpetually purchase. The savvier among us realize that the real pleasure is in terms of *prospective* satisfaction. This is probably part of the reason why the 'unboxing phenomenon' is so pervasive on YouTube (see, e.g. Marsh, 2016). Yes, we are cyberflâneurs but there is a logic of sorts behind what presents as aimless web surfing.

Competition. Entrepreneurs tend to covet the monopoly as their desired market position. The fewer competitors, they think, the better. However, in practice, the opposite can yield higher rewards, particularly in specialist markets. This is what I refer to as the *paradox of competition*. As a teenager in the mid-1990s I was a dedicated audiophile. If I wanted, say, a new amplifier, I got on the number 43 bus and headed to Tottenham Court Road in London's West End. Here, I found dozens of Hi-fi shops all vying for my hard-earned cash. Real estate in this part of London was—and remains—pricey, and competition steep, but—paradoxically—the shrewder retailers knew this was the best way of securing customers. This was an example of 'economic clustering' and is what some theorists (see, e.g. Chung & Cheng, 2019) describe as 'coopetition', a hybrid form of competition and cooperation. Notably, discussions of coopetition have parallels in the natural sciences, too. In a rebuttal of Darwinian orthodoxy, Briggs and Peat (1985: 208), for example, note that:

> rather than competing with each other for survival ... chemical matter structures actually evolved through a kind of cooperation. They flowed into one another, sharing the information of their chemistry. Cooperative exchanges led eventually to the formation of chemical structures containing nucleic acid (ultimately DNA) and the first appearance of 'living' forms.

They continue:

> So far as scientists know, only oxygen-breathing cells with a nucleus can form cell tissues and link with each other to create multi-cellular organisms. In the era of the bacterial dominance of earth, there was no

free oxygen. Some of the bacteria responded to the fluctuations of their own genetic macrosystem (the gene pool) and to the fluctuations of the larger macrosystem of the earth by restructuring into forms capable of photosynthesis. For some 2000 million years, photosynthetic bacteria performed the enormous task of totally transforming the atmosphere. According to Jantsch, there was a curious selflessness and vision in the way they went about it.

(ibid.: 210)

On the one hand, then, evolution *is* about competition; on the other, evolution demands cooperation. Briggs and Peat go on to remind us that

in the late nineteenth century, 'social Darwinism' was used to justify cutthroat business practices, and even today a 'survival of the fittest' attitude prevails in many areas in society. At this point, one can only wonder about the possible effect of a theory which emphasizes the cooperative aspects of evolution and depicts us as intimate participants in the fate of all nature.

(ibid.: 217–218)

Russian naturalist Peter Kropotkin had already made a comparable observation, 80 years earlier in his 1902 book *Mutual Aid: A Factor of Evolution*. As natural scientists, presumably Briggs and Peat hadn't come across economic clustering. This of course is one way in which texts such as the one you are reading—which celebrate transdisciplinary understanding—seek to add value.

Prosperity. Nietzschean scholar Jill Marsden (2002: 27) reflects on the difficulty of determining a recipe for creativity when she asks, pointedly, 'is it hunger or superabundance that has here become creative'? Nietzsche himself explores this very bind, and it is something we might refer to as *the paradox of economic success*. Nietzsche reminds us that suffering elicits creativity:

The discipline of suffering, of great suffering—do you not know that only this discipline has created all enhancements of man so far? That tension of the soul in unhappiness which cultivates its strength, its shudders face to face with great ruin, its inventiveness and courage in enduring, persevering, interpreting and exploiting suffering, and whatever has been granted to it of profundity, secret, mask, spirit, cunning, greatness—was it not granted to it through suffering, through the discipline of great suffering?

(Nietzsche, 1886: s225; 1989: 154)

A revealing parallel is the empirical observation that the most ambitious and entrepreneurial individuals are likely to have struggled when younger through some form of deprivation. This is, of course, the root of the much celebrated truism associated with *overcoming adversity*.

More broadly, we can discern a *paradox of prosperity*. For Morris and Salamone (2011), for example, such a paradox is revealed if we reflect on the alternating levels of economic predisposition *between* generations. If one generation is characterized by hard work, they suggest, that very generation will produce its opposite in the generation that follows. A diligent generation tends to yield a licentious one since the progeny who are the very beneficiaries of the prosperity 'develop a diminished capacity to produce wealth' (Morris and Salamone, 2011: 54). '[W]e live with a constant, unrelenting paradox: the more prosperous we become, the more susceptible we are to abandoning the very values, principles and conduct that created the prosperity in the first place' (ibid.: 51). This paradox of prosperity is reminiscent of the intergenerational paradox we identified as part of our earlier discussion of politics in respect of the dialectical attitudes between generations. It is also reminiscent of (albeit patterned slightly differently) the paradox of plenty. All, it seems, are implicated in evening out experience.

Economic ideology. Thus far we have considered paradoxes which manifest in observed economic behaviour. Pertinently, however, the very mechanics of the free market itself reveal some extraordinary paradoxes. Adam Smith's apposite observations in respect of the division of labour, discussed earlier, are buried deep inside *The Wealth of Nations*. It is most likely for this reason that they are rarely acknowledged. Smith is undoubtedly better known for his observation that ostensibly self-interested behaviour in a free market economy will in effect elicit care for others, what I call *the paradox of egoism*. Clearly, we want to keep our customers happy. We care for them, then, not out of self*less*ness, but because they make us money. Smith's infamous utterance in this vein is worth reproducing:

> It is not from the benevolence of the butcher, or the baker, that we expect our dinner, but from their regard to their own interest. We address ourselves, not to their humanity, but to their self-love, and never talk to them of their own necessities but of their advantages.
>
> *(Smith, [1776] 1900: 11)*

Smith was a remarkable scholar not least because he acknowledged the complexity of social life. Indeed, for any student of economics who has studied his canon as part of a Bachelor of Arts—rather than as part of Bachelor of Science—programme, they will almost certainly recall that Smith is not the free market poster boy he is so often portrayed as. His economic philosophy is more sophisticated than this. Furthermore:

> The pursuit of self-interest has to be balanced, as Adam Smith ... remind[s] us, by sympathy, a fellow feeling for others which is, he argues, the real basis of moral behaviour. Only if we are conditioned by this 'sympathy' will we want to take any risks with our fellow men and women, will we trust them farther than we can count them .... the 'invisible hand' needs to be accompanied by an 'invisible handshake'. Self-interest, unbalanced, can only lead to a jungle in which any victory will mean destroying those on whom our survival ultimately depends. That would be the paradox to end all paradoxes.
>
> *(Handy, 1994: 81–82)*

Beyond discussions pertaining to the tensions inherent to our egoist predisposition, there is an interesting paradox in respect of the dynamic between government and economic agent. Despite the prevalent libertarian rhetoric which paints government intervention as the nemesis of free enterprise, markets and the state have a deeply symbiotic relationship. In his wonderfully titled book, *The Utopia of Rules: On Technology, Stupidity, and the Secret Joys of Bureaucracy*, the late anthropologist David Graeber argues that markets did not emerge as some autonomous domain of freedom independent of, and opposed to, state authorities. 'Exactly the opposite is the case', he says.

> Historically, markets are generally either a side effect of government operations, especially military operations, or were directly created by government policy. This has been true at least since the invention of coinage, which was first created and promulgated as a means of provisioning soldiers.
>
> *(Graeber, 2016: 8)*

Furthermore:

> [W]hile the idea that the market is somehow opposed to and independent of government has been used at least since the nineteenth century to justify laissez faire economic policies designed to lessen the role of government, they never actually have that effect. English liberalism, for instance, did not lead to a reduction of state bureaucracy, but the exact opposite: an endless ballooning of legal clerks, registrars, inspectors, notaries, and police officials who made the liberal dream of a world of free contract between autonomous individuals possible. It turned out that maintaining a free market economy required a thousand times more paperwork than

a Louix XIV-style absolutist monarchy. This apparent paradox—that government policies intending to reduce government interference in the economy actually end up producing more regulations, more bureaucrats, and more police—can be observed so regularly that I think we are justified in treating it as a general sociological law. I propose to call it the iron law of liberalism. The iron law of liberalism states that any market reform, any government initiative intended to reduce red tape and promote market forces will have the ultimate effect of increasing the total number of regulations, the total amount of paperwork, and the total amount of bureaucrats the government employs.

(ibid.: 9)

As Graeber acknowledges, noted sociologist Émile Durkheim ([1893] 1984) had observed this tendency a century earlier, and it is something several other contemporary contributors, including Paul L. Wachtel, have also identified. As we saw earlier, Wachtel's work presents a rich source of the paradoxical. However, for my money, his most remarkable contributions are in respect of economic ideology. For Wachtel (1989: 146), neither capitalism nor socialism will triumph, because each sees economics as the primary metric for happiness.

Further analysis of Graeber's text yields yet another economic paradox related to economic ideology: *the paradox of economic deregulation*. Simply by labelling a new regulatory measure 'deregulation', Graeber argues, you can frame it in the public mind as a way to reduce bureaucracy and set individual initiative free,

even if the result is a fivefold increase in the actual number of forms to be filled in, reports to be filed, rules and regulations for lawyers to interpret, and officious people in offices whose entire jobs seems to be to provide convoluted explanations for why you're not allowed to do things.

(ibid.: 17)

Those most determined to eliminate bureaucracy are, paradoxically, the most likely to enact it. This is something I have explored myself (see Vine, 2021), and something we pick up in more detail in Chapter 4.

Homo psychologicus

Some paradoxes of psychology are so ingrained in popular parlance they hardly warrant explication. These include *Stockholm Syndrome* (the predisposition for hostages to develop a psychological bond with their captors; see, e.g. Adorjan et al., 2012); the *good enough mother* (the notion that a parent should respond to their baby's needs in a way that is just 'good enough' such that the infant's needs are met but that the child also learns to tolerate frustration when its needs are not immediately satisfied, a variation of the broader 'cruel-to-be-kind' thesis; see Winnicott, 1973); and the *paradox of character* (the observation that exhibited behaviour is very much at odds with felt experiences; the 'sad clown' is a case in point, as too was surrealist Salvador Dali; outwardly eccentric but inwardly timid; see Janus, 1975; Ando et al., 2014). In recent years, and in line with its growing popularity as a therapeutic technique, numerous *paradoxes of mindfulness* have attracted attention, too. Of particular note is the observation that mindfulness is concurrently a prospective goal, but one which ostensibly—and paradoxically—requires us to live in the present. (For an excellent assessment of the relationship between mindfulness and paradox, see Sauerborn et al., 2022.) Pop psychology firmly aside, then, this subsection is delineated as follows. We begin with a brief exploration of the manner in which paradox characterizes *psychoanalysis*, before training our attention on paradoxes in respect of *self, dependency, anxiety, intimacy, professional practise*, and *emotion*.

Psychoanalysis. Paradox vis-à-vis psychoanalysis extends back to—and almost certainly beyond—Freud's infamous and far-reaching argument that repression is imperative to the effective functioning of society, an argument he advances in his 1930 book, *Civilization and its discontents*. Indeed, for Freud ([1930] 1991: 286), 'It is impossible to overlook the extent to which civilization is built upon a renunciation of instinct'. If we were unable to suppress our carnal urges, for example, we would most likely inhabit a world characterized by sexual violence, and our kin relations would be devoid of stability. As Dickson (1991: 246) stresses in his interpretation of Freud's thesis, 'The main theme of the book [is] the irremediable antagonism between the demands of instinct and the restrictions of civilization'. For Freud, it was through a process of sublimation (i.e. the re-articulation of socially unacceptable impulses or urges—such as sexual predation—into acceptable ones) that this antagonism was avoided. But here, too, we find a tension: *the paradox of buried objects*. Celebrated French philosopher Gilles Deleuze ([1968] 2004: 16) makes the following observation:

> [F]rom the standpoint of a certain Freudianism, we can discover the principle of an inverse relation between repetition and consciousness, repetition and remembering, repetition and recognition (the paradox of the 'burials' or buried objects): the less one remembers, the less one is conscious of remembering one's past, the more one repeats it.

The more we repress an unpleasant experience (i.e. 'bury' it), the more likely we are to repeat it. Herein lies a highly problematic paradox. However, this should not imply that the alternative is always more desirable. Consider for a moment the pragmatic conviction—certainly in the West—that the more we 'bring something out into the open' to discuss and share it, the better. This rationale is rarely challenged. However, as this predisposition becomes subsumed into the dominant cultural discourse it may well elicit a potential problem. On the one hand, it is certainly desirable to talk through harrowing experiences so as to process those experiences. On the other—and conscious that we *co-construct* the world in which we inhabit (which of course includes the experiences thereof)—at the very least we need to consider the possibility that the therapist (as a catalyst of behaviour) could actually cause further harm. The concepts of anti-psychiatry (e.g. Cooper, 1967; Foucault, 1973), overdiagnosis (e.g. Coon et al., 2014), and pathologization (e.g. Brinkman, 2016) are broadly relevant here. Although none suggest that repression is desirable, they all point to the possibility of a countervailing force. Potentially, at least, there is a disconnect between a shared sociocultural discourse (however noble it may be) and the highly personal psychological manoeuvrings demanded of an individual to process a traumatic experience.

By way of a (nonpsychological) example, suppose your nephew has just failed his driving test. It is tempting to offer your commiserations and make a bit of fuss of cheering him up. But is this necessarily what he wants? He'll more than likely be pissed off that he failed and, although your intentions are no doubt good, you are—in effect—drawing attention back to this negative experience. On your part, then, it is a backward-looking rather than a forward-looking gesture. Arguably, a more efficacious and disarming means by which to offer your support is to briefly and sincerely acknowledge the incident, before swiftly directing his attention elsewhere. This is not to make light of the experience but to enable him to recognize the salience of a broader context. Now, while the failed driving test example won't have much traction in discussions of psychology, we can at least speculate on how something similar may well play out in a comparable (albeit, significantly more serious) psychological situation.

Such is the controversial nature of this next example, readers are urged to approach it tentatively and with due sensitivity. For the purposes of prising open the analytical potential of paradox, I am assuming the unenviable position of Devil's advocate. In an analogous vein, then, something similar might be said of the dispensation of regard towards victims of, say, sexual predation. This is controversial, and it is something that I grappled with in the early drafts of this book, but there is—I think—an argument that a climate which reinforces the tragedy of abuse might actually aggravate the subjective experience of that abuse. Indeed, this is of course precisely what discourse analysts argue more generally about public opinion; our voices and weight of opinion co-construct the reality around us. While this is in no way intended to make light of what are undeniably horrific experiences or discredit conventional talking therapies, it may be that we can become so all-consumed by particular ideas—in this case that sexual assault is a heinous crime—that some victims might actually find it more difficult to recover psychologically because they are perpetually bombarded with messages that sexual assault is a heinous crime. While backpacking in Australia in the late 2000s, I recall press coverage about child abuse in aboriginal communities. While, on the one hand, Australian authorities were keen to address decades of imperial oppression by reinstating the rights of self-determination to indigenous communities, on the other, they expressed concern at what was apparently widespread incidence of sexual relations between male elders and ostensibly underage girls in these communities, many of whom live in very isolated parts of inland Australia. From what I could gather, the indigenous communities were arguing that such relations were a long-established part of their culture and tradition and—as far as they could see—caused no problems. They felt that the age of consent advanced by the white settler community was arbitrary, unrelated to the body's biology and constituted yet another form of imperial oppression. Of course, I would imagine the male elders had more of say as regards what's considered part of their culture/tradition than did the girls. A tricky one—but that of course is the point. In any event, hypothetically at least, victims of sexual assault may actually suffer more in a subjective sense if they grow up in countries or cultures where such abuse is perpetually vilified in the public discourse (because they grow up acutely aware that something horrific has happened to them). In cultures where the significance of such abuse is not recognized or downplayed, victims might focus their attention elsewhere, and perhaps on aspects of their lives with a firmer forward-looking orientation. In a very recent piece of research about child sexual abuse, Howells (2022) consciously and deliberately shifts the nomenclature used to describe those who have experienced abuse from 'victim' to 'survivor'. This apparently minor semantic gesture assists, at least in part, with a broader transition from backward-looking to forward-looking attitudes, as well helping to preclude the possibility of the individuals in question developing a troubled identity underscored by victimhood. And interestingly, in her celebrated novel, *Oryx and Crake* (2003), Margaret Atwood's characterization of Oryx, a young girl viewed and lusted after by the novel's protagonist, Snowman, feels aggravated by the latter's preoccupation with the pathological casting of her early—and ostensibly tragic—experiences of abuse. We might call this extremely controversial idea a *paradox of support*.

The works of both Lacan and Jung, too, are a rich source of the paradoxical. Lacan rejects the idea of an autonomous unitary Self, in favour of a subject mediated by the pre-existing world of the Other, or as Bowie (1979: 135) says: 'The subject is made and re-made in his [sic] encounter with the Other'. Carl Jung's work is relevant in terms of paradox, in at least three respects. First, Jung contended that any dimension of human behaviour can also be expressed in its opposite form (see, e.g. Harvey, 1988). Second, Jung argued that what he referred to as collective consciousness is determined by recurring primordial behaviour over the course of an unfolding history. In this sense, Jung was fascinated with the occult, religion, and parapsychology, not because he felt there was merit to their specific ontologies, but because their very existence as cultural artefacts reveals so much about humankind and its predispositions. As such, any attempt to educate ourselves out of these artefacts is likely to be existentially troubling; hence Jung implies what we might describe as a *paradox of education*. Ignorance, as the trite saying goes, may well turn out to be bliss. Finally, Jung's conception of archetypes is fruitful in discussions of paradox, particularly in terms of the ego component and its counterpoints, anima and animus (as vital aspects of the collective unconscious). In my role as a father of a young child, the archetype that currently interests me most is that of the monster. Although not one of the archetypes Jung explicitly tackles, it is arresting in terms of paradox. The infantile preoccupation with monsters, it seems, transcends culture. Children are concurrently scared of—but perversely fascinated by—monsters. For Christie (2020: 2) this fascination serves a vital practical purpose: 'children commonly use this fear as the foundation upon which to develop their bravery in order to confront their monster in later childhood, or later life'.

Professional practise. The practise of both psychiatry and psychology hinges on a peculiar tension. In the case of the former, where drug-based intervention prevails, there exists what I refer to as the paradox of psychiatric drugs (many of which initially exacerbate underlying conditions before ultimately improving them; drugs known as Selective Serotonin Reuptake Inhibitors are a good example). I have first-hand experience of precisely this. I was prescribed numerous antidepressants in the early 2000s, all of which elicited conflicting experiences. The drug Fluoxetine was especially discordant: the first few weeks were marred by discombobulation and truly terrifying dreams until one morning I woke up to an all-consuming sense of warmth and well-being. In the case of the latter, where non-drug-based intervention prevails, this tension is often referred to as paradoxical intention (the accepted wisdom that for a therapist to treat anxiety, the client is encouraged to engage in the anxiety-inducing thought patterns or behaviour as a means of—ultimately—improving them, known colloquially as 'facing one's fears'). My mother-in-law's recent experience of cognitive behavioural therapy to treat her anxiety revealed precisely this. She noted that a core principle of the therapy is to worry deliberately. To this end, the client is asked to record their worries in a notebook (or 'worry box') where they are stored until such time as there is an appropriate opportunity to confront them. She found that the very process of identifying and recording her worries this way significantly exacerbated her feelings of anxiety. However, she explained that ultimately the therapy was beneficial. These tensions are explored in more detail in Chapter 8 as part of a broader exploration of the paradoxical dynamic between pleasure and pain.

Self. One of the most pervasive paradoxes inherent to discussions that take place among curious social scientists is that which centres on the question of individuality. Political philosopher Isaiah Berlin reveals a sense of naivety when he makes the following declaration: 'I wish my life and decisions to depend on myself, not on external forces of whatever kind' (Berlin, 1958: 131). Although perfectly reasonable—and indeed compelling—at first glance, Berlin overlooks the complexity inherent to the dynamics of agency, autonomy, and identity. Upon closer scrutiny, we are compelled to conclude that each of us is inescapably dependent on others to determine our own sense of 'self' and—by implication—our sense of agency and independence. Paradoxically, individuality can only be achieved in relation to others. This is something Knights and Willmott (2002: 62) recognize:

It is difficult to imagine how the construction of Berlin's sovereign self is possible without engaging the 'forces' that he would regard as 'external'. Thinking and willing, whether in respect of 'autonomy' or anything else, is learned and developed through processes of interaction within traditions of thought through practices of will formation in which 'subjects' are participants, not observers or consumers. The very process of self-identification as a subject who is differentiated from its 'object' is a social process. The practices—of thinking, willing, choosing, bearing responsibility, etc.—to which Berlin attributes 'autonomy' are socially embedded or situated; they are not, in our view, plausibly conceptualized as the manifestations or possessions of a sovereign, cognitive being.

This paradoxical dynamic between individual and collective identity has fascinated a wide range of contributors including Bowie (1979), Dixon (1980: 24), Eco (2001), Handy (1994: 41), Keen (1982: 116), (Rieff (1959, 1966), Solomon (2004: 1023), Toffler (1970: 292), and Wachtel (1989: 198). Perspective is crucial here. In her reflection on Rousseau's work, for example, Einspahr (2010) stresses that each of us needs an alternative perspective to come to the realization that they are a 'self'. She thus affords us a more exacting interpretation of Rousseau's infamous remark in *The Social Contract*, itself a rich source of the paradoxical: 'Man is born free, and everywhere he [sic] is in chains. Those who think themselves the masters of others are indeed greater slaves than they' (Rousseau [1762] 1998: 5). A century later Kierkegaard further advanced this line of thought implying an evident paradox between the individual and the collective. As Robinson and Zarate (2006: 30, 56) comment:

> [For Kierkegaard] the individual is not a real person unless related to other persons. [...] He who lives ethically expresses the universal in his life. It is only by being part of a community that one can become fully realised as a human being.

Drawing on research by Ricoeur (1992, 2005), Wallace (2002), and Pellauer (2007), Larsen (2020: 110–111) examines this tension and its reciprocal character:

> It is only through being recognised by others that we understand and thereby recognise ourselves. And others recognise themselves only through our recognition of them. Recognition involves particular people realising themselves through and with the other [...] We can never fully understand or account for ourselves, though. The self will always be, at least partly, 'other' to itself because we do not have full access to how we have been formed by others. [...] [I]dentity is [thus] experienced as a dialectic between sameness and otherness.

As Larsen implies, then, the concept of 'self-as-other' is fundamentally paradoxical. And—perhaps unsurprisingly—this tension between self and other transcends individual psychology. For example, it has broader traction when reflecting on group behaviour. In *The Human Swarm*, Moffett (2019) illustrates this idea by explaining that our sense of personal security and certainty is strongest when we belong to a group perceived as distinct from outsiders. Moffett goes on to provide an extraordinary example. He notes that 'Native Australians became Aborigines and developed a sense of otherness and self-awareness as a race *only after Europeans populated Australia*' (ibid.: 122, emphasis added). It seems, therefore, that a sense of togetherness only emerges when an identifiable 'other' presents itself. Moffett proposes a rule: the more societies interact with different competitors, the greater the number, complexity, and conspicuousness of the identity markers they display (ibid.: 184).

Let us now consider an application of this paradox with which many of us will be familiar. According to celebrated sociologist Georg Simmel (1904), it is the interaction between individual and collective drives that underpins human behaviour in respect of fashion. His central thesis was summarized a century later by Benvenuto (2000) who notes that fashion (i.e. 'non-cumulative change in cultural features') derives from a basic tension specific to the social condition of the human being. On the one hand, each of us has a tendency to imitate others. On the other, we each also have a tendency to distinguish ourselves from others. Undoubtedly, some of us tend more towards imitation (and thus to conformism) while others tend to distinction (and thus to eccentricity and dissidence), but fashion's flux needs both of these contradictory tendencies in order to work. In short, Simmel argues, we are compelled to postulate two contradictory radical drives, each of which is inherent to the human condition.

Finally, upon immersing herself in the discipline, the perceptive psychology student quickly realizes that there is a separate paradox related to the paradox of other. This we can refer to as *the paradox of cognitive dissonance.* Reflecting on Durkheim's work, Šubrt (2019: 118) notes that 'human beings are dual and internally contradictory; they are antagonistic units of individual egoism and internalised social regulators of action'. This contradiction is described as cognitive dissonance, that is, the ability to endure contradictory information without 'powering down' or 'crashing'. For Harari (2014), tensions, conflicts, and irresolvable dilemmas are the spice of every culture. A human being, he insists, must hold contradictory beliefs and be riven by incompatible values.

> Cognitive dissonance is often considered a failure of the human psyche. In fact, it is a vital asset. Had people been unable to hold contradictory beliefs and values, it would probably have been impossible to establish and maintain any human culture.
>
> *(ibid.: 184)*

Quite simply, it seems, contradictions create cultures. This of course hints at a deeper ontological paradox between agency and structure, which we go on to explore in Chapter 9.

Dependency. Related to—but distinct from—paradoxes of self is what I describe as *the paradox of dependency.* As we grow up, Homans (1988) argues, we strive for an ever higher degree of separateness, individuality, and autonomous self-regulation. Crucially, however, it is this very autonomy that demands a long period of dependency upon authorities, including of course our parents.

> At the psychological heart of all family life is a paradox so obvious that its mere mention may well appear gratuitous; but this paradox, which is as profound in psychological resonance as it is simple, sometimes escapes unnoticed. I call this paradox 'the psychological core' of family life and also of the situation comedy. The family is the child's first social setting and in it occurs the life-long struggle between two fundamental modes of inner, psychological organization—autonomy and dependency.
>
> *(ibid.: 111)*

The thorny question is how autonomy can grow from its logical and psychological opposite, dependency, for that is precisely what does happen over and over again. It is at this point that we usher in another aspect of dependency, which I describe as the *paradox of voluntarism*. In a similar vein to that explored earlier as part of our discussion of political theory, Salancik (1977: 6–7) makes the following observation in respect of commitment.

> One of the simplest ways to commit yourself to a course of action is to go around telling all your friends that you are definitely going to do something. You will find yourself bound by your own statements. The same commitment will not develop from proclamations to strangers you meet on trains. The publicity of one's action places the action in a social context which is more or less binding and, as we shall describe, contributes to directing the effect of those behaviors on subsequent behaviors.

Crucially, our determination to act in a particular way in certain instances only comes about through the validation of others; we thus become dependent on others to animate our own convictions. Our compulsion to act autonomously (voluntarism) is thus determined by others. Salancik goes on to draw attention to another aspect of this idea, suggesting that people become what it is they do:

> [Another] simple truth ... is that people become what they do. When people behave certain ways, they develop conceptions of themselves which are consistent with their behavior. A person who helps another sees himself as a benefactor and a humanitarian. A President who has impressive papers placed in front of him for signing comes in time to see himself as an important person.
>
> *(ibid.: 22)*

This very behaviour (which Salancik describes as 'cognitive consistency') is plain to see in Philip Zimbardo's infamous prison experiment (Haney et al., 1973; Zimbardo, 1991). Philip George Zimbardo is an American psychologist and Professor Emeritus at Stanford University. He is known best for the *Stanford Prison Experiment* (in which he demonstrated that our sense of personhood actually changes when randomly assigned a particular role) and *The Lucifer Effect* (in which he sought to explain how 'good' people can do 'bad' things). Whereas we might logically assume that behaviour precedes role, Zimbardo's social experiment was the first to demonstrate—unequivocally—that it is all-too-often the other way round, i.e. if somebody is furnished with the markers (e.g. attire, uniform, equipment, etc.) of a particular role, identity, or occupation, the behaviour we associate with that role will almost certainly follow. In Zimbardo's experiment, although participants were allocated either the role of prisoner or of prison guard at random, both sets of participants very quickly adopted the expected behaviour of each (authoritarian, in the case of the prison guards; submissive in the case of the prisoners).

Anxiety. In the UK, in recent years there has been a determined campaign to raise awareness about mental health problems. Both depression and anxiety, we are told, have been suffered by many for too long in silence. To defeat them, we need to talk about them. But is there a *productive* side to mental ill health? For Dostoevsky, Nietzsche, and the Manic Street Preachers (all of who we met briefly in Chapter 2) this seems beyond doubt. I'm not entirely convinced all would agree (certainly, my own experience of mental illness in my 20s and 30s was deeply unpleasant). Nevertheless, this should not suggest that there may be an all-too-often overlooked silver lining to these conditions. Is it mere coincidence that brilliant minds are so often plagued by mental illness? In her book, *Creative and psychotic states in exception people*, Magagna (2015) pieces together the unpublished work of the late psychiatrist Murray Jackson to explore the constructive impact of psychosis in four remarkable individuals: mathematician John Nash, ballet dancer Vaslav Nijinsky, novelist José Saramago, and artist Vincent van Gogh. The insights are extraordinary. More recently still, the BBC ran a piece on the celebrated artist Edvard Munch which revealed a similar inclination.

> For as long as I can remember I have suffered from a deep feeling of anxiety which I have tried to express in my art. Without this anxiety and illness I would have been like a ship without a rudder.
>
> *(Munch, cited in BBC, 2021a)*

Intimacy. Couples therapist Esther Perel refers to what we can describe as a *paradox of intimacy*. For my own part, I have long felt a tension between sexual desire on the one hand, and the widely shared societal expectation of monogamy on the other. I had always assumed this was part and parcel of the sense of guilt cultivated by my Catholic education. The Immaculate Conception is immaculate, we were instructed, precisely because it involved no intercourse. The problem, as I saw it, was that love and eroticism were mutually exclusive, i.e. sex was dirty; love wasn't. As I've matured I've realized that this tension is far from peculiar to those unfortunate enough to have been educated by the Catholics. During the research for this book, my wife, a clinical psychologist, suggested that I read Perel's work. Perel writes about intimacy, sexual desire, and eroticism in the context of long-term stable and committed relationships, and discusses the challenges of retaining desire and separateness whilst also creating stability, security, and care for one another. In short, she speaks to the tension between egalitarianism and eroticism:

> The belief in democracy, equality, consensus building, compromise, fairness, and mutual tolerance can when carried too punctiliously into the bedroom, result in very boring sex. Sexual desire and good citizenship don't play by the same rules. American men and women, shaped by the feminist movement often find themselves challenged by these contradictions.
>
> *(Perel, 2007: 55–57)*

Emotion. We conclude this discussion of paradox in psychology with a cursory mention of what we can legitimately label *the paradox of emotion*. This paradox calls attention to the fundamental incommensurability between the experience of emotion and the study thereof. Academic commentary aside, we turn once again to television sitcom, *The Big Bang Theory*, for a playful illustration of this final psychological paradox:

Sheldon: Let me see if I understand this correctly. Her missing you is an emotional state you find desirable?
Leonard: Yes, obviously.
Sheldon: All right. Well, given that missing you is predicated on you leaving, logic dictates you must leave.

> *(The Big Bang Theory, Series 2, Episode 23:*
> *The Monopolar Expedition)*

Homo sociologicus

A second incident from the aforementioned backpacking trip in Australia is worth sharing. I had been travelling for a few weeks, and had just arrived in Alice Springs. It had been a long bus trip, and I was in need of refreshment. I bought a coffee and copy of *The Age* newspaper, and then headed towards a local park to settle down. En route, I passed an Aboriginal Australian man walking in the opposite direction. As he passed me, he said, under his breath, 'ya white cunt'. He was, of course, quite right. Despite my best efforts, I am probably both those things. But the question that irks me is why he said these specific words. Was it, quite simply, because I was white? Or—perhaps he took cues from some subtler clues. I had a copy of *The Age* newspaper under my arm, a liberal rag, akin to *The New York Times* or *The Guardian*. I was also holding a cappuccino and heading to a park in search of soaking up—rather than finding shelter from—the morning sunshine. These signs almost certainly painted a picture of privileged apologetic metropolitan. Is there anything more abhorrent?

For Šubrt (2019: 77), 'sociology [only] gets interesting and becomes useful when uncovering and analysing the unintended or unplanned side of things'. By far the most pervasive paradox that is normally—but by no means exclusively—explored within the realm of sociology is that concerning the agency/structure conundrum. However, this constitutes our overarching concern in Chapter 9. In the present discussion, then, I restrict coverage to sociological paradoxes distinct from that one. We begin with a brief discussion of what I refer to as *paradoxes of proximity*, before going on to consider some extraordinarily controversial *paradoxes of diversity*. These include contradictions inherent to discussions of feminism, racism, minority representation, cultural nuance, and genocide.

Proximity. My ongoing research has revealed a pervasive—and yet routinely overlooked—paradox in the field of sociology: *the paradox of proximity*. In *Civilization and its discontents*, Freud makes the following observation:

> [I]t is precisely [those] communities with adjoining territories, and related to each other in other ways as well, who are engaged in constant feuds and in ridiculing each other—like the Spaniards and the Portuguese, for instance, the North Germans and South Germans, the English and Scotch, and so on. I gave this phenomenon the name of the narcissism of minor differences.
>
> *(Freud [1930] 1991: 305)*

This tension plays out the world over. Consider the rivalry between Finland and Sweden, between Canada and the United States, between Morocco and Tunisia, or between Australia and New Zealand. And—of course—think about enmity between specific sports teams. Derby matches are those sports competitions between rival teams from the same area or city—and they tend to be the most competitive. The paradox of proximity can also be understood in terms of demographic strata more generally. Think about social class. It is frequently—but mistakenly—assumed that the most vehement rivalries exist *between* classes (this is certainly the sentiment that Marx and his followers have advanced), and yet—in practice—the most fervent rivalries exist *within* specific classes. A classic case in the United Kingdom concerns the middle classes. This stratum encompasses both *The Guardian* readers and *Daily Mail* readers, who maintain mutual—and far-reaching—disdain for one another. Yet another way of approaching this tension is courtesy of Granovetter's theory of the *strength of weak ties*: it is those associates we know least well that move in social circles and professional networks distinct from our own that represent the best networking opportunities.

Diversity. A critical assessment of progressive sociological sentiment reveals some more controversial paradoxes. These include, in particular, *the paradox of feminism.* As feminism advances, does it—paradoxically—disadvantage some of the most marginalized women? As Lois from the animated American sitcom *Family Guy* quips, 'I'm all for equality, but if you ask me, feminism is about choice. I choose to be a wife and mother—and now I'm choosing to end this conversation' (*Family Guy*, Season 2, Episode 8: "I Am Peter, Hear Me Roar"). Growing up I distinctly recall one of my aunties defending her identity as a homemaker over a family meal in which some of the younger members of the tribe were championing the conventional feminist cause. I can't recall the exact words my auntie used, but it went along the following lines: 'Hang on a minute. I enjoy being a homemaker. Feminists make me feel as though my role—as homemaker—is something I should feel ashamed of. That's not fair'! Approached differently, Harari (2014: 178) asks us the following question: 'If … the patriarchal system has been based on unfounded myths rather than on biological facts, what accounts for the universality and stability of this system'? I'm not entirely sure I agree with Harari that patriarchy is either universal or stable, but his broader point ought not to be overlooked: will biology necessarily yield to all-too-ephemeral cultural sensibilities?

And does paradox play a role in discussions of racism? This is an especially difficult discussion to have, not least of course because racist sentiment has underpinned all sorts of abhorrent human behaviour. For Moffett (2019), however, it is important not to overlook the anthropological purpose of ethnocentric tendencies. He notes, for example, that '[e]vidence suggests that learning markers and using them to categorize people, places, and things is instinctive—organized in advance of experience' and that '[e]ven a three-month-old hones in on faces of its own race' (ibid.: 191). But more extraordinary still, he regales us with a story about Alex Todorov who he describes an exuberant Bulgarian from Princeton University:

> [Todorov] has shown that a face glimpsed at for a tenth of a second, a span of time too short to enter our awareness, is subconsciously assessed in terms of the person's emotional state, sex, race, and ethnicity and society too. Our nimbleness with markers must reduce our cognitive load—the conscious effort we expend.
>
> *(ibid.: 199)*

Moreover, it seems that drawing attention to our prejudices can have unintended consequences. Of this, Moffett (2019: 208) says, '[a]ttempts to suppress our own negative views can backfire through a "don't think of an elephant" effect, where we end up thinking of something—such as an elephant—even more after we try to force our attention on something else'. Ironically, he suggests, this occurs because the energy we burn in attempting to circumvent stereotypes can wear us out, with the result that we can slip up and in so doing exhibit even less desirable behaviour. It would be truly exhausting—in a cognitive sense—to be genuinely racially inclusive. This is because of what is known as decision fatigue (see, e.g. Pignatiello et al., 2020). Clearly, we need to expend some effort getting to know individuals but—equally—we do not want to fall victim to the psychological damage caused by evaluation overload. Our brains have finite capacity which is, of course, why we are required to make generalizations. And let us not forget: ours is a world based on generalizations, otherwise known as science.

Related to both paradoxes of feminism and racism is what I refer to as *the paradox of minority representation.* In his highly influential text, *The Disuniting of America: Reflections on a Multicultural Society,* historian and social critic Arthur M. Schlesinger (1991) argues that the liberal rhetoric of diversity and multiculturalism reinforces separatism and in so doing undermines the metaphorical 'melting pot'. In this way, minority groups are paradoxically further marginalized from becoming part of (and contributing to) an integrated community. We can conceptualize this as part of a broader *paradox of progressive thought.* As part of my evolving role at the University of Suffolk, I became pivotal in brokering relations with universities in Indonesia. In my discussions at Ciputra University in Surabuya, following one of my guest lectures in which I sought to champion diversity in organizations, one of the Indonesian faculty approached me. She explained to me that trying to encourage Indonesians to accept LGBTQ+ lifestyles was difficult because marrying and starting a family is seen as a responsibility to the community in Indonesian cultures, whereas—she noted—it is seen as a choice in the West. This struck me as interesting. Presented this way, LGBTQ+ cultures are, in effect, an articulation of free market choice. This of course means they exhibit a bias towards prioritizing the individual, as opposed to the collective, as the primary unit for analysis. Such a bias is immanent to the practice of psychology and has, notably, been subject to comprehensive critique (see, e.g. Carrette, 2007). Interestingly, I suspect most advocates of critical theory would probably side with LGBTQ+ causes while at the same time express concern at the encroachment of the ideology of the free market into social domains. Were critical theorists aware of this tension, I pondered, as I returned that evening to my hotel in Jakarta.

Yet another way of exploring tensions inherent to discussions of diversity is by recourse to what I refer to as *the cultural nuance paradox.* As academics we urge our students to acknowledge the socially constructed nature of our lives and in so doing enable them to see how short-sighted many of our deep-seated convictions really are. And yet, at the same time, we actively encourage them to recognize and respect the salience of community, culture, and a sense of belonging. The tension here, then, is that in acknowledging the socially constructed nature of our beliefs we end up undermining or betraying our own culture. This is, perhaps, a derivative manifestation of the tension between attachment and transcendence. Approached from an even broader perspective, the concept of globalization reveals a further tension vis-à-vis diversity. Hirsch et al. (2013: 232), for example, question whether globalization leads to an increase or decrease in consensus over cultural symbols. This, they say, is 'the most intriguing aspect of globalization' (ibid.). They point to the fact that some authors (e.g. Hamelink, 1994; Latouche, 1995) have argued that globalization leads to increased homogeneity, while others (e.g. Featherstone et al., 1995) have argued that diversity actually increases in the wake of globalizing tendencies.

> In the twenty-first century, we are currently witnessing vigorous debates about whether the spread of common symbols and cultures across nations contributes to their unification and solidarity or to the loss and isolation of particular regions', nations', and ethnicities' distinctive identities. The growing universality of media formats, including TV news and entertainments, restaurant specialties, and clothing styles support the view that people across nations participate in an increasingly global popular culture. Are the artisans and other representatives of local traditions being eclipsed and downgraded by these developments? Or is the common appreciation of the same music, movies, and other global icons uniting people across cultures, promoting solidarity, and reducing anomie?
>
> *(ibid.: 240–241)*

For their part, Hirsch et al. do not subscribe to the suggestion that globalization will eventually lead to a universally shared culture. However, they do concede that the global spread of certain cultural forms facilitates increased levels of interaction due to shared values and vocabularies. But, of course, increased levels of interaction can be both beneficial (in terms of developing mutual understanding) and detrimental (in terms of reinforcing prejudice or a heightened sense of existential threat). Seemingly, then, globalization represents a very wide-angle macrosociological 'experiment' that puts our paradox hypothesis to the test. And, yes, even here paradox prevails.

Finally, and most controversial of all, discussions of diversity might also include what I tentatively describe as a *paradox of genocide*. Here we invoke the contribution of the late Polish sociologist Zygmunt Bauman. For Bauman, the oppressed (in this case, the *Judenrat*) unwittingly become co-conspirators in their own destruction during World War II:

> Paradoxically ... the situation of the Jews during the preliminary stages of the Final Solution was more akin to that experienced by a subordinate group within a normal power structure, than by the victims of an 'ordinary' genocidal operation. To some remarkable extent, the Jews were

part of the social arrangement which was to destroy them. They provided a vital link in the chain of co-ordinated actions; their own actions were an indispensable part of the total operation and a crucial condition of its success. 'Ordinary' genocide splits the actors unambiguously into the murderers and the murdered; for the latter, resistance is the only rational response. In the Holocaust, divisions were less clear. Incorporated in the overall power structure, given an extended set of tasks and functions within it, the doomed population had apparently a range of options to choose from. Cooperation with their sworn enemies and future killers was not without its own measure of rationality. The Jews could therefore play into the hands of their oppressors, facilitate their task, bring closer their own perdition, while guided in their action by the rationally interpreted purpose of survival. Because of this paradox, the Holocaust records offer a unique insight into the general principles of bureaucratically administered oppression.

(Bauman, 1989: 122)

This is an especially troubling insight, and not least because it has the potential to be co-opted, misrepresented, and then championed by rabid anti-Semitic supremacists. Paradoxical thinking, it seems, demands a formidable responsibility and acute sense of curatorship.

Postlude

Like the arts, then, societal relations are underscored by paradox. Our coverage has of course been restricted to the principal disciplines in the social sciences: politics, economics, psychology, and sociology. However, a glance at advanced research sensitive to complexity in adjacent fields mirrors the same predisposition to paradox—for example, anthropology (e.g. de Castro, 2011; De Carolis, 2018; Schippers, 2013), geography (e.g. Oakes, 1997; Longhurst, 2006; Minca, 2007), and history (e.g. Cohen, 2014; Hoffer, 2008; Ten Dyke, [2001] 2014). Stirred—and doubtless unsettled—by these observations vis-à-vis society, in the next chapter we train our attention on the prevalence of paradox in organizational life more specifically.

4
PARADOX AND ORGANIZATION

The study of organization is of course a social scientific endeavour. However, and unlike the more traditional areas of social science explored in Chapter 3, organization studies (and the related discipline of management science) are consciously multidisciplinary; that is, they build upon both empirical and theoretical advances from those more traditional quarters but do so with a distinct conceptual visage. This multidisciplinary heritage means the study of organization is inevitably rather challenging. Ever the sage, Charles Handy passes the following comment in respect of his—and my—native field:

> We used to think we knew how to run organisations. Now we know better. More than ever they need to be global and local at the same time, to be small in some ways but big in others, to be centralised some of the time and decentralised most of it. They expect their workers to be both more autonomous and more of a team, their managers to be more delegating and more controlling.
>
> *(Handy, 1994: 37–38)*

Suffice it to say, organizational life is staggeringly complex. Moreover, and unlike comparable units of analysis such as, say, 'society' or 'culture' (over which few would dare to suggest they comprehend in full technicolour), there remains a stubborn insistence on the part of both practitioners and many academics that organizational life *can* be understood and controlled. Nothing could be further from the truth. As will become clear, paradox is endemic to organizational life (see, e.g. Mowles et al., 2015). Even the very semantics reflect this. As Cooper and Law (1995: 240) note, dictionary definitions marshal organization both as 'the state of being organized'

DOI: 10.4324/9781003203339-5

and 'the act of organizing'. The first definition tells us that organization is an effect, while the second suggests it is an active process of organizing that has not yet solidified into an effect. This is important when exploring and critiquing the linear logic associated with cause and effect (one of our objectives for Chapter 6).

This chapter is configured around four broad areas of organizational paradox. These are *control* (including paradoxes of bureaucracy, structure, and leadership), *performance* (including paradoxes of success and commitment), *group dynamics* (including paradoxes of group composition, consensus, and organizational identity), and *operations* (including paradoxes of quality, risk, and technological interaction).

Control

Control is the cornerstone of classical management theory. Etymologically, the word management traces its origins to the 1500s, in particular, to the Italian word maneggiare, which implies 'to control' and is used especially in respect of the control of horses. The rather ominous assumption here, of course, is that if we can control a horse, we can control a human being. Yet, and as we shall see, there is an incontrovertible propensity for increased levels of control to yield increased levels of resistance. This is something we are all intuitively—though not always consciously—aware of. Indeed, it is something we all too often forget, sometimes at great expense.

> By overemphasising the duties and the rules of the core, organisations unintentionally breed distrust ... Obsessed by the need to control, organisations create self-fulfilling prophecies when their people find the only way to be independent is to break the rules. My children learnt to smoke because the schools they went to made non-smoking a rule. They justified the rule with all the lessons about the dangers of nicotine, but the implicit message was, 'We don't believe that you will heed these warnings so we will make it a core obligation'. Such a denial of responsibility made it legitimate, in the eyes of the students, to ignore the rule. Smoking became a symbol of free choice, a personal space.
>
> *(Handy, 1994: 79)*

The more organizations seek to control something, the greater the propensity for resistance. There are echoes here of Newton's Law of Politics, encountered in Chapter 3. However, it is in Streatfield's work from 2001 that the nail is hit squarely on the head:

> Business leaders are expected to be in control of the situation in which their businesses find themselves. But how can organizational leaders and

managers control matters entirely out of their hands; such as the next action a competitor takes, or the next law a government may pass?

(Streatfield, 2001: ii)

As I stress to my MBA students, effective management is at heart not a science but a duplicitous art. In any event, as soon as we try to control that which cannot be controlled, we become an incredibly anxiety-prone society (see, e.g. Biroc, 2008). This presents what we might label, alliteratively, a *control conundrum*, or, in our preferred vocabulary, a *control paradox*. From this generic control paradox, we can identify multiple permutations. The first of these is found in relation to the much derided—but frequently misrepresented—concept of bureaucracy.

Bureaucracy. I have published previously on complexity in relation to bureaucracy (see Vine, 2018c, 2021) and do not plan to rehearse the detail advanced in those texts. Nonetheless, for the purposes of this current discussion, I have gleaned—and summarized—the relevant paradoxes. The first of these is one of (and arguably the most important) species of the broader *paradox of unanticipated consequences*.

This paradox emerges via the contradiction of how a large and powerful bureaucracy, a necessary component of the administrative means of the nation-state or any organization, will itself become a force of such dominance that it threatens the very aim of that state or organization.

(Symonds & Pudsey, 2008: 235)

In a similar vein, Clegg et al. (2016: 72) ask how we might restructure unwieldy organizations without succumbing to the bureaucratic temptations of the audit society. The authors are unable to provide a clear response to this question because, candidly, such an end can only exist in hypothesis. From this very bind, I have advanced what I call, quite simply, *the paradox of bureaucracy*. In the aforementioned publications (Vine, 2018c, 2021), I suggested that organizational problems are both created *and* purportedly solved by an appeal to greater proceduralization. I arrived at this conclusion by a combination of events, notably from a re-reading of March and Simon's ([1958] 1984) 'The dysfunctions of bureaucracy', and then reflecting on my own organizational experience. When exploring this with my students, I sketch a basic diagram on the whiteboard to help illustrate the paradox (see Figure 4.1.).

Suppose rectangle 'A' represents the scale of your operational procedures. All is going well. Then one day, one of your clients discovers a problem. The problem is one you've yet to encounter, and your operational procedures are not set up to detect it. The solution? You incorporate a check into your

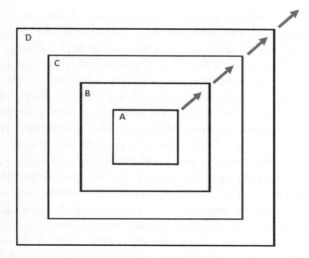

FIGURE 4.1   The Paradox of Bureaucracy.

procedures to detect this problem, should it arise again in the future. Your system expands accordingly, and is now represented by 'B'. All goes well from here for a few weeks. And then another client reports another problem. Again, it was unanticipated and your procedures are not set up to detect it. The solution? Once again, you incorporate another check into your procedures so as to detect it, should it arise again in the future. Your system expands accordingly, and is now represented by 'C'. All goes well again, for another few weeks. But then, yet another problem! And so the cycle continues. I would bet what little hair I have left that most of us are familiar with this bind. Over time, our bureaucracies slowly expand to incorporate additional system checks to remedy unanticipated problems. The unforeseen difficulty, however, is twofold. First, despite what we might like to think, this expansion will continue perpetually; we will never create a perfect, foolproof system. This is of course because we inhabit a world underscored by perpetual change. Second, the expansion of the system (or bureaucracy) compounds the problem. As it grows larger and larger we place more and more faith in it to deliver in the face of uncertainty. We become *reliant* on the system to such an extent that we grow complacent. Counterintuitively, then, if we really want to minimize the chances of our clients experiencing problems we are probably better off dispensing with the procedures altogether and addressing client needs on an *ad hoc* basis. Of course, in practise, this approach would most likely fail to gain commercial traction because we'd be unable to secure economies of scale. We are therefore compelled to engage in the ever-expanding system we call bureaucracy.

While this portrayal of bureaucracy as a manifestation of the paradox of unintended consequences draws attention to a negative aspect of the phenomenon, other paradoxes reveal greater potential. Consider, for example, what I call *the paradox of bureaucratic flexibility*. Paradoxically, bureaucracy becomes imperative in the emergent, dynamic world in which we so often claim to reside. Bureaucracy is vital when faced with uncertainty. Karreman et al. (2002: 87–88, cited in Styhre, 2007: 99) argue that since complex environments produce situations wherein ambiguity and uncertainty are endemic, to cope with these ambiguities bureaucratic procedures are enacted to provide a sense of closure, control, and predictability in organizations and work relations. We are used to associating non-bureaucratic networked management techniques with complex, evolving organizational environments. But it appears to be precisely the opposite that is warranted; bureaucracy is crucial if we are to successfully weather change and maintain a sense of existential stability in a dynamic, fast-changing environment. Is it any surprise, then, that supposedly post-bureaucratic organizational forms, while superficially appealing to a rhetoric of fluidity, actually retain the central practices of the bureaucratic form? As Willmott (2011: 75) notes, 'detailed regulations, record keeping and provision of information in standardized forms are crucial constitutive features of many ostensibly "post-bureaucratic" practices'.

Finally, it is worth considering the associated and potentially paradoxical argument that bureaucracy is flexible not in spite of its characteristics but precisely because of them. As Kallinkos (2004: 23) notes:

> Despite its common sense and, to a certain degree, justified associations with rigid and inflexible behaviour, bureaucracy is the first and perhaps sole organizational form capable of addressing the demands that incessant social, economic, and technological change induces ... [T]he organizational involvement of individuals qua roles implies the dissociation of the process of organising from the emotional and cognitive complexity of agent qua persons. By contrast to persons, roles can be adapted, modified, redesigned, abandoned or reshuffled to address the emerging technical, social and economic demands the organization is facing.

For Styhre (2007: 168), large organizations are frequently assumed to adapt poorly to emergent conditions and new demands imposed by either new forms of competition or regulatory authorities. In fact, he suggests, it is quite the opposite. Large organizations have typically established a series of mechanisms for identifying such external changes and orchestrating responses to them. Of the examples Styhre invokes, there is no intrinsic bureaucratic logic that prevented action being taken. Instead the companies developed responses to deal with the new challenges. While small start-up businesses can capitalize on the *zeitgeist* and hit the ground running with a fresh commercial flavour, a few years on (and when the market shifts again) they have no experience of managing change. Compare this to the long-established firm. Although it is probably unable to compete with a start-up in terms of an emergent 'flavour of the month', it will almost certainly be in a stronger position when the market next changes (since it has experience of multiple changes). Ironically, then, it is the smaller, younger, and supposedly dynamic firm that has only every known 'one way of doing things' that is at the disadvantage.

Structure. We might also approach the dynamic between organization and control from the perspective of structure. Here I invoke several *paradoxes of organizational structure*. The study of organizational structure remains a core part of the curriculum on business degree programmes. Students are typically presented with different types of organizational structures (depicted as *organograms*) and urged to recognize and scribe to memory their relative strengths and weaknesses. Codswallop. Not only are such abstract renderings precisely that, but the more interesting if often overlooked aspect of organizational structure is its relationship with control. The 'tall' structure has been increasingly lambasted in recent decades as outdated and little more than a vessel via which authoritarian power can be administered with impunity. In rhetoric, at least, it has given way to the penchant for 'flatter' organizational structures in which there are fewer layers in the hierarchy. Such a configuration, it is suggested, improves communication and rids the organization of 'unnecessary bureaucracy'. But as we have already seen bureaucracy brings with it a vital sense of stability and existential reassurance. And we ought not to overlook the fact that its metaphorical dressing implies that 'organizational structure' has important edificial property. This is part of the reason why we might express concern at the so-called 'structureless' rhetoric that has underpinned recent commentary both within and beyond the academy. Here structure is seen as deadening, a relic of more bureaucratic times. Drawing on the work of Jo Freeman, one of the leading American feminists of the 1970s, Keith Grint pointedly reminds us that 'the consequence of structurelessness is not freedom from structure or authority (patriarchal or any other variety) but a shift from formal to informal structure—with all the potential for tyranny that informal groups and militant sects can muster' (Grint, 2010: 115). And if structure is characterized by paradox, might we say the same for routine? As a condition of joining an organization, Jackson and Carter (1985: 22) argue that the individual surrenders discretion over the structure of his or her time.

The first characteristic our worker needs, then, is the desire to have his life ordered by some authority figure—the recreation of the parent-child dyad, the organisation acting in loco parentis. The worker must adopt as his own the organisational structure of time that is already established. Typically, starting and finishing times, when breaks may be taken, hours per week etc.—i.e. in general, quantity of time—are determined by the organisation and nominated 'working time', in separation from and opposition to any other form of time.

(Jackson & Carter, 1985: 22)

This is relevant in terms of paradox because, on the one hand, we resent the nine-to-five grind, but on the other, we desire the sense of 'structure' it brings. Here then we posit a *paradox of routine*.

Inevitably, discussions of routine will eventually elicit concerns about repetition. As we have become ever more consumed by the neoliberal agenda in recent decades, there has been growing concern about the rise of the much derided 'McJob' and the deadening nature of repetitive, routine work. This, of course, stems back to early recognition about the existential threats posed to humankind by the repetition inherent to the division of labour, as outlined by Adam Smith in a rarely read part of *The Wealth of Nations* (see Chapter 3). On the one hand, we lambast contemporary employers for not doing more to offer interesting, creative work. On the other, perhaps there is something to be said for routine work? Consider, for a moment, what I have referred to as 'temping bliss' (see Vine, 2021). Could it be that we are today conditioned or perhaps even encouraged to embrace careers, change, and dynamism because this is what ostensibly 'successful' people are expected to do? A very good friend of mine launched a successful career as a nutritionist. Soon, however, it became apparent that many of her clients had needs that went far deeper than nutrition. They were plagued by mental illness and self-doubt—and began placing their faith in modifying their diet as a potential panacea. She felt torn. On the one hand, she welcomed the work and the income it generated. On the other, it became a thorny question of integrity. It also placed her in a very difficult position in which she was compelled to weigh up the rights of her clients to confidentiality with legislative concerns related to safeguarding. Ultimately, she withdrew from the work altogether and took a temporary contract as administrator for a local firm. She describes her new role as a delight. It is virtually free from stress and not badly paid. In any event, and practicalities aside, there is something deeper here, something that goes to the heart of the temping experience. As I have noted previously, 'It is no coincidence that so many hobbies (which are, of course, undertaken as a form of relaxation or escapism), follow a repetitive/routine logic: stamp collecting, bird-watching, knitting, model-making and so on' (Vine, 2021: 104). And it is at this point that we might consider Chandler's (2012) paper, 'Work as dance'. Controversially, Chandler makes a rare concession: that repetitive work *can* be desirable:

I have no wish to romanticize work, to ignore the degradation of labour ... or to argue that repetitive work produces pleasure as frequently as dance does. I do, however, want to suggest that this is at least a possibility—and that even degraded work might, by the very nature of its repetitiveness and rhythmic qualities, be experienced by those doing it as more or less pleasurable at times. At the very least we might be drawn along in work, and remember the distinction ... made between tedium and traction— with the opportunities for traction provided by repetitive, cyclical work providing a degree of satisfaction (or at least pseudo-satisfaction) as an alternative to tedium.

(Chandler, 2012: 9)

This sort of conclusion flies in the face of some much self-described 'critical literature'. In the case of my native discipline this is known as 'critical management studies', and takes its conceptual cues from Marx. It is rarely challenged. However, perhaps we ought to do precisely this. We critical scholars routinely take aim at capitalism for rendering modern work overly routinized and yet, in some cases, this is precisely that which is desired.

Hierarchy is another principal consideration vis-à-vis organizational structure. There are four paradoxes of hierarchy that demand our attention. Despite the prevalent analysis that represents the employment relationship as a rigid configuration between managers, on the one hand, and workers, on the other, such a division is difficult to sustain in practice. One reason for this is that in a hierarchical organization most employees exhibit characteristics of *both* manager and worker, although not at the same time (Jackson and Carter, 1985: 21). Think about it. It is only at the very top of the hierarchy, and at the very bottom, that 'pure manager' and 'pure worker' actually exist (and even here they do so only in the abstract). The vast majority of intermediate roles are manager *and* worker. They are 'manager' in so far as they involve some sense of responsibility for people at lower levels of the hierarchy. Equally, they are 'worker' in so far as they involve reporting to higher levels of the hierarchy). Interestingly, for Wortman and Linsenmeier (1977: 38):

an individual may be dependent not only on those at his [sic] own level in the hierarchy, but also on those individuals who report to him. Evaluations of a department manager by higher management are linked to the performance of those who work in his department.

Second, and in a vein comparable to one of the paradoxes we noted in respect of a division of labour as part of our discussion of economics in Chapter 3, we might very well posit another: *a paradox of delegation*. For March and Simon ([1958] 1984: 34), for example, '... delegation has both functional and dysfunctional consequences for the achievement of organizational goals. It contributes both to their realization and to their deflection'. Third, I advance what can be described as a *promotion paradox*. Of the paradoxes explored in this subsection, this is probably the one most readers (of a certain age!) will relate to best. As many of us eventually realize, promotion at work often amounts to a pyrrhic victory. This is because in most industries promotion necessitates a move away from the trade or profession we signed up to in the first place; promotees typically transition into some sort of management role. The academic profession, particularly in its neoliberal guise, is a case in point. For the academic looking to climb the ladder, no longer is it a case of demonstrating your mettle as a scholar. No. Today, you are expected to exhibit income-generating abilities, as well as a willingness (and, increasingly, downright enthusiasm) to take on student recruitment, course management, and programme administration responsibilities. As alt-rock band, Jesus Jones, quipped in their song, 'The Right Decision': *the problem with success is you become what you detest*. Finally, and in response to knee-jerk concerns about the imbalance of power in cases of hierarchy,

> [d]ominance has its advantages, even for those who fail to achieve it. Certainly once a hierarchy is set in place, influenced by each individual's physical and mental endowments—and in some species, based on the status of its mother—conflict may decline, a bonus for all.
>
> *(Moffett, 2019: 40)*

This lends important conceptual context to the purported stability associated with *Pax Brittanica* (historically) and *Pax Americana* (more contemporaneously), explored in the subsection on war and conflict in Chapter 7. As we will see in that chapter, conflict itself is bound by paradox.

Leadership. For Manz et al. (2008: 35), 'Irony and paradox are woven into the very fabric of contemporary business leadership'. Broadly speaking, I have gleaned two key tensions vis-à-vis leadership. First, it seems, the concept of leadership has attracted more research than any other in the field of business and yet it remains one of the most poorly understood. Second, although the prospect of control is forever unrealizable, the perception of control remains fundamentally important. Let's explore each, in turn.

Celebrated leadership theorist Ralph Stogdill (1974) noted in the 1970s that leadership is the single most popular topic of research in the field of business and management and yet it remains arguably the least well understood. For Calder (1977: 181), 'this view is probably shared by a majority of social scientists, with research on leadership being held in vague disrepute. Nor does there appear to be any great optimism that the accumulation of research is really heading anywhere'. And so he asks:

> What is to be made of this paradox? On the one hand, even a superficial examination of the history of leadership research conveys the sense of steady progress in theoretical sophistication and data collection. Yet there is little sense of really having achieved anything in the way of a new or profound understanding of leadership beyond that available from everyday knowledge.
>
> *(Calder, 1977: 181)*

It is this very paradox that probably explains why it is that leadership remains such a difficult topic to teach. Indeed, Calder goes on to argue that leadership cannot be taught as a skill because leadership is so much more than a skill, or even a set of skills. Crucially, it demands of its practitioners an ability to recognize and react to the perception of others. And this cannot be reduced to a discrete teachable 'skill'.

> To teach leadership is to sensitize people to the perceptions of others—that is, to sensitize them to the everyday common-sense thinking of a group of people. The transfer of leadership from one group of actors to another thus becomes highly problematic. The would-be leader must respond to attributions based on the meaning of leadership for each group with which [s]he interacts.
>
> *(ibid.: 202)*

The big question here, of course, is: do business degrees effectively sensitize students to the perceptions of others? I really do hope so, but—honestly, and on the basis of my own experience and observations—I don't think that they do. Another way to approach this is to recognize that the concept of leadership makes no sense without followership and yet the latter concept is rarely used and attracts virtually no research. In a very practical sense this is astonishing, not least because the vast majority of us would (conventionally, at least) be described as followers, rather than leaders.

Second, there exists a peculiar tension between leadership and effect. In 2016, I penned a brief piece for the British Chartered Management Institute in which I argued that 'strong leadership' is a false idol. In times of crisis, I argued, we regularly hear calls for 'strong leadership'. In recent years, examples include the aftermath of the Volkswagen emissions scandal and 2016's European Union referendum result. Indeed, after the Brexit vote, the Chartered Management Institute itself called for strong leadership: 'With the UK facing a period of political and economic uncertainty, strong and inclusive leadership is more important than ever'. But is strong leadership, I asked provocatively, all it's cracked up to be? Every organization is subject to multiple forces—politics, economics, society, and technology—over which the leader has no discernible control. The business leader has no control over labour laws, exchange rates, the zeitgeist, or the speed of the telecoms revolution. But these factors, and countless others, have a direct bearing on the future of the organization she leads. Indeed, organizations are driven and directed not by will, but by the environment in which they operate—a sort of 'organizational Darwinism'. Of course, a leader may believe they still have a discernible input in terms of how they interpret and/or react to their environment. But even here we face problems. Take decisions about recruitment or promotion. There is a tendency for people to be attracted to those who are similar to themselves. Even in the post-selection period, recruits are subjected to pressure to conform. This means, ultimately, that leaders are a homogeneous bunch. And, in turn, this leads to stasis. So should we just accept the limitations of leadership? After all, many of the businesses highlighted for their strategic and managerial excellence in Tom Peters and Robert Waterman's bestselling *In Search of Excellence* were in dire straits a few years after the book's publication in 1982. Leaders—political and organizational alike—are not, it seems, in control. Interestingly, while cases of leaderless organizations are rare, they do show a common theme: Belgium, for example, went without an elected prime minster for a year and a half (*The Telegraph*, 2011), and it didn't seem to make the remotest difference to the performance of the country; worker cooperatives in South America—businesses without traditional leadership structures—also appear to be flourishing (Heras & Vieta, 2020).

So does this mean we should dispense with leaders altogether? No—and our growing appreciation for the subtle mechanics that underpin paradox should support this. Indeed, and although the effective control of organizations is almost certainly beyond the power of their leaders, the *perception of control* is likely to be beneficial to the well-being of subordinates. Leadership provides certainty and security for those lower down the ladder. Our fears of the UK descending into nuclear war are, at least in part, alleviated by our confidence that the British prime minister has the requisite skills of diplomacy to prevent this.

Performance

As Umberto Eco (2011: 420) hints gracefully in his novel *The Prague Cemetery*, achievement elicits paradox: 'There's a certain melancholy when a duty is completed—a melancholy greater and more impalpable than the sadness of a steamship voyage'. Here then we explore two areas of paradox vis-à-vis performance: success and commitment.

Success. It is sometimes quipped that people become 'victims of their own success' or that 'success breeds contempt'. In this sense success is self-limiting because it renders us complacent. Pahl's work from 1995 is perhaps most instructive here: 'In a competitive society to be neurotic is normal. The highly successful may simply reveal neuroses in a more extreme form' (Pahl, 1995: 78). One of Pahl's research participants, David, reflects on his career: '[W]hat the hell shall I do next ...? I'm actually roughly where I want to be and I can't see a good place to go on from here ... In a way I'm hooked on the treadmill...'. He continues:

My life has become so dominated by work ... that I can't get off the treadmill at the moment ... I don't know what else I can do. I don't know what else I can be and so [I ask myself] 'What are you'? [I respond] 'I am my job'.

(ibid.: 80)

By way of interpretation, Pahl suggests that David has lost touch with any 'real' self. He has become a machine for getting jobs done. He lives a life of fictions trying to live up to his idealized self. Is he a victim of his own success or, in his striving for super success, has he created for himself a kind of monster which is devouring him? Depressingly, Pahl concludes that David's only option is to carry on achieving. While there is certainly an element of ideological conviction (in the form of an anti-corporate bias) to this interpretation, there is an all-too-familiar ring of truth about it. Pahl draws on the insightful work of Karen Horney in suggesting that the pursuit of success is intrinsically unrealizable: 'Self-idealization turns into a comprehensive drive—what Horney calls *the search for glory*. The drive towards external success is fuelled by neurotic ambition' (ibid.: 83). And more emphatically still, '... the whole pursuit of success is intrinsically unrealizable (Horney, 1991: 26)' (ibid.: 84). Here, then, is an instructive example of how paradox constitutes an immanent dimension of the human condition. Horney continues:

[L]ike any other compulsive drive, the search for glory has the quality of insatiability. It must operate as long as the unknown (to himself) forces are driving him. There may be a glow of elation over the favourable reception of some work done, over a victory won, over any sign of recognition or admiration—but it does not last.

(Horney, 1991: 30, cited, in Pahl, 1995: 90)

In a less existential—more prosaic—sense, Frost and Brockmann (2014) advance what they describe as *the performance paradox*. In their study of the academic profession—but their conclusions are more than likely applicable in other industries—they argue that since measurement of qualitative performance dictates the use of quantitative metrics, it ends up having a negative effect on actual performance:

> [D]ue to the increasing implementation of governance logic of entrepreneurial universities, there is a growing tendency within the public sector to equate qualitative productivity with quantitative productivity. This makes scholars behave less like homo academicus and more like homo stratigicus and [thus] encourages them to pursue a gaming strategy and play safe. A performance paradox then occurs.
>
> *(Frost & Brockmann, 2014: 25)*

Osterloh and Frey (2020: 5) put it simply: the paradox emerges when people focus on 'performance indicators but not on the performance they are supposed to indicate'. There are, of course, echoes here of the paradoxes we have explored in respect of bureaucracy, that is, while bureaucracies are designed to administer a particular end, they do so through process and quantification, and eventually these processes displace the envisaged end as the overriding logic.

Finally, we can discern contradictions when exploring the psychology of organizational performance. Here, I advance two further paradoxes: *the organizational norms paradox* and *the pretence paradox*. In delineating each, I take empirical cues from Wortman and Linsenmeier (1977: 151):

> Because creativity and independence are important traits in organizational settings, a person who slavishly conforms to the opinions of his superiors, or to the norms and values of the company, may run the risk of eliciting negative reactions. [...] [I]ndividuals who accept all the values and norms of an organization should be regarded as socialization failures.

In this sense, 'successful' organizational men and women will challenge and in many cases violate the rules, norms, and values of their organization. 'Unsuccessful' organizational men and women including the proverbial and much derided 'jobsworth' (see Vine, 2021) are those who adhere doggedly to organizational rules. Similarly, Wortman and Linsenmeier suggest that we inevitably become what we 'pretend' to be. This is pertinent. In pretending to be somebody we are not in the present, we are laying the foundations for our 'real' selves in the future.

> [If somebody] receives positive reinforcement from others after employing a particular self-presentation, he [sic] is likely to take this feedback from others quite seriously and come to believe the things he has said about himself. Thus, any differences between the real person and the façade are

likely to diminish over time. The ingratiatory will unwittingly become what he is pretending to be.

(Wortman & Linsenmeier, 1977: 173)

Commitment. Closely related to paradoxes of success are tensions related to commitment. In an instructive book chapter published first in the 1970s, Salancik reviewed the extant literature and concluded that levels of commitment among subordinates are inversely proportional to the affability of their boss. In other words, in order for subordinates to enjoy their work, superordinates must be unpleasant. The example Salancik used described the working relationships between students and supervisors.

When students are led to believe they worked very hard for a nasty supervisor, they enjoyed the task more than when they worked very hard for a nice supervisor. When they work for a nice person they attribute their effort to their liking for him, not the job. This would be an unrealistic attribution to a nasty boss, so they like the job more.

(Salancik, 1977: 18)

This example invites a broader consideration of behaviours vis-à-vis attitudes. A good instructor can ask her class: which comes first, our behaviours or our attitudes? Most students will probably conclude that our attitudes come first, and yet we'll all be familiar with the saying 'he's stuck in his ways'; that is, he's used to doing it a particular way and that, for him, becomes the 'right' way of doing it. Conservatism is founded on the very notion of behaviours preceding attitudes. The truth is we are unable to disentangle behaviours and attitudes. There is, it seems, a cyclical relationship between beliefs and behaviour. In all probability they are self-reinforcing. Salancik goes on to draw attention to Lieberman's (1956) extraordinary research about the relationship between role and behaviour. Lieberman documented how dramatically attitudes change with organizational roles. In his research, he assessed the attitudes of workers towards management and unions at one point in time. A year later, he interviewed the same individuals, some of whom had become foremen and some of whom had become union stewards. Those who had become foremen expressed more pro-management attitudes than previously, while those who had become stewards expressed more pro-union attitudes. Still some time later, the company demoted some foremen when an economic recession forced a cutback in personnel. Those returned to the ranks of workers expressed the same attitudes they had held as workers before.

Ideology, it would seem, is related to role; it has very little, if anything, to do with conviction. And this peculiar dynamic between role and behaviour sheds light on Zimbardo's infamous Stanford Prison Experiment, discussed in Chapter 3. Contributing to the school of thought first advanced by phenomenological sociologists, Pfeffer (1977: 238) reminds us that the meaning of behaviour is inferred *ex post*. Rather than having behaviour directed by or toward some goal or preference, the goal is constructed after the action occurred in order to rationalize the behaviour.

> While, in this framework, behaviour is always goal-directed and, hence, rational, it is clear that this view of human behaviour is in conflict with the notion that persons have well-defined goals and preference orderings that they use to evaluate ex ante possible actions.
>
> *(Pfeffer, 1977: 267)*

In that same publication, Salancik goes on to describe another organizational paradox related to commitment, this time in terms of participation.

> In many ways, participation is an elaborate form of co-optation, regardless of whether such intentions are present. [But] in many cases managers who use participation do so intentionally as a co-optation; that is, as a means of getting employees to carry out the objectives of management ... The important fact is that committing someone to do something places constraints around him so that he is more likely to do it. By having a person choose to do something, you create a situation that makes it more difficult for him to say that he didn't want to do it. And the ironic thing is that the more freedom you give him to make the decision, the more constraining you make the subsequent situation. In the literature published about participatory programmes, it is generally the case that the goals workers decide on are goals set by management. The boundaries of the decisions are always controlled and defined by management.
>
> *(Salancik, 1977: 35–36)*

This is extraordinary. One of the defining themes of contemporary (i.e. 'human relations') approaches to management is that of empowerment, not just of subordinates but of stakeholders more generally. In involving stakeholders in decisions from the outset, we naively think we are ensuring we value and take on board their views. In reality, what we are doing is securing 'buy in' and precluding the possibility of later resistance. It is connivance. Power is thus wielded, paradoxically, by involvement. Drawing on research by Selznick (1949) and Pfeffer (1972, 1973), Salancik himself notes how

> boards of directors are used by organizations to coopt the support of the organization's critical interest groups. Outsiders are invited into the

organization, given a sense of participating, and over time find themselves supporting the organization and defending it to other outsiders .... The most ironic aspect of participation is that the more the appearance of freedom is given, the more coopted one becomes.

(1977: 45)

Group Dynamics

A fundamental consideration on most organizational behaviour modules is that of group dynamics. Of course, and in line with the prevailing progressive sentiment (and despite the conciliatory efforts of the likes of Schlesinger, 1991), a rarely challenged outcome of these discussions is that *diverse* groups are most effective. Certainly, there is strong evidence to suggest that businesses that recruit a diverse workforce are more likely to prosper, not least because a diverse workforce can reflect—and understand—the consumer behaviour of the diverse marketplace they serve. However, there exists a rarely acknowledged *paradox of group effectiveness*. On the one hand, we live today in a world which champions diversity and proclaims, somewhat tritely, that 'opposites attract'; on the other, we tend to gravitate towards and collaborate most effectively with 'like-minded individuals'. This is understood as the tension between 'heterophily' and 'homophily', and is something my business ethics undergraduates, in particular, struggle to come to terms with. A recent assignment brief I set them read as follows:

> We regularly hear calls for greater diversity both in the political realm and—increasingly—in business. In this assignment, we would like you to consider how you might go about determining the optimum level of diversity in an organisation? What issues do you think need to be taken into account? Please note that this assessment requires you to think critically and to navigate some potentially controversial ideas.

Despite this priming to encourage students to challenge the ethical status quo in respect of diversity, not a single respondent was prepared to explore the possibility that diverse groups might be problematic. And, this, despite the fact that in the lecture theatre the students predominantly sat in groups in accordance with specific demographics: towards the front sat a large group of international African students; a little further back three groups of all-female students, and then right at the very back the jocks: all male, broad-shouldered, and most donning varsity tops, coincidentally markers of their kin. In their written work, however, *all* felt that diverse groups were desirable and none were prepared to concede that although this is something we currently see as desirable, in fact, many of us tend to solicit companionship and support with those most like us.

Organizational identity. We have, of course, already explored identity vis-à-vis paradox in Chapter 3. However, there exists a peculiar relationship between identity, authenticity and organization. On the one hand, we are taught from a young age about the purported virtues of honesty. On the other, being honest about our foibles in organizational life rarely translates into a successful strategy; bullshitting tends to yield more favourable results. What else is the curriculum vitae (or résumé, if you're reading this from the other side of The Pond) but an exercise in writing bullshit? Arguably, job applicants are screened *primarily* on their ability to bullshit. This of course amounts to what we might regard as a sort of *authenticity paradox*. In an influential article in *Harvard Business Review*, Hermina Ibarra (2015: online) presents the following examples to illustrate what she refers to as the authenticity paradox:

> Consider Cynthia, a general manager in a health care organization. Her promotion into that role increased her direct reports 10-fold and expanded the range of businesses she oversaw—and she felt a little shaky about making such a big leap. A strong believer in transparent, collaborative leadership, she bared her soul to her new employees: 'I want to do this job', she said, 'but it's scary, and I need your help'. Her candor backfired; she lost credibility with people who wanted and needed a confident leader to take charge. Or take George, a Malaysian executive in an auto parts company where people valued a clear chain of command and made decisions by consensus. When a Dutch multinational with a matrix structure acquired the company, George found himself working with peers who saw decision-making as a freewheeling contest for the best-debated ideas. That style didn't come easily to him, and it contradicted everything he had learned about humility growing up in his country. In a 360-degree debrief, his boss told him that he needed to sell his ideas and accomplishments more aggressively. George felt he had to choose between being a failure and being a fake.

'[G]oing against our natural inclinations', Ibarra continues,

> can make us feel like impostors, we tend to latch on to authenticity as an excuse for sticking with what's comfortable. But few jobs allow us to do that for long. That's doubly true when we advance in our careers or when demands or expectations change, as Cynthia, George, and countless other executives have discovered.
>
> *(ibid.)*

You will more than likely have your own experiences of something similar (you don't need the badly drawn characters of Cynthia or George to illustrate the point). I have numerous examples myself. For instance, I have felt irritation at the suggestion that academics should now routinely attend training sessions. My counterargument is that the best professors bring a sense of individuality and quirkiness to the lecture theatre. The last thing students want is to be presented with a fleet of identikit 'knowledge-brokers' all jostling for the student body's attention. *Fuck that!*, I thought. In any event, I felt that the training on offer was hackneyed, patronizing, and a waste of resources. Advocate training on an exceptional basis, I suggested. I was outvoted. I resist no longer. I play the game, and dutifully complete the training session, complement the coordinator and the university department arranging the session, and keep my head down. My boss is happier. Her boss is happier. And, honestly, I'm happier too. But— yes—and to Ibarra's point—I'm faking it.

Consensus. The concept of consensus has an unmistakable allure. However, its scrutiny reveals several tensions. The first of these relates to the phenomenon described as groupthink (see Janis, 1972). Most students enrolled on business management degrees will at some point study the 1986 Challenger Shuttle Disaster. It has become a staple on organizational behaviour modules because it illustrates—better perhaps than any other case study— the problems associated with groupthink which arise when our collective desire for consensus overrides the reservations harboured by individual members of the group. Ultimately Challenger exploded shortly after take-off because political aspirations trumped practical reservations. A second—more familiar—tension in respect of consensus has become known as *The Abilene Paradox* (so called because its illustration involves a flawed plan to travel 50 miles to have dinner in a town called Abilene; see Harvey, 1988). It is an example of the all-too-familiar scenario in which a decision is made which is apparently consensual when, in actual fact, it is what nobody wants.

Paradoxically, it is frequently by recourse to conflict—not consensus— that progress is achieved. A familiar derivative is the popular dictum: *we learn through our mistakes*. Arguably, catastrophe or disaster (particularly when described as 'apocalypse', a word which literally means 'to reveal') can be considered paradoxical since without disaster, we do not learn and hence become complacent, which in turn leads to further catastrophe. We can describe this as the *conflict-consensus paradox*.

Operations

In the field of operations, we can discern at least three paradoxes: the paradoxes of quality, risk, and technology. All, it seems, are in some way related to anxiety.

Quality. Modern cars contain huge amounts of advanced technology, much of which is geared towards improving reliability. But with more technology, the more there is to go wrong and the more complex repairs are when things *do* go wrong. A popular anecdote regaled by used cars sales staff (at least in the UK, but most likely elsewhere too) is that brand new cars are *less* reliable than those that are a few years old. This is apparently because the car will have been taken in to the main dealer by the first owner to correct production recall errors, and address any niggling issues that the owner has noticed. This is almost certainly an anecdote that has helped used car dealers shift plenty of stock. Think about the number of new car owners complaining about the catalogue of faults they have had to have repaired. This rarely ever happens in the case of second or third owners of vehicles. This is of course partly because those who buy used cars do so precisely because they are not going to fuss over minor imperfections. The car is already several years into the atrophying phase and, subconsciously, used car owners know this. When buying a brand new car, the buyer expects flawless perfection—but the laws of physics prohibit this.

Anecdotes aside, there is a separate tension related to quality that demands our attention. In a rarely cited but absolute gem of a book—*Fundamentals of Management*—Mike Smith touches upon a *paradox of quality management*, and uses the instructive example of teacher feedback to illustrate his point:

> Quality systems work well in production environments where the outcome was an objective, measurable product. However, they are more difficult to implement in personal services where there is an interaction between the provider and the customer. For example, a quality system may evaluate a teacher partly on the basis of questionnaires from students. Hence, a teacher will have a vested interest in giving high marks so that students will rate them highly. Unfortunately, this may lead to the quality of education being driven downwards rather than upwards as the designers of the system intend.
>
> *(Smith, 2007: 258)*

Something similar is gleaned more broadly from an examination of the much hailed Total Quality Management (TQM) methodology, particularly in terms of the methodology's desire to achieve zero defects. In my own consultancy work, I have heard on more than one occasion that a culture of TQM which famously demands complete commitment on behalf of an entire organization can paradoxically lead to a culture in which one's mistakes are concealed. Consequently, these mistakes are likely to be repeated by others in the organization because their suppression means there is no learning feedback loop. Furthermore, there may be a reluctance on the part of the TQM-wedded business to try anything new. This is because the all-consuming aspiration for zero defects means it is better off sticking to techniques/product lines and so on with which the business is familiar. Finally, Beardwell and Holden (1997: 640) argue that while schemes such as TQM begin life for the most positive reasons they will almost certainly become distorted by factors which turn them into 'something more unworkable and, from the employee point of view, into a sinister attempt to gain more commitment, work and productivity, without the concomitant reward, control or empowerment'. Unsurprisingly, while it enjoyed comparative success in the 1980s, TQM began to yield to alternative methodologies in the 1990s, the most notable of which was Lean Manufacturing (and the closely related concept of Just-In-Time Manufacturing). This facilitated a shift away from the all-consuming focus on quality, in part because of the tensions described. However, while dodging one set of paradoxes, this shift elicited another:

> Just-In-Time Manufacturing was developed in Japan, and later copied everywhere. The idea of a constant stream of deliveries to your factory door, as and when you needed them, was blindingly obvious when you thought about it. Cut out the warehouse and all those storage costs. Let the suppliers carry the inventory costs instead, or rather, eliminate them completely, provided always that you can guarantee that the lorries with the bits will arrive 'just-in-time'. Unfortunately, the idea became too popular. They tell me that the delivery vehicles now jam all the freeways around Tokyo, meaning that just-in-time often gives way to just-too-late. The costs of the traffic jams are beginning to outweigh the costs of the original warehouses, to say nothing of all the environmental damage caused by those idling exhausts. You can have too much of a good thing, or, curvilinear logic strikes again.
>
> *(Handy, 1994: 58)*

I daresay you could take any one of the numerous management methodologies out there—both those trained on quality, and those on alternative panaceas—and none would be resistant to the curvilinear logic Handy describes; all would eventually succumb to paradox.

Risk. A casual glance at the literature on risk reveals a wealth of paradoxes, several of which demand our attention. First, and as Hardy and Maguire (2016) stress, risk paradoxes often emerge because of the tensions between commercial (or 'realist') and more advanced (or 'critical') readings of risk. A commercial focus prioritizes an evaluation of risks which are quantifiable. In effect, this means that extremely large risks such as nuclear plant disaster or a financial crash get overlooked because they are simply too large and complex to accurately conceptualize, measure, or model. Second, a pertinent paradox emerges when we consider the example of the relationship between risk and health. As Slovic (1994: 63) explains, as people in industrialized nations have become healthier and safer on average, they have become more—rather than less—concerned about risk, and they feel increasingly vulnerable to the risks of modern life.

If risk is both prevalent and ever-present, we simply don't have time to worry about it. All our existential resources are ploughed into managing that risk. It is only when the real risks are alleviated that we have the time—that is, *the resource*—to worry about them. Of all the paradoxes we have examined so far, this is probably the most insightful in respect of our broader argument about how paradox helps even out inter- and intra-personal experience, and is something we pick up on in the concluding chapter of this book. Third, a preoccupation with risk (as a negative) precludes the opportunity for learning. When I lecture on project management modules, this is something my students are often pleasantly surprised about. Risk tends to imply negativity whereas uncertainty implies the possibility of both positive and negative outcomes. Indeed, any decent instructor of project management will instil in her brood a focus not on risk management, but on 'uncertainty management' (Ward & Chapman, 2003) or, better still, 'opportunity management' (Hillson, 2003). And this is much more than semantic chicanery. There is something at its heart. As Ward and Chapman note, the term 'risk' encourages a threat perspective because risk has become associated with events rather than more general sources of significant uncertainty. They therefore advocate 'a focus on "uncertainty" rather than risk [as a means of enhancing] project risk management, providing an important difference in perspective' (Ward & Chapman, 2003: 97). By way of illustration, Maylor (2010) regales his readers with some corporate folklore:

> One of 3M's most successful and enduring projects has been the Post-It note. It is well described in 3M folklore how this was the by-product of another research project which had produced an adhesive that was not sufficiently sticky. Had there not been a process for exploiting such a finding, the discovery might have been lost.
>
> *(Maylor, 2010: 231)*

If the example of the Post-it note strikes you as trivial, you may be interested to learn that Apple Inc. presents a comparable case: the extraordinary failure of one of their earliest models, the Apple Lisa. The Apple Lisa was a commercial flop and yet Steve Jobs credited that early experience as a key part of the learning curve which laid the groundwork for the subsequent and enormously successful Macintosh range of computers. Indeed, and as Milano (2022) notes wistfully in reflecting on the brief life of Apple Lisa: 'the rest, as they say, is history' (Milano, 2022, online). Arguably, had the Apple Lisa been more successful, Jobs and his team at Apple wouldn't have had the necessary pedagogical experience to transform the world of consumer electronics. Indeed, had things been different, you might still be touch-texting on your Nokia. The horror.

Technology. In a popular and well-cited blog post, Larsen (2015) lists 16 paradoxes related to technology, the most notable of which is 'The more time-saving devices we have, the less time we have'. This is what I refer to as *the paradox of labour-saving technologies*. It is a historical truism. As our technologies slowly advance and more and more is automated one would expect us to be working fewer and fewer hours; but both documented observations (e.g. McGregor, 2015) and a reflection on our experiences more often than not suggest that precisely the opposite has happened. What's also interesting is that some critics appear to point both to the job displacement effects of new technologies and to the fact that we appear to be working ever longer hours, in spite of technological innovation. Related to the paradox of labour-saving technologies, in their discussion of the sociomaterial mangle of connection in contemporary organizational life, Symon and Pritchard (2014) hint at the *paradoxical nature of connectivity in respect of smartphones*. On the one hand, smartphones distance us from other people (at least in a co-present sense); on the other, they embody technological connectivity par excellence. This is something we can all relate to as we sit, stand, or lie next to our loved one, each utterly absorbed in our phone. Controversial artist Banksy has captured this in his piece *Mobile Lovers* (see Figure 4.2.)

Postlude

As with the earlier discussions on arts (Chapter 2) and society (Chapter 3), in this chapter we have documented a dizzying array of paradoxes inherent to considerations of organization. Such is the prevalence of paradox in the context of organization there are signs that even the ostensibly benign practice of management consultancy is beginning to take seriously the role of paradox (see, e.g. Cheal, 2020; Sarra et al., 2023). Of course, we have assumed in this chapter that 'organization' is a social phenomenon. However, the concept of organization is also relevant in discussions of nature, and here too we face comparable paradoxes. Briggs and Peat (1985: 170, 173), for example, ask: '[h]ow can life appear, sustain itself, and display organizational growth in the face of a universal march of entropy'? It was Russian physical chemist Ilya Prigogine who finally found an answer.

> [For Prigogine] life and nonlife both appear in nonequilibrium situations— and such situations are everywhere. Nineteenth century thermodynamics had portrayed a universe in which entropy increases and structures inevitably break down. Prigogine discovered a thermodynamics which

FIGURE 4.2 Banksy's *Mobile Lovers*.

describes how in far-from-equilibrium situations structures will inevitably form. He called the dynamics of such structures 'order through fluctuation'.

(ibid.: 179)

In nature, then, organization only emerges when natural systems are *out of equilibrium*. This is remarkable. It is thus to the broader relationship between nature and paradox that we now turn.

5

PARADOX AND NATURE

We have now examined paradox vis-à-vis the arts, society, and organization in Chapters 2, 3, and 4, respectively. In this chapter we turn our attention to the manifestation of paradox in nature. Here, I build on previous contributions in respect of the paradoxes in the sciences (see Vine 2018b, 2018c, 2020). In the interests of expedience, I subdivide this chapter by discipline. But as in previous chapters, this should not imply that such subdivision reflects a natural state of affairs. We begin by tackling paradox in the numerical and physical sciences, before turning our attention to paradoxes in the life sciences. We then examine paradoxes vis-à-vis ecology and environmental sustainability. In the concluding part of the chapter, we explore the manner in which paradox emerges *between* science and its 'non-scientific' counterparts: art, mystery, and religion.

Mathematics, geometry, and physics

In Chapter 3, we cited Nicholas Mosley's *Paradoxes of Peace*. Notably, the subtitle for Mosley's book is *The presence of infinity*. In Chapter 4, we encountered Cooper and Law's work in which the pair note that '[p]roximal thinking deals in the *continuous* and *"unfinished"*; it's what is forever approached but never attained' (Cooper & Law, 1995: 239, emphasis added). Broadly speaking, the concepts here invoked—infinity, continua, and the unfinished—help frame our discussion of mathematical paradoxes. Almost certainly the best known mathematical paradoxes date back to the Ancient Greek philosopher Zeno of Elea. Zeno's *paradoxes of motion* are extremely popular in discussions of paradox, so much so that they have become rather clichéd. But this should not distract from their significance. There have been

DOI: 10.4324/9781003203339-6

numerous attempts to illustrate Zeno's paradoxes with varying success. In my own classes, I have developed the hypothetical example, below. I make no claims to pedagogical elegance, but it has proven to be reasonably effective.

Imagine you are tasked with walking along a tightrope which is, say, 12 metres in length. (We'll assume you have a head for heights and excellent balance!). However, the specifics of the steps you take are determined by the following rule: for each step you take, you only move a distance equal to half of the remaining length of the rope. It follows, then, that in your first step you move 6 metres (we'll also assume you have long legs!), your second step will be 3 metres, your third 1.5 metres, your fourth 75cm, and so on. With each step you move forward further and yet, since you only ever cover half the remaining distance on rope, you never—ever—reach your destination. You thus move perpetually but never actually arrive, even though the overall distance of your prospective journey is only 12 metres.

For some mathematicians I discussed this with over the course of the research for this book, this is not really a paradox. Rather, they say, this is an issue with not being able to measure (or 'perform') infinity. In this vein, motion is, I'm told by esteemed colleagues in the hard sciences, notoriously difficult to pin down (if you'll excuse the paradoxical pun). Consider, for example, Galileo's infamous thought experiment. Galileo urges us to imagine we are on a ship, below deck, and without a window. In this scenario, we are unable to determine whether we are moving or stationary (although we can of course tell if we are accelerating). The key point here is that there is no experiment you can do to determine your motion without an external frame of reference (or, in this case, a window and—ideally—a proximate landmass).

Ancient philosophy aside, more recently set theorists Georg Cantor and Bertrand Russell have explored the relationship between paradox and mathematics. Notably, both implied that with mathematical perseverance paradox can be either solved or, at the very least, transcended. While the German mathematician was interested foremost in what he referred to as 'transfinites' (a species of infinites), and believed that his work demonstrated techniques that could help solve Zeno's paradoxes, mathematician-turned-philosopher Bertrand Russell noted the following: 'Philosophical antinomies ... find their counterpart in mathematical fallacies' (Russell, 1990: 52). Sorensen reflects on Bertrand Russell's experience of studying mathematics at university:

At Cambridge, the vast majority of mathematicians seemed [to Russell] narrow and uncultured. Students crammed to pass the Tripos examination, a marathon of tricky mathematics. To make a respectable showing, you had to train intensively. So teachers and students focused on competitive, time-sensitive problem-solving. This shallow regime did not encourage ruminations on the philosophical difficulties posed by infinitesimals, continua, and infinity. But when Russell encountered mathematicians in France, Germany, and Italy, he no longer pictured the whole profession as hurriedly sweeping its contradictions under a rug.

(Sorensen, 2003: 318)

Indeed, for Sorensen (ibid.: 319): 'Part of Russell's project was to show how contradictions led from mathematics to physics, and from physics to metaphysics, and then onto the Absolute'. In one sense, then, and given the transdisciplinary objectives of our current thesis, Russell's work is a precursor—of sorts—to that you are reading.

Although considerations of paradox are peppered throughout Russell's canon, in discussions of paradox he has become best known for what is termed, quite simply, *Russell's Paradox*. Technically, it belongs to set theory and, as such, can be illustrated most precisely using algebra. However, and rather helpfully for non-logicians, Russell presented an alternative, more accessible illustration of the paradox known as the barber paradox: 'The barber is the "one who shaves all those, and those only, who do not shave themselves". The question is, does the barber shave himself'? (Russell, 1986: 228). Despite significant effort to 'solve' this esoteric paradox, none has succeeded. Paradox, Russell demonstrated, is also inherent to discussions of infinity: 'The number of finite numbers is infinite. Every number is finite. These two statements seem indubitable, though the first contradicts the second, and the second contradicts [the first]'. (Russell, 1994: 123). Russell also noticed that the diagonal argument is really another manifestation of the liar paradox. As Sorensen (2003) notes:

> A set that contains everything must contain itself. Now consider a set that includes all and only those sets that do not contain themselves as members. If this set contains itself as a member, then it does not contain itself as a member. But if it does not include itself as a member, then it does include itself as a member.

Russell feared that at least part of the confusion in respect of these sorts of paradox came down to the vagaries, ambiguities, and redundancies of everyday language (Sorensen, 2003: 321), and hence could be addressed if a logically perfect language (i.e. algebra) could be substituted for our linguistic meandering mess. He tried, and failed. Indeed, and as we learn from Sorensen:

> Time lost on 'the contradiction' made the deadline for his book Principles of Mathematics more pressing. The systematic nature of the book made it

more difficult the dodge the question whether his set contained itself. Russell become more and more fretful. He sought advice from fellow logicians. Once he telegraphed [fellow mathematician] Alfred North Whitehead reporting that he had found a solution. After Whitehead congratulated him, Russell's indescribable relief collapsed under the weight of a minor variation of the original paradox.

(Sorensen, 2003: 328–329)

This anecdote is revealing in two senses. First, it provides a real sense of how preoccupied we have become in *solving* paradoxes. Second, it illustrates part of the broader 'patterned' thesis we are advancing in this book: as one paradox is apparently solved another materializes to take its place, in this case a minor derivative. In any event, and as one mathematician quipped as he reviewed an early draft of this chapter, we would be foolish to overlook the fact that some misguided men actually choose to grow beards.

Related, of course, to mathematics is the study of geometry. As we noted in our exploration of paradox in the arts in Chapter 2, the simple concept of symmetry represents a rather elegant paradox. Symmetry is, concurrently, both the same *and* the opposite. In a very loose sense, the tensions we associate with Escher's sketches represent geometrical paradoxes that can be deliberately created when rendering three-dimensional shapes on a two-dimensional medium. But there is much more to geometrical paradox than this. Indeed, at its most arresting, Barbour builds on tensions inherent to discussions of geometry to argue that time cannot exist in the wake of the relativity of simultaneity (don't worry—we'll come on to this): 'Time does not exist. All that exists are things that change. What we call time is—in classical physics at least—simply a complex of rules that govern the change' (Barbour, 2000: 137). To lend credence to his argument, Barbour invokes the work of German mathematician and physicist Carl Gauss:

Gauss's most important insight was that the surface in three dimensional space is characterized by two distinct yet not entirely independent kinds of curvature. He called them intrinsic and extrinsic curvature. The intrinsic curvature depends solely on the distance relationships that hold within the surface, whereas the extrinsic curvature measures the ending of the surface in space. A surface can be flat in itself—with no intrinsic curvature—but still be bent in space and therefore have extrinsic curvature.

(ibid.: 158)

Here we might very well postulate a practical implication, and in so doing invoke a *paradox of geography*. If we travel along a Roman Road (which were, of course, notoriously straight) in an *intrinsic* straight line, we would—in effect—take off into the air, since the surface of the earth is curved. It is only if we travel in an *extrinsically* curved line that we 'stay on the straight and narrow'. And here, of course, is the paradox; one we might label *the paradox of straight line travel*. Interestingly, and as Barbour notes, it was building on the work of Gauss in 1912 that Einstein became aware of the possibilities unlatched by non-Euclidean geometry hence ushering in a whole new paradigm for physics. What is especially arresting about Barbour's thesis is that it provides for us a fresh vista from which to appreciate Zeno's paradoxes of motion. Barbour arrives at a formidable conclusion:

> I now believe that time does not exist at all, and that motion is pure illusion. What is more, I believe there is quite strong support in physics for this view. [...] Space and time in their previous role as the stage of the world are redundant. There is no container. The world does not contain things, it is things. These things are Nows that, so to speak, hover in nothing.
>
> *(Barbour, 2000: 4, 16)*

Barbour thus further advances Parmenide's (and latterly Zeno's) claim that there is no motion. At any rate, and as both my father and my father-in-law are fond of reminding me: time flies like an arrow, but fruit flies like a banana.

Heated discussions of mathematics and geometry eventually transport us to the realm of physics. Non-scientists could be forgiven for making the naïve assumption that physics is immune from paradox. None less than the highly decorated Israeli historian Yuval Noah Harari falls into this very trap. In his otherwise excellent book *Sapiens*, he suggests that the laws of physics are free of inconsistencies (see Harari, 2014: 182). Prior to undertaking the research for this book, I too made a similar assumption. Ultimately, nothing could be further from the truth. Indeed, it was in my study of physics that I finally felt a sense of conviction in respect of my broader thesis: if paradox can be found in this, the 'hardest' of hard sciences, then there is almost certainly a potential for the transcendental application I was seeking to advance with the book. Over the course of my research, I met with numerous physicists and grappled with some truly perplexing concepts. Initially, I struggled to get my head around some of the conundrums with which I was presented. In the event, it was really only when I let go of those deeply held convictions about 'hard science' that I began to properly appreciate the field's potential. Of the numerous extant accounts of paradoxes in physics I read, it was actually biologist Gunther Stent's coverage from 2002 that articulated these complex ideas most effectively. I thus rely heavily on his contributions in this subsection. He begins by reminding us that we are schooled in the methods of Galileo and Newton and it is difficult—and for some downright impossible—to break away from the deep-seated assumptions they have embedded in our cognitive apparatus. Part of the challenge, Stent (2002: 199) says, is that '[t]he classical physics of Galileo and of Isaac Newton are visualizable because they are based on our innate categories of space and time ...'. In classical physics, Stent continues, both space and time are absolute and independent realities that can be measured by use of yardsticks and clocks. 'But this basic tenet regarding space and time had to be abandoned at the turn of the twentieth century upon the emergence of Einstein's relativity theories' (ibid.). So in actively moving beyond the certainties of Galileo and Newton, Bronowski (1976: 353) suggests that:

> [W]hat physics has done now is to show that ... there is no absolute knowledge. And those who claim it, whether they are scientists or dogmatists, open the door to tragedy. All information is imperfect. We have to treat it with humility. That is the human condition; and that is what quantum physics says.

The paradoxes of physics we are compelled to consider include wave-particle duality, the uncertainty principle, and the theory of relativity, all of which become part of a broader—truly astounding—phenomenon. Like so many of the paradoxes we have explored, the paradoxes inherent to the study of physics are encountered at the *extremes*: in this case, nuclear physics (the study of extremely small particles) and astrophysics (the study of extremely large objects).

Wave-particle duality is the idea that every particle or quantum entity may be described as either a particle or a wave. On first glance this may seem rather inconsequential. It is in fact extraordinary. The idea pertains to the fundamental inability of the existing vocabulary we associate with classical physics to convey with any degree of accuracy the observed behaviour of atomic and subatomic objects. As Albert Einstein himself noted as part of a collaborative paper,

> It seems as though we must use sometimes the one theory and sometimes the other, while at times we may use either. We are faced with a new kind of difficulty. We have two contradictory pictures of reality; separately neither of them fully explains the phenomena of light, but together they do.
> *(Einstein & Infeld, 1938)*

Heisenberg's Uncertainty Principle refers to the observation that we cannot know both the position and speed of a particle, such as a photon or electron, with perfect accuracy; the more we nail down the particle's position, the less we know about its speed, and vice versa. Sufferers of eye floaters will be familiar with this scenario: the more you try to focus on the floater, the further away it drifts. For Stent (2002: 244), Heisenberg's uncertainty principle asserts that the variables p and q represent quantities that cannot be measured jointly to any arbitrary degree of accuracy in a single experiment or have their exact magnitudes inferred from successive experiments. This is because it inheres in the nature of these experiments that when an experimental arrangement is set up that is designed to measure the magnitude of one of these variables, information is necessarily lost concerning the magnitude of the other. The double slit experiment, first conducted by British polymath Thomas Young (see Young, 1804), illustrates this paradox most effectively. Space prohibits a meaningful discussion of Young's complex—but extraordinary—experiment. Suffice it to say, Young has been described as 'the last man who knew everything' (Robinson, 2006).

Relativity theory has probably attracted more attention outside the world of physics than either wave-particle duality or Heisenberg's uncertainty principle. For Stent (2002: 197–198), 'one of the first contraventions of classical physics was Albert Einstein's development in 1905 of his *relativity theory*, which tampered with the categories of time and space. Stent continues:

> The point of departure of Einstein's relativity theory was a then recent, to physicists very surprising, discovery by Albert Michelson and Edward Morley. They had found that the speed of propagation of light is the same for all observers, regardless of their own motion relative to the light flow. Einstein attributed the inconsistency of this fact with our intuitive concept of relative motion to our evidently false intuition that the flow of time is absolute, i.e. independent of how it is observed. So he developed a theory of relative motion—later designated as the 'special theory of relativity'— which does not invoke the concept of an absolute flow of time. Instead, Einstein's theory posits that the time of occurrence of an event depends on the frame of reference of the event's observer, so that there does not exist just one universal, or pancosmic time, but many times to each observer his own. Einstein thus dissolved the intuitive conceptual independence of space and time.
>
> *(ibid.)*

Similarly, for Barbour (2000: 129):

> Two aspects of Einstein's work ensured its triumphant success. First, he took the relativity principle utterly seriously. It was the bedrock, repeatedly exploited. Second, he took for real a local time that [Dutch physicist, Hendrik Lorentz] had introduced as a formal device to describe phenomena in a reference frame moving relative to the aether. Events simultaneous in the 'local time' were not so in the real time of the aether frame. But Einstein, committed to relativity, regarded one as just as real as

the other. He made a virtue out of an apparent vice, and saw that the key to the entire mystery lay in the concept of simultaneity.

Making a virtue out of a vice is of course precisely what I am trying to achieve in respect of paradox in this book. The concept of the relativity of simultaneity that Einstein advanced suggested that time is relative to space, and so it is impossible to lay claim to accuracy in respect of time without a frame of reference. The infamous 'train and platform' thought experiment illustrates this extremely well: Imagine two people, one midway inside a speeding train carriage and another observer standing on a platform as the train moves past. A flash of light is emitted at the centre of the carriage just as the two observers pass each other. For the observer on board the train, the front and back of the train carriage are at fixed distances from the light source and as such, according to this observer, the light will reach the front and back of the train carriage at the same time. For the individual standing on the platform, on the other hand, the rear of the train carriage is moving (and hence catching up) towards the point at which the flash was given off, and the front of the train carriage is moving away from it. As the speed of light is finite and the same in all directions for all observers, the light headed for the back of the train will have less distance to cover than the light headed for the front. Thus, the flashes of light will strike the ends of the train carriage at different times.

In a more prosaic—and non-technical—sense, comparable paradoxes associated with time can be gleaned by reflecting on our own experiences. For example, there is an interesting dynamic between time and utility. Most of us will be familiar with several such truisms. First, there is the suggestion that time flies when you're having fun vis-à-vis time drags when you're not. Second, time passes slowly when you're young (during which time you are desperate to be older) vis-à-vis time passes more quickly when you're older (during which time you are desperate to be younger). According to some commentators, experientially, we are half way through our lives by age 20 (see, e.g. *The Guardian*, 2007). It's a sobering thought. Beyond these we can add a third: time passes slowly when we are bored vis-à-vis time passes quickly when our lives are configured around routine (see, e.g. Riggio, 2012). This third one is interesting because if we accept received wisdom regarding routine (i.e. that it is mind-deadening, as Adam Smith and countless others have argued) it must therefore represent a form of boredom. We are now getting dangerously close to virtual insanity, an experience some refer to as an endless loop of déjà vu (see, e.g. BBC, 2015b).

Complementarity. Perhaps unsurprisingly, at least one physicist has brought together these paradoxical observations in a bid to generalize: Danish physicist Niels Bohr. Bohr, Stent (2002) explains, had noticed that the parade of counterintuitive findings of the early twentieth century presented the field of physics with some deeply troubling epistemological problems. These findings included those of Max Planck (in respect of quantum theory), Albert Einstein (in respect of wave-particle duality), and Heisenberg (in respect of the uncertainty principle) and his own discovery (in respect of the discrete character of the electron orbits around the atomic nucleus). Was there more to this, Bohr pondered, than coincidence?

> By 1927, Bohr had realised that all these strange phenomena could be traced to a common epistemological root, which he called complementarity. In his use of the term complementarity Bohr did not refer to its ordinary, everyday meaning, namely the aspects of two different parts of an entity that make it a whole, as the two 'complementary' polyynucleotide chains make the DNA double helix a whole. Rather, Bohr gave 'complementarity' a special, esoteric meaning, namely the relation between two rationally irreconcilable (or in Kantian terminology, antinomial) descriptions of the world whose factual irreconcilability no experiment can ever demonstrate. Bohr's prime example of complementarity was the description of electrons in terms of both waves and particles. The irreconcilability of these two antinomial descriptions is not experimentally demonstrable, because a critical test of either the wave or of the particle nature of the electron demands mutually exclusive observational arrangements.
>
> *(Stent, 2002: 244–245)*

Bohr's concept of complementarity represents an attempt of sorts to erect a conceptual umbrella to make sense of the various paradoxes physics was throwing up. What characterizes them all, Bohr argued, is nature's point-blank refusal to yield its innermost secrets. Scientists repeatedly find themselves pushed up against the parameters of life in a manner in which any and all attempts to transcend them are met with a sardonic chuckle. Bohr himself referred to this as the *conspiracy of nature*.

Chemistry, biology, and medicine

It seems clear, then, that paradox is marbled throughout both the numerical sciences and physical sciences. But what about the life sciences? Unsurprisingly, here too we find numerous, pervasive contradictions.

By way of a gentle—and familiar—introduction, an accessible source of paradox in the life sciences is what I refer to as the *paradox of medication*. We have encountered this already as part of discussion of psychology, in Chapter 3, but it is worth revisiting again here: this time from the point of view of biochemistry. Experience of psychotropic substances lends further credence to the paradox thesis. The group of drugs known as

Selective Serotonin Reuptake Inhibitors, for example, are routinely used to treat mental health conditions. But—and as any bewildered reader of the often lengthy guidance notes packaged with the medications regarding side effects knows—they are also linked to the exacerbation of the same. Indeed, and I speak from my own experience here, the first couple of weeks on Selective Serotonin Reuptake Inhibitors is often a truly dark and foreboding experience. In effect, the symptoms - depression and anxiety - actually worsen before actually improving. What I find most striking about this paradox is that it mirrors the paradox we see in respect of non-drug-based therapies. In Chapter 3, as part of our discussion of paradox in psychology, we touched upon what is sometimes known as *paradoxical intention* (the accepted wisdom that for a therapist to treat anxiety, he or she will seek to rehearse the anxiety-inducing thought patterns or behaviour as a means of—ultimately—improving them; known colloquially as 'facing one's fears'). Stop for a moment. This is extraordinary. What the paradox of medication and paradoxical intention suggest is that irrespective of our method of intervention, there can be no panacea to that black dog clinging to one's shoulder.

A similar dynamic can, of course, be discerned in respect of recreational drugs. Just as a drinker of alcohol will have stories of hangovers, a smoker of cannabis will regale you with tales of paranoia, or a user of ecstasy will describe the horrors of 'comedowns', every high inevitably—and *without exception*—elicits a low. Even coffee drinkers know when they've had too much. Your first coffee in the morning is typically a delight; that third coffee later in the day typically tastes bitter and is accompanied by frustratingly loose stools. This very bind was covered by the BBC in a piece which examined the science of addiction. It concluded that we do not always 'like' the things we 'want' (such as that third coffee of the day) (BBC, 2020). Looked at slightly differently, recreational drugs that have routinely been regarded as fundamentally problematic in terms of mental health (e.g. LSD) are now being used to treat mental health conditions. Timothy Leary was clearly on to something (see BBC, 2016b).

But experiences of drugs aside, chemistry reveals at least two more fundamental paradoxes. The first relates to oxygen and antioxidants. Here exists what we might describe as *a paradox of metabolism*, that is, the tension between the demands for oxygen required for any living organism vis-à-vis the damage caused by that oxygen in the form of the reactive chemicals the oxygen itself introduces to those living organisms. These reactive chemicals include peroxides, superoxide, hydroxyl radical, singlet oxygen, and alpha-oxygen. Such chemicals can damage both DNA and RNA, as well as necessitate harmful oxidation processes (see, e.g. Brooker, 2011). A second fundamental paradox is gleaned from microbiology. While common sense might suggest that resource scarcity would elicit competitive behaviour, the empirics suggest that precisely the opposite happens: bacteria exhibit cooperative behaviour in terms of scarcity, and only compete in times of abundance. This of course is directly comparable to the paradox of plenty which we touched upon in Chapter 3.

But, of course, paradoxes in chemistry are inevitably rather abstract. It is at the point at which chemistry meets biology that we can more readily attract the attention of non-scientists. One such example with which we can more readily relate is what I refer to as *the paradox of disease prevention*. Vaccinations involve administering a small dose of the disease being treated. This is something we know all too well in the wake of the global pandemic. Many—perhaps most—people reading this book will have their own experiences of ill feeling following a COVID-19 vaccination. Personally, while each of my booster shots attracted no discernible unpleasant side effects, my very first vaccination was a different story. A few hours after the shot, the muscles throughout my body began to spasm uncontrollably. My 43-year-old body was experiencing a mild dose of this global disease and didn't much like it. But this of course is precisely how vaccinations work; a little pain is required if we are to yield broader benefits. Vaccinations involve, paradoxically, a small dose of the disease. We see the same pattern as we saw first in *paradoxical intention* (psychology), and then in *the paradox of psychiatric medication* (chemistry). Here again, it seems some pain is required in order to address the underlying problem. This biological dynamic can be understood more colloquially, too. Complete avoidance of germs as part of a will to cleanliness renders us more vulnerable to serious infection. This has become known as the 'hygiene hypothesis', and is captured best by British epidemiologist David Strachan:

> Over the past century declining family size, improvements in household amenities, and higher standards of personal cleanliness have reduced the opportunity for cross infection in young families. This may have resulted in more widespread clinical expression of atopic disease, emerging earlier in wealthier people, as seems to have occurred for hay fever.
>
> *(Strachan, 1989: 1259)*

Paradoxically, then, cleanliness exposes us to disease. Interestingly, there is a saying in Indonesia, a country I visit regularly on business, that Western food tastes bland because Western kitchens are too clean.

Over the course of my research into biological paradoxes, I eventually discerned what appear to be two deeper-seated paradoxes: these I refer to as *the paradox at the crux of life* and *the paradox of Darwinian evolution*. The paradox of at the crux of life is the tension between order and chaos. For Nietzsche, as Marsden (2002: 99) notes, 'order is emergent'. However, as Handy points out:

Scientists call this sort of time the edge of chaos, the time of turbulence and creativity out of which a new order may jell. The first living cell emerged, some four million years ago, from a primordial soup of simple molecules and amino acids. Nobody knows why or how. Ever since then the universe has had an inexorable tendency to run down, to degenerate into disorder and decay. Yet it has also managed to produce from that disorder an incredible array of living creatures, plants and bacteria, as well as stars and planets. New life is forever springing from the decay and disorder of the old.

(Handy, 1994: 16)

This tension between order and chaos is fascinating and implies, of course, a will to power (in a Nietzschean sense), or, at the very least, a determining logic for survival. It is relatively straightforward to wrap your head around. The paradox of Darwinian evolution, however, is a little trickier. It is not, as one might imagine, to do with the tensions between science and religion (although this is certainly relevant to broader discussions in respect of paradox). No—it is something quite distinct. On the one hand, many of us take Darwin's theories as gospel (if you'll excuse the paradoxical pun), but in another sense the supposed thrust of evolution—that is, adaptation, improvement, and survival—is undermined by a simple thought experiment. Drawing on the work of astrophysicist and system theorist Erich Jantsch, Briggs and Peat (1985: 206) note that:

the usual way of looking at evolution views each level of ... progress as a move towards adaptation. But is it? Curiously, human beings are in many ways not as well adapted as bacteria .... [I]f the principle of evolution is adaptation, why did organisms grow steadily more complex? Consider the fact that your human complexity, which makes you extremely adaptable in one sense, also makes you as delicate as a piece of high technology. If you live in northern latitudes, think of all the trouble you had to go through to keep warm last winter. A bacterium never shivers! [...] The earliest life forms were by far the best adapted. If the meaning of evolution was in adaptation and increasing the chances of survival, as is so often claimed, the development of more complex organisms would have been meaningless or even a mistake. Darwinian evolution emphasizes adaptation to competition. In contrast, co-evolution emphasizes evolutionary cooperation—cooperation of a remarkable kind.

Jantsch was an extraordinary scholar, a borderline polymath. His work is especially appealing to me because he deliberately transcended the divide between the natural and social sciences, and expressed a particular interest in the relationship between organization theory and biology.

Briggs and Peat continue: 'Co-evolution says that changes which take place on the micro scale instantaneously effect changes which take place on the macro scale and the reverse. Neither really "causes" the other in the usual sense' (ibid.: 207). However, beyond the parallels between biology and systems theory identified by Jantsch, we might also reflect on the tension between heterophily (love of the other; or 'opposites attract') and homophily (love of the same; or 'birds of the feather flock together'). Both are 'common sense', but imply precisely opposite outcomes. This was a tension we first explored in respect of organizational behaviour in Chapter 4, but what has this got to do with biology? Well, in biology we see a comparable paradox—in this case, between inbreeding depression and homophily, on the one hand, and outbreeding depression and heterophily, on the other. Homophily (or love of the same) can lead to inbreeding depression, that is, a reduction in the genetic fitness of the offspring due to inbreeding. But this should not imply that outbreeding (love of the other) is necessarily advantageous, despite common assumptions that it is. Indeed, heterophily (love of those distinct from ourselves) can—and does—lead to outbreeding depression, a reduction in the genetic fitness of the offspring due to outbreeding.

Finally, let us briefly consider some of the paradoxes incumbent upon discussions of modern medicine. According to Hofmann (2001: 369),

> Modern health care appears to be rich in contradictions, and it is claimed to be paradoxical in a number of ways. In particular health care is held to be a paradox itself: it is supposed to do good, but is accused of doing harm.

Hofmann documents some key paradoxes related to healthcare, including the arguments that as medical treatment improves, we become less satisfied (Barsky, 1988) feel worse (Knowles, 1977), and experience increased levels of anxiety (Solbakk, 1995; Le Fanu, 1999). As healthcare improves, so do our expectations, as well as our awareness of what constitutes 'good health'. Another paradox is elicited in respect of what has become known as medicalization. In a very simple sense, naming a condition (say 'chronic fatigue syndrome') simultaneously establishes a community of support (desirable) *and* pathologizes the condition (undesirable). It's a double-edged sword. It's a paradox. As Greenwood and Nunn (1994) so pertinently observe, unless we make place for the paradoxical, we will never truly understand health and illness.

Ecology and environmental sustainability

According to Fox (2021), agriculture marked the beginning of a long journey in which we separated ourselves from nature and tried to control it; and yet, he says, we have never been more at its mercy. This of course invokes the paradoxes we saw in Chapter 4 in respect of control; the more we attempt to control something, the more anxiety prone we become. On the other hand, it is almost certainly erroneous to assume—categorically—that nature always knows best. Indeed, beyond this all-encompassing existential posturing in respect of agriculture, there exists a much more familiar paradox that those of my readers with green fingers will be all-too-familiar: you need to cut back plants in order to encourage further growth.

But this *gardener's paradox* aside, it is in our interrogation of the concepts of climate change, sustainability, and resilience that things get really interesting. Such discussions—particularly in respect of climate change—represent extremely contentious subject matter and so once again, readers are cautioned to approach the arguments with due sensitivity. Let me begin by noting that there is an expectation—a duty even—for academics to lend their research faculties to support *any* cause which draws attention to the 'climate crisis'. Nonetheless, we discern paradox even here. So, for example, one of the widely accepted universals associated with life is that it is underscored by change, an observation we trace back to Heraclitus. Indeed, as Harari (2014: 73) stresses, 'the truth is that earth's climate never rests. It is in constant flux'. With this in mind, a much more significant concern would surely be if climate *wasn't* changing (as this would violate one of the few universals we have discovered). A fair retort from the climate change activists would go along the lines of: *well, yes, climate change is inevitable, but our principal fear is the degree to which human activity is shaping that change.* Point taken. But we might well venture a counter-response to this: *Surely Homo sapiens is part of nature!* Admittedly, however, this is a rather trite counter-response. A more persuasive counter-response can be advanced by actively acknowledging what it is that distinguishes *Homo sapiens* from other species. For Bronowski (1976: 19),

> nature—that is, biological evolution—has not fitted man [sic] to any specific environment. On the contrary, by comparison to any other animal he has a rather crude survival kit; and yet—this is the paradox of the human condition—one that fits him to all environments. Among the multitude of animals which scamper, fly, burrow, and swim around us, man is the only one who is not locked into his environment. His imagination, his reason, his emotional subtlety and toughness, make it possible for him not to accept the environment but to change it.

Humankind's distinguishing feature, then, is her ability not simply to accept the prevailing environment but to shape it. In this respect, the semantics of climate change activism must evolve significantly if the movement is to gain genuine traction. We must de-emphasize concerns at *change* and, instead, harness those shaping abilities to improve its course. This is a minor—but not insignificant—point brought to our attention by considerations of paradox.

There are also multiple complexities associated with the study of sustainability that demand our attention. For example, on several occasions I have heard the argument that when presented with a recycling bin and general rubbish bin it is always better to put recyclable items in the general rubbish. This, I am told, is because until such time as we can harness energy directly from the sun (and no longer burn fossil fuels which of course provide the energy for the recycling process) it is preferable to deposit recyclables in landfill and allow them to degrade naturally. But, of course, this doesn't amount to a paradox—rather it is the question of refining our utility function, that is, it would appear that at least some of the decisions we make regarding sustainability are contingent on a rather poor understanding of the underlying science. It seems the 'recycling mindset' is less a scientific axiom and more a political concept packaged and propagated without much thought for efficacy.

The concept of resilience is similarly problematic. In 2011, the final year of my doctoral programme, my university won a research grant to explore ecological, social, and organizational resilience from critical perspectives. I was recruited as part of the team and tasked with reviewing existing research data in this field from a critical management perspective. Unexpectedly, my review of the data revealed that small-scale organic farming methods can be more destructive than large-scale non-organic methods. It seemed that economies of scale—in one sense at least—gave rise to ecologies of scale. More generally, I argued that the extant body of knowledge appeared to prioritize convictions about desirable states, rather than empirically grounded realities. My report was rejected on the basis that it 'did not contribute to the message that we want to send'. I was flabbergasted. I knew this sort of thing happened in newsrooms, but at universities? The project organizers assumed, of course, that my report would bolster support for the argument that small-scale, indigenous techniques were preferable to those associated with large-scale capitalist enterprise. My report concluded instead that many of the case studies we were presented with were premised on problematic assumptions. Although applauded by several other people involved on the project for drawing attention to both ideological assumptions and underlying conceptual tensions, ultimately my contribution was withdrawn by the project leads.

I tell this story not to vent my frustrations (those have, thankfully, long passed), but in a bid to demonstrate that ecological discourses can—and should—be interpreted via the prism of paradox. In 2017, I presented this same research at a conference in Crete organized by the European Group of Organization Studies (see Vine, 2017). The conference was billed as follows: *Food organizing matters: Paradoxes, problems and potentialities.* My arguments were undoubtedly better-received here, but I got the sense that at least some members of the audience were uncomfortable with the findings. Looking back on the report I produced at the time, my analysis revealed an overwhelming tendency on behalf of the extant academic literature on resilience, ecology, and eco-cultures (as well as the case studies we were tasked with reviewing) to assume—unreflexively—that small-scale food production represents *the* sustainable choice. The critique I presented was levelled at five distinct, but apparently related, assumptions.

Problematic assumption #1. Indigenous peoples are inherently 'in tune' with nature. There is a tendency in the relevant literature to assume indigenous people are (or at least, were, prior to Western influences) 'in tune' with their environs. For example, Cullen-Unsworth and Wallace (2011: 6) declare that: 'Aboriginal people ... are acutely aware of the biophysical changes in the landscape'. Similarly, Hayashi (2011: 1) suggests that hunting has traditionally been an integral way of life in the Arctic communities of North Greenland and so with the changes brought about by climate change, they have been coping 'by drawing on Inuit cultural practices, such as trans-generational environmental knowledge ...'. In his conceptual paper, Pretty (2011: 10), meanwhile, goes to lengths to critique historical stereotypes of hunter-gatherers, foragers, and farmers and prejudice thereof. However, each of these declarations requires corroboration, without which they remain conjecture. Indeed, this predisposition to assume that indigenous peoples are invariably 'in tune' with nature clouds the accuracy of the research presented. In their fear of being cast as the oppressor, Western academics must be careful not to lose sight of producing accurate and efficacious research. Notably, however, Clifton (2011: 4) is more measured. He suggests of his indigenous Indonesian subjects, the Bajou, that they conceive the passage of time as consisting of a series of unrelated events, described ... as 'living in a frozen moment'. Current actions are envisaged as acting only by future deeds. 'This belief system clearly nullifies the basic ecological rationale of fishery management, hence it should not be surprising that awareness and understanding of marine conservation regulations amongst the Bajou is consistently low'. Clifton does point out that the Bajou are by no means the sole culprits, but—in addition to demonstrating fundamental differences between knowledge systems—the important point is that it is imprudent to unreservedly assume that traditional techniques are *necessarily* sustainable.

Problematic assumption #2. 'Fair Trade' is universally beneficial. Later in his paper, Pretty (2011: 16) claims that 'initiatives that protect biological and cultural diversity include the Fair Trade movement'. But this too is an assumption that begs further enquiry. The Fair Trade movement is a form of branding and so—inevitably—carves up the market and in so doing creates insiders and outsiders. It discriminates between those who have access to the 'right' information and can afford the investment to fulfil the requisite product and marketing criteria and those who cannot. In this sense, the Fair Trade movement might plausibly be considered alienating. Interestingly, Hayashi (2011: 22) gives an example of how supposedly 'ethically minded' consumption in one part of the world damages the traditional livelihoods in another, hence highlighting a potential tension between ecological resilience and ethical practice: '[R]ecent animal rights campaigns in Europe have made it difficult for Greenlandic hunters to ... earn money by selling sealskin and fur'.

Problematic assumption #3. Social and ecological resilience go hand in hand. Adger (2000: 347) suggests that 'there is a clear link between social and ecological resilience, particularly for social groups or communities that are dependent on ecological and environmental resources for their livelihoods'. Indeed, this is a conceptual position common to all the case studies that were presented in this broader research project. However, and once again, this relationship needs to be re-examined and its complexity acknowledged. In making an assumption that social and ecological resilience are directly proportional, there is an inevitable predisposition to identify causal relationships between people and their environment. More judiciously, Warner (2001) reminds us that 'people-environment' systems *cannot be deconstructed into their causal components*. Beyond such reservation, the assumption that social and ecological resilience are directly proportional is more tangibly constrained by the inclusion of a specifically socio-*economic* perspective, a fundamental concern of assumption #4.

Problematic assumption #4. Small-scale activities are more resilient than large-scale activities. In a hypothesis dating back at least to Schumacher's (1973) seminal text *Small Is Beautiful*, alternative, ecologically minded initiatives have based their revisionist objectives on reducing the scale of human activities. In this way, the virtues of traditional re-skilling (in a subsistence sense) represent a common thread throughout the literature examined. For example, in Cullen-Unsworth and Wallace's (2011: 11) study of an aboriginal community, they suggest that their indigenous subjects '... have retained and/ or regained their connection to the local environment primarily by moving back to their traditional lands and reconnecting with "country"'. This re-skilling (or 'reconnection') is an apparent response to what Pretty (2011: 3–4) refers to as 'the crisis of disconnection' precipitated by commercial enterprise. Similarly, as Mustonen et al. (2011: 2) suggest of their subjects: 'The traditional knowledge developed within local communities is grounded in the close interaction between people and their local ecosystems over periods of hundreds or even thousands of years'. The implication here is that 'small is beautiful' because small-scale operations mean that participants have a first-hand, practical knowledge of their environs. In the event of economic or natural disaster, it is implied, skills of subsistence will constitute a key part of our resilience. However, this shift 'back' to small-scale human activities overlooks an alternative—and apparently inconvenient—interpretation. As Sedlmayr and Boehm (2011) concede, small agricultural businesses (which they consider invaluable in terms of ecological resilience) folded at the first sign of an exogenous economic shock, in their case a recession. In this sense, apparently ecologically *resilient* initiatives have proven in at least one case to be economically *vulnerable*. The same authors note that the principal challenge is related to the availability of 'cheap convenience foods, which have been produced with significant social and ecological impact'. But, once again, this is an assumption that requires unpacking. There is actually a convincing argument that quite the opposite is true, that is, that the much derided 'cheap convenience foods' have most likely been produced with *lower* ecological impact. Schlich and Fleissner (2004), for example, align what they refer to as 'ecologies of scale' with economies of scale. They say that 'people assume that the regional [i.e. small scale] production and distribution of food requires less energy turnover, compared with global transports of food' (ibid.: 219). However, their empirical data '... demonstrate a strong regressive relation of the specific energy turnover and the business size ... the efficiency and logistics of the production and the operations determine the specific energy turnover' (ibid.) In this sense, the ecological benefits accorded to large-scale production outweigh the ecological benefits accorded to proximity to the customer. With this in mind, does the civic practice of artificially sustaining small-scale ethical businesses, for example, through tax concessions and other financial incentives (such as those examined by both Sedlmayr & Boehm, 2011 and Accorigi, 2011), further compound the problems associated with this assumption? At the very least, the influence of scale on sustainability— and by implication resilience—warrants further impartial investigation.

Problematic assumption #5. Resilience should become a universal objective. Resilience is frequently contrasted to vulnerability. But again, this presupposes too much. We must ask broader questions: Does resilience in one region confer vulnerability in another? Does resilience in one sphere confer an opportunity cost in another? Is resilience is a zero-sum game? Furthermore, will today's resilience prove to be tomorrow's vulnerability? Pilgrim (2011: 4) acknowledges that 'what is resilient and adaptive in one place and at one point in time, may be vulnerable at another point along spatial or temporal trajectories'. Of his indigenous subjects, the Bajou, Clifton (2011) corroborates this. He argues that historically the Bajou demonstrated resilience in adapting to an exchange economy, but latterly, this has proven to be a source of vulnerability since—to some extent at least—they are now exposed to the will of the market. Similarly, Lokgariwar (2011: 13) writes of the studied indigenous Himalayan community: 'A shift to a cash economy means a reliance on the market'. The salience of this point cannot be overstated. In discussing resilience, we invariably do so to *contemporary* challenges. Does this represent a form of myopia? Rather than simply implementing strategies to respond to these challenges, might a focus on *prospective* challenges represent a good use of intellectual/empirical resources? Indeed, all the case studies appeared to assume—categorically— that resilience is a desirable objective. Only Regibeau and Rockett (2011), writing from an economics perspective, question this assumption. They write: 'It should be pointed out that while we focus on resilience as a concept … we do not present [an] argument that policies that increase resilience are necessarily desirable' (ibid.: 1). Furthermore: '[S]ustainability and resilience as concepts are very broad and do not reflect all that one would want in terms of narrowing down a policy choice' (ibid.: 3). Environmental resilience certainly proclaims to be conservational, but—I wonder—is also unwittingly rather *conservative*? Its adherents (few of whom I suspect would be happy to be labelled as conservatives) certainly seem to assume that human behaviour vis-à-vis ecology was markedly more responsible in times past. In any event, as Harari (2014: 82) notes:

Don't believe the tree-huggers who claim that our ancestors lived in harmony with nature. Long before the Industrial Revolution, Homo sapiens held the record among all organisms for driving the most plant and animal species to their extinctions. We have the dubious distinction of being the deadliest species in the annals of biology.

Science contra art, magic, and religion

We turn now to explore the manner in which paradox characterizes the dynamic between the sciences, on the one hand, and its oft-cited counterparts (specifically art, magic, and religion), on the other. Ask yourself a simple question: why exactly is the scientific method considered desirable? Science is regarded as desirable precisely because it seeks to abstract and isolate variables for analysis. And yet it is this very act of abstraction and isolation that disengages the enterprise of science from the all-important context. This methodological tension is explored in detail in Chapter 6. For the purposes of our current discussion, however, we focus instead on the *existential* tensions between science, on the one hand, and art, magic, and religion on the other. For Marsden (2002: 32), there is an enduring allure to art and mystery: 'For the human animal, the eruption of "new worlds" into being is glimpsed all too fleetingly in exhilarating experiences which defeat explanation in familiar terms—hence the devastating allure of erotic adventures, mystical revelations, and, of course, dreams and intoxication'.

> [W]e might even say science is 'our' magic. This assertion is amply borne out by the history of the most aggressively modern ideological formation, science, in relation to magic; numerous historical studies have shown how early modern science, while disavowing magic by that name, borrowed heavily from its ideology (an anthropocentric exercise of power), imagery (the powerful male magus), and techniques (alchemy and natural astrology).
>
> *(Curry, 2012: 77)*

Science—and certainly *scientism*—contends that we can know everything; it's just a matter of research. But to know everything would rob us of mystery and the 'unknown' and, perhaps, what it means to be human. Later in her tome, drawing on the work of Hölderlin, Marsden (2002: 79) continues: 'art is the bloom, the perfection of nature, for nature only becomes divine by its connection with art which harmonizes with nature as it differs'. In this sense, art is not the antithesis of nature or science, but its catalyst. And later still, this time drawing on the Immanuel Kant's vast canon, Marsden (2002: 82) poses a rather esoteric paradox:

> that nature [must] be judged as if it were art (that is, as if intentionally ordered and hence consonant with the power of judgement to discern systematic unity) and that fine art is only to be judged as fine when it 'looks to us like nature'.

Furthermore, Marsden eloquently argues that 'art emerges as the consequence of knowledge driven to its limit, as if creativity erupts at the very point where "natural cognition" is surpassed' (ibid.: 101).

In a similar vein, and once again drawing on the ideas of astrophysicist, Erich Jantsch, as well as chemist, Ilya Prigogine, Briggs and Peat (1985: 213) identify some pertinent parallels between physics and art:

> Jantsch wasn't suggesting that a co-evolutionary universe is a universe unfolding according to some fore-ordained, deterministic or God-given plan. He and Prigogine compared their theory to the Greek idea of the world as a work of art, and compared it to the usual scientific idea of the world as automaton. A work of art is a creative order. For Prigogine, what happens at the bifurcation point where dissipative structures are formed is the creative moment, a macroscopic 'uncertainty principle' equivalent to Heisenberg's microscopic uncertainty principle. The observer must accept

he [sic] is no longer dealing with a mechanical order that can be totally determined. He inhabits an indeterminate whole which exists beyond formulation of any particular level. In this way, the universe is as free from ultimate interpretation as a Bach cantata or a poem by Blake.

Comparable to—but most certainly distinct from—the peculiar dynamic between science and art is that of science and religion. Science and religion purportedly occupy polar ends of an analytical scale. For science, testable explanation reigns, while for religion it is a case of unfettered faith. But paradox rears its head here too. The existence of a deity is regularly invoked and conceptualized as the 'ultimate cause' in the case of the latter. *Causa sui*, or 'something that is its own cause', is a term routinely applied to God. Like scientists, then, theologians are all too often seduced by cause-and-effect epistemologies. For example, linear logic is clear to discern in *The Book of Genesis*: God, we're told, created the heavens and the earth. But as atheists are only too keen to point out (and usually in the terms of the specified gender bias): it is man that has created God who has, in turn, created man.

For Robinson and Zarate (2006: 75), 'Some philosophers and theologians suggest that reason and faith together can form solid foundations for religious belief. Others insist that the two are inherently incompatible.' A belief in god and a belief in science are each contingent on cause and effect. However, 'one obvious problem for 'compatibilists' is that Christianity's doctrines seem utterly beyond rational justification—God created the world from nothing; He is both one and three persons; and, as an infinite being, He took on a brief historical and finite existence in human form. Clever theologians can try to explain away these paradoxes. But a more radical way of dealing with them is to celebrate their very absurdity' (ibid. 79). This further cements our case that paradox is to be celebrated, not resolved. In any event, Robinson and Zarate insist that for Kierkegaard the problem is not to understand Christianity but to understand that it cannot be understood. Faith, they explain, is more like sight than knowledge—something immediate and vital—which means that to prove Christianity would actually make it emotionally vacuous (ibid.: 98).

Most perplexing of all is the significant overlap we find between scientific conviction and spiritual certainty. The eccentric artist Salvador Dalí once quipped: 'And now [we have] the announcement of Watson and Crick about DNA. This is for me the real proof of the existence of God' (Dalí, [1964] 1990, cited in Stent, 1978: 115). This peculiar union of science and spirit was something I discerned when I undertook the ethnographic research for my PhD. I was studying organizational behaviour in a remote commune based in Scotland, or 'intentional community', The Findhorn Foundation. Ostensibly, the community was underpinned by a synergetic blend of ecological and spiritual credentials. Early on in the fieldwork, and to my surprise, I realized that a (very) large proportion of participants who engaged in the spiritual practices themselves came from scientific backgrounds. Initially, I interpreted this on the basis of a naïve assumption: I assumed that the participants had become disillusioned with the 'godlessness' of the scientific world, and had instead found solace in the mysticism on offer at Findhorn. I was wrong. The numerous in-depth discussions I had with the participants revealed a very different explanation. What the participants suggested is that there was a vital—if often overlooked—continuity between physics and metaphysics. During my time living and working in the community, I began to spend more time in the community library. Perusing the shelves revealed a bibliographical penchant for the esoteric literature from the 1970s that transcends science and spirituality. There were, for example, dozens of books about Carl Jung, but also several haggard paperback copies of Capra's *The Tao of Physics* and Zukav's *The Dancing Wu Li Masters*. A fascination with science, particularly at an advanced level, must it seems eventually engage with—rather than stubbornly discount—considerations of religion and spirituality. In short, 'Dawkins is a douchebag', as another Findhorn participant joked (after a little too much camomile tea). At any rate, and as Dostoevsky reminds us: 'God sets us nothing but riddles' (Dostoevsky, cited in Marsden, 2002: 49). In the introduction to his rather quirky discussion of what he refers to as the 'holographic paradigm', Ken Wilber reflects on the character of this science/spirituality transcendence:

> [In] the 1970s, some very respected, very sober, very skilled researchers—physicists, biologists, physiologists, neurosurgeons … were not talking with religion, they were simply talking religion, and more extraordinarily, they were doing so in an attempt to explain the hard data of science itself. The very facts of science, they were saying, the actual data (from physics to physiology) seemed to make sense only if we assume some sort of implicit or unifying or transcendental ground underlying the explicit data.
>
> *(Wilber, 1982c: 1)*

'Either way', Wilber continues,

> modern science is no longer denying spirit. And that, that is epochal. As [Swiss Catholic Priest] Hans Küng remarked, the standard answer to: 'Do you believe in Spirit'? used to be, 'Of course not, I'm a scientist', but it might very soon become, 'Of course I believe in Spirit, I'm a scientist'.
>
> *(ibid. 1982c: 1, 4)*

And then later in the same text, at the point at which he goes on to advance his specific holographic metaphor, Wilber notes that the last thing religion or mysticism should seek is validation by science! This is really interesting: we are used to thinking of religion or mysticism as ephemeral and temporary, while scientific belief is permanent; in the event, it seems, it's quite the opposite.

> [A]s Jeremy Bernstein professor of physics at the Stevens Institute explains (1978), 'If I were an Eastern mystic the last thing in the world that I would want would be a reconciliation with modern science'. His point is that it is the very nature of scientific discoveries is that they ceaselessly change and alter, that last decade's scientific proof is this decade's fallacy, and that no major scientific fact can escape being profoundly altered by time and further experimentation. What if we said that Buddha's enlightenment just received corroboration from physics? What happens when, a decade from now, new scientific facts replace the current ones (as they must)? Does Buddha then lose his enlightenment? We cannot have it both ways. If we hitch mysticism to physics now, mustn't we ditch it then? What does it mean to confuse temporal, scientific facts with timeless contemplative realms? 'To hitch a religious [transpersonal] philosophy to a contemporary science', says Dr Bernstein, 'is a sure route to its obsolescence'.
>
> *(Wilber, 1982a: 167–168)*

Similarly, and casting physics in the wake of Heisenberg as an equivalent (for the natural sciences) of interpretative social science, Capra notes the following:

> We know in physics, since Heisenberg, that the classical ideal of scientific objectivity can no longer be maintained. Scientific research involves the observer as a participator and this involves the consciousness of the human observer. Now this insight, which is, by the way, one of the main parallels to mystical knowledge, implies that science can never be value free.
>
> *(Capra, 1982: 228)*

The classic idea of objectivity in science can no longer be maintained. From here, of course, we can consider the concept of belief, and here again we see paradox. In his excellent book *Subjectivity and paradox*, Thomas (1957) notes that Kierkegaard went to significant lengths to show that the devout are not dependent on any external sense of security:

> If faith's certainty were a philosophical matter, that meant for Kierkegaard that there was something wrong with it. The point that [Kierkegaard] had grasped so surely was that faith begins when its certainty is inward. If it

were certainty that resulted from a metaphysical scheme then it could be held only as long as that metaphysics is held. Now this is patently not true of faith.

(Thomas, 1957: 16)

There is an arresting parallel here with Wilber's point in *The Holographic Paradigm* where he argues that if physics eventually validated New Age spiritual endeavours this would be terrible news for the latter as in time that validating physics would be displaced by a newer physics. Thomas continues, on this occasion drawing upon the German philosopher Johann Georg Hamann (popularly known as 'The Wizard of the North'):

Hamann (1730–1788) was a firm opponent of the eighteenth-century Enlightenment in Germany. His work is little known, mainly because it is completely unsystematic, indeed chaotic, and written in a tortuous and difficult style. In his very first work which he called The Memorabilia of Socrates, he opposed his standpoint of faith to the rationalism of Enlightenment and the philosophy of Kant. His contention quite simply is that belief is more important than knowledge and understanding. [...] Our own existence and the existence of all objects without us must be believed, and can in no other way be made out ... What a man [sic] believes, therefore, does not need to be proved, and a proposition may be proved ever so incontrovertibly without on that account being believed. Faith is no operation of the Reason, because faith comes as little through argument as tasting or seeing.

(ibid.: 54–55)

Hamann was greatly influenced by David Hume. This is most evident in Hamann's conviction that faith and belief, rather than knowledge, determine human actions (Kinnaman, 2022). And, perhaps, most pertinent of all 'When faith asks for proof it sells its birthright for a mess of pottage. Its birthright, its very essence, is the absence of proof. Indeed, religion has no room "for proof"; it is subjectivity' (Thomas, 1957: 60). This is beyond dispute. If faith were ever proven to be correct, it would cease to be faith and would—thus—be stripped of its definition, value, and purpose. Thomas thus advances Kierkegaard's paradox of faith: 'For Kierkegaard the object of faith must by definition be something uncertain—that is, objectively uncertain. This contrasting certitude (inner certainty) and uncertainty (objective lack of certainty) of faith he called the paradox of faith' (ibid.: 103). Looked at another way, sociologist Gregor McLennan (2010: 5) suggests of postsecular endeavours: 'There is a bitter irony: secularism requires and even produces "religion" as its own discourse and political condition of existence'.

Postlude

For Bronowski (1976), an exploration of the contradictions nature itself yields brings us face to face with what he describes as 'the crucial paradox of knowledge'. With each year that passes we devise more precise instruments with which to observe nature. And yet when we look at the observations, we are discomforted to see that they are still just as fuzzy, and as uncertain as ever. We seem to be running after a goal which lurches away from us to infinity every time we come within sight of it. And Bronowski's paradox of knowledge is not confined to the small, atomic scale; on the contrary, it is as cogent on the scale of humankind, and even of the stars. He puts it in the context of an astronomical observatory. When we look at the position of a star as it was determined 200 years ago and compare that to now, it seems to us that we are closer to finding it precisely.

> But when we actually compare our individual observations today, we are astonished and chagrined to find them as scattered within themselves as ever. We had hoped that the human errors would disappear, and that we would ourselves have God's view. But it turns out that the errors cannot be taken out of the observations. And that is true of stars, or atoms, or just looking at somebody's picture, or hearing the report of somebody's speech. The world is not a fixed, solid array of objects, out there, for it cannot be fully separated from our perception of it.
>
> *(ibid.: 356)*

Just like eye floaters, the world shifts under our gaze, it interacts with us, and the knowledge that it yields must be interpreted by us. '[W]hatever fundamental units the world is put together from, they are more delicate, more fugitive, more startling than we catch in the butterfly net of our senses' (ibid.: 354). It is thus timely that we turn our attention now to the very paradoxes upon which our knowledge of the world is premised.

6

PARADOX AND ONTOLOGY

The preceding chapters explored paradoxes in specific fields. In this chapter, we deliberately draw back to secure a wide-angle vantage point. The coverage in this chapter represents our first tentative steps towards advancing the argument that paradox is a transcendent phenomenon. A primary means of accomplishing this is to recognize and explore the manner in which the very foundations of knowledge are themselves subject to paradox.

Ontology is the study of reality. Invariably, existential enquiries such as those pre-empted by discussions of ontology are often regarded as 'tosh' (a term my salt-of-the-earth dad uses to describe anything that is even remotely intellectual). Certainly, when I usher in a discussion of ontology among my MBA students, I am almost always met with a barrage of protestations. 'We didn't sign up for a degree in philosophy!', they holla. No—they didn't. But in order to meet the expectations of *any* academic research, instruction in ontology is imperative. While I have no intention of delineating a comprehensive discussion of the concept, it is important that we posit a working definition. Barbour (2000: 138) suggests that ontology is 'the branch of knowledge that considers what exists'. Quite simply, ontology refers to the concept of *being*. It is distinct from epistemology (which describes what we decide to designate as 'knowledge' or 'data'), but—crucially—both ontology and epistemology feed into a researcher's declared methodological position; that is, the assumptions they make about the process of research.

The first part of this chapter examines the manner in which ontology is characterized by paradox. This is illustrated by presenting the controversial argument that subjective methods (specifically ethnography) have a more convincing claim to objectivity than their hypothetical-deductive counterparts. We also demonstrate how hypothetical-deductive methods can actually be

DOI: 10.4324/9781003203339-7

more sensitive to subjective concerns than the former (hence illustrating the bi-directionality of the paradox). The latter part of the chapter then explores the manner in which ethnographic research puts paradox at the centre of its enterprise, and thus represents an exemplar from which future academic endeavours might take inspiration.

The definitive methodological paradox

In a radical departure from convention, Alvesson and Deetz (2000: 66) have suggested that

> interpretivists and others labelled as 'subjective' frequently have the *better claim to objectivity* given that they allow alternative language games and the possibility of alternative constructions arising from existing communities denying both research community conceptions and preferred methods as privileged and universal.

Part of the problem, of course, and as Hühn (2019: 4) points out is that life is characterized by disorder. And disorder rarely gels with objectivity: 'Who wants to deal with messy observable facts, when…. clean "stylised facts" are accepted by the hypothetico-deductive crowd'? Mannheim [1936] (1955: 4, 5) draws attention to the complexity of these ontological tensions and in a comparable vein to Alvesson and Deetz speculates on the potential for subjective sensitivities to yield objective insight.

> Just as pure logical analysis has severed individual thought from its group situation, so it has also separated thought from action. It did this on the tacit assumption that those inherent connections which always exist in reality between thought on the one hand, and group and activity on the other, are either insignificant for 'correct' thinking or can be detached from those foundations without any resultant difficulties. [...] It is, of course, true that in the social sciences, as elsewhere, the ultimate criterion of truth or falsity is to be found in the investigation of the object, and the sociology of knowledge is no substitute for this. But the examination of the object is not an isolated act; it takes place in a context which is coloured by values and collective unconscious, volitional impulses. In the social sciences it is this intellectual interest, oriented in a matrix of collective activity, which provides not only the general questions, but the concrete hypotheses for research and the thought-models for the ordering of experience. Only as we succeed in bringing into the area of conscious and explicit observation the various points of departure and of approach to the facts which are current in scientific as well as popular discussion, can we hope, in the course of time, to [understand] the unconscious motivations and presuppositions

which, in the last analysis, have brought these modes of thought into existence. A new type of objectivity in the social sciences is attainable not through the exclusion of evaluations but through the critical awareness of them.

This final sentence is extraordinarily pertinent for the purposes of our current thesis; we are best off, it would seem, side-stepping hackneyed contests between objectivity and subjectivity, and instead delineating terms for a new objectivity which is—itself—sensitive to hitherto subjective concerns. In marshalling the contemporary philosophy advanced by celebrated philosophers of science Thomas Kuhn and Paul Feyerabend, biologist Gunther Stent (1978: 212–213) opines along similar lines:

> [The] impersonal and objective science on behalf of which authority is claimed is only a myth and does not, in fact, exist. Since scientists are human beings rather than disembodied spirits, since they necessarily interact with the phenomena they observe, and since they use ordinary language to communicate their results, they are really part of the problem rather than part of the solution. That is to say, scientists lack the status of observers external to the world of phenomena, a status they would have to have if scientific propositions were to be truly objective.

Finally, in his excellent preface to Mannheim's *Ideology and Utopia*, Wirth (1936: xv) says the following with regards to objective thought: 'In the language of the Anglo-Saxon world to be objective has meant to be impartial, to have no preferences, predilections or prejudices, no biases, no preconceived values or judgements in the presence of the facts.' Contrariwise, those who approach academic research more subjectively recognize that impartiality is impossible. Consequently, we are better off acknowledging— and then reflecting on—our inevitable prejudices. Since interpretivists (of whom ethnographers are perhaps the most notable given the up close and personal engagement they seek with their subjects) are assumed to be more sensitive to social constructions and research bias, they ultimately produce more 'objective' data than their positivist counterparts. And this lays the foundations for what I refer to as the *definitive methodological paradox*. Addressing the related discourses of truth, objectivity and cause-and-effect in turn, I seek now to establish the foundations for a more comprehensive rendering of this definitive paradox.

Truth. Truth and methodology have a screwed-up relationship. I have lost count of the number of substandard undergraduate dissertations I have read in which the student's methodology chapter reads something like this: *I have selected a positivist epistemology because I am interested in the truth.* Although this sort of utterance is all-too-often the inevitable outcome of a failure to understanding the purpose of methodological framing, it is hardly surprising that students fall into this trap. We are primed to think of objectivity as 'good' and subjectivity as 'bad'. Objectivity (associated foremost with positivist research), we assume, means truth. But even the hardest of hard sciences has no legitimate claim to the truth. We continue to teach Newtonian physics in our schools even though—by the perspectives of Einstein or quantum theory—Newtonian physics is wrong. But does this mean that Einsteinian or quantum theoretical approaches are correct? No. Semiotician Umberto Eco hints at as much in his novel *The Name of the Rose:* 'Perhaps the mission of those who love mankind is to make people laugh at the truth, *to make truth laugh,* because the only truth lies in learning to free ourselves from insane passion for the truth' (Eco 1984: 491, original emphasis). Significantly, Nietzsche (1887: III, s24; 1989: 151) has said, 'Strictly speaking, there is no such thing as science without any presuppositions'. Rather, (ibid.: 119)

> there is *only* a perspective seeing; *only* a perspective knowing; and the *more* affects we allow to speak about one thing, the *more* eyes, different eyes, we can use to observe one thing, the more complete will our 'concept' of this thing, our 'objectivity', be.

As we will see, ethnographers are among the best placed to be the myriad eyes Nietzsche describes, each—in turn—contributing by way of a unique perspective to the collective ethnographic record. In this way, truth is more legitimately described as something subjective; something *emotional* (Bochner & Ellis, 2016: 85), and as something we *feel* rather than acknowledge (ibid.: 218).

Generalizability. Celebrated management theorist, Henry Mintzberg (1979: 583), asks us some pertinent questions:

> What is wrong with small samples? Why should researchers have to apologize for them? Should a physicist apologize for splitting only one atom? A doctoral student I know was not allowed to observe managers because of the 'problem' of sample size. He was required to measure what managers did through questionnaires, despite ample evidence that managers are poor estimators of their own time allocation. Was it better to have less valid data that were statistically significant?

Three decades on we are *still* forced to apologize for the same. In spite of the ideographic orientation of their research, Thomas and Southwell (2018) were forced to apologize for their 'small sample' of 20. And what of the circumstances when we conduct case study research where we typically have a sample size of one; a single datum? Is case study research therefore a waste of time? In qualitative research methods classes, I am asked this question perhaps more than any other: *How many interviews do I need to do?* Inevitably, I respond with three pieces of advice. (1) I ask the student 'How long is a piece of string?' (2) I suggest they revisit the concepts of ontology and epistemology. (3) I direct them to this brief passage in Holliday's (1995: 17) ethnography of a small business:

> At the very outset [of my research] I began to worry that I had not really seen the inside of a small manufacturing firm and so had no idea what kind of questions I would need to ask when I began my fieldwork. If I had been researching by questionnaire, of course, I might never have seen the inside of a small business.

These three pieces of advice are normally enough for the student to figure out that a small sample size is frequently *advantageous*. For Gelsthorpe (1992: 214)

> a rejection of the notion of 'objectivity' and a focus on experience in method does not mean a rejection of the need to be critical, rigorous and accurate; rather, it can mean making interpretive schemes explicit in the concern to produce good knowledge.

It is surely better to impose a caveat (and say 'this is my story') than to control for variables (and so deny the existence of a 'story'). As Becker (1967: 239) explains, it is impossible 'to do research that is uncontaminated by personal and political sympathies'. But aside from paradoxes associated with epistemology, it may be that the very 'stuff' of knowledge itself is subject to the mediating influence of paradox. Put simply, we'd do well to consciously shift our emphasis from 'explanation' to 'understanding'. As Marsden (2002: 100) notes, at its heart, the problem here is that any bid to explain will inevitably undermine the phenomenon in question: 'knowledge is victorious at the price of vanquishing its object'. In any event, she continues, 'Nietzsche insists that in spite of this "will to know" understanding can be conducted further than explanation' (ibid.).

Causality. As acknowledged at the outset of this book, we are schooled from an early age to think in terms of 'cause-and-effect' or—in the humanities—'beginning-middle-end'. Such instruction is, of course, an oversimplification. For Marsden (2002: 60), cause-and-effect thinking is useful only as a descriptive device. It is useless as a purported ontological fact. Drawing on the work of Arthur Schopenhauer [1819] (1966), Marsden argues that rather than viewing causality as 'objectively valid', it actually exists only 'in the understanding'. Furthermore, she notes, the epistemological vocabulary which supports its metaphysical reasoning is a fabrication. Certainly—and despite our dogged attachment to linear 'scientific' methods in schools and everyday discourse—there is growing disquiet trained on its limitations. For example, drawing on the work of both Nowotny (2005) and Tsoukas (2005), Styhre (2007: 9) notes the following:

> The climax of high modernity with its unshakeable belief in planning (in society) and predictability (in science) is long past. Gone too is the belief in simple cause-effect relationships often embodying implicit assumptions about their underlying linearity; in their place is an acknowledgement that many—perhaps most—relationships are non-linear and subject to ever changing patterns of predictability. Equally, [let us consider] 'changing patterns of unpredictability' as an 'open-world ontology': An open-world ontology assumes that the world is always in a process of becoming, of turning into something different. Flow, flux and chance are the fundamental processes of the world. The future is open, unknowable in principle, and it always holds the possibility of surprise.

Sagacious though these observations are, it is imperative to stress that paradox is more than mere flux. What I think all three of these authors are hinting at is complexity; but in training their focus on complexity they overlook the paradox. Briggs and Peat (1985), however, are closer to the mark. In their bid to precipitate a move beyond cause-and-effect thinking, they invoke the nineteenth-century German poet-philosopher-scientist Wolfgang von Goethe. von Goethe, they say, objected to the scientific revolution of his day because he said it didn't explain 'becoming' in nature. Science was at that time and to a large extent still is 'too engrossed in explaining cause-and-effect relationships on the surface of things and missed the dynamic creative activity beneath' (Briggs & Peat, 1985: 165). More pointedly still, they go on to argue that linear systems are really just approximations.

> Not all systems are linear—in fact, very few real ones are—but physicists could assume that, provided systems stayed very close to equilibrium, a linear approximation would be a good one. Because linear equations were so well understood and because linear systems behaved as they could be broken apart into independent units, scientists throughout the nineteenth century grew increasingly confident about a linear world. Of course, there were problems that remained stubbornly nonlinear, but, wherever possible, mathematical physicists would attempt to 'linearize' a system and treat the nonlinear parts as corrections. The mathematical treatment of nonlinear differential equations is far more forbidding than that of linear ones. Their solutions are not always obvious or straightforward, and obtaining one

solution may not be much help in obtaining others. Most important is how these solutions change when interaction terms are modified. In a linear system a small change in an interaction will produce a small change in solution. This is not the case with a nonlinear differential equation. The solution may change slowly as a parameter in the equation is varied and then suddenly change to a totally new type of solution.

(Briggs & Peat, 1985: 186)

Put another way, when we ask the world simple questions we get simple answers. The questions asked at the cutting edge of academic disciplines today are far from simple. We are thus in need of a fresh approach.

The active embrace of paradox in ethnographic research

For those unfamiliar with ethnography, it is the preferred method of fieldwork anthropologists. In recent decades it has also started to gain traction elsewhere in the social sciences. It is even beginning to make waves in the natural sciences (e.g. Strudwick, 2018). When teaching ethnographic methods to my students I typically begin class with a discussion of ethologist, Jane Goodall. Unlike her contemporaries, Goodall did not graduate from university and had no formal training in primatology. It was for precisely these reasons, however, that her research was so ground-breaking. Unlike her Victorian predecessors (for whom 'scientific research' meant dissection) or her contemporaries (who studied chimpanzees in captivity), Goodall chose to travel to their natural habitat in Africa. She lived among them and gradually gained their trust. In this way, she made some extraordinary discoveries. For example, she noted that chimpanzees experience emotion and mourn their dead. She documented not only that inter-troop conflict can and does arise, but that it can rapidly descend into war which spans generations. Perhaps most remarkable of all, however, Goodall gathered unequivocal evidence that chimpanzees used tools. This was extraordinary because until this point it was assumed by the scientific community that a distinguishing characteristic of humankind was an ability to use tools. In a manner analogous to Goodall's study of primates, I explain to my students that ethnographers do likewise but with *Homo sapiens* as their research subjects. Ethnography is thus anathema to experiment. Ethnographers do not dissect. Ethnographers do not distribute questionnaires. Ethnographers do not even schedule interviews. At its heart ethnography involves participant observation. Quite simply, the researcher immerses herself in 'the field' (be that field a specific culture, community, kinship group, or organization) and studies it from the inside out. To this end, the researcher both participates and observes. And as Bochner and Ellis (2016: 243) argue '...ethnography shares with fiction the desire to produce the effect of reality, verisimilitude, which seeks a likeness to life'. Put simply, ethnography helps shift our analytical emphasis from explanation to understanding.

For Denzin and Lincoln (1994: 15), research endeavours are 'defined by a series of tensions, contradictions and hesitations'. However, and unlike other research methods, ethnography has embraced this complexity. In Vine (2018b), I presented the case that since ethnography involves a sensitivity to paradox it is a more accurate reflection of the 'real world' than are abstract objective methods. In this subsection, I present—in abridged form—the arguments I advanced in that text. Inclusion of this coverage is important for two reasons. First, it is more than likely that it was my training as an ethnographer that has enabled me to embrace paradox. Second, it constitutes an important preamble to the chapters that follow this one in terms of enabling a fresh perspective vis-à-vis our understanding of ethics, pleasure, and agency.

So where does ethnography fit into the broader chronology of research methods? Well, since the publication of Burrell and Morgan's text on sociological paradigms in 1979 (itself a re-articulation of Thomas Kuhn's influential 1966 book), the framing of social science research methods has remained largely unchanged. Though illuminating in so many ways, their thesis had the effect of entrenching ideological positions (see, e.g. Hammersley, 1992: 182). If we are to propel our understanding of human behaviour to new pastures, we thus need to initiate an analytical shift away from paradigms. Ethnography represents an excellent opportunity to expedite the desired move from paradigms to paradox. As Atkinson and Hammersley (1994: 256) have previously observed, 'paradox lies at the heart of the ethnographic endeavour and of the ethnography as a textual product'. Contemporary ethnography 'explores the discontinuities, paradoxes, and inconsistencies of culture and action [and does so] not in order to resolve or reconcile those differences' (ibid.). To this end, it is argued that paradox must be celebrated rather than concealed or maligned since it is, for the most part, representative of social interaction itself. I here expand on this interpretation and in so doing identify nine paradoxes inherent to the ethnographic experience. These are: the participant–observer paradox, the familiarization paradox, the insider–outsider paradox, the honesty paradox, the consensus paradox, the all-too-human paradox, the plagiarism paradox, the linguistic construction paradox, and the autoethnographic paradox. The overriding aim here then is to draw the reader's attention to the extraordinary value of the ethnographic method as an approach which sensitizes its practitioners to the potential of paradox.

1. The participant-observer paradox. The expectation that the ethnographer must, concurrently, participate *and* observe is itself paradoxical. As Boncori (2018) has observed this essence of ethnography is a contradiction *par excellence.* Barnes too (2018), echoes Punch's (2005) concern as regards the ethnographer's capacity for observation when preoccupied with participation: 'One of the key objections to relying upon participant observational data is that it raises the question about how effectively a "participant observer" can observe the group if they are participating fully'. This dilemma is brought into relief if conceptualized slightly differently: Is it possible to internalize an 'exotic' culture while simultaneously maintaining professional distance? Boggis (2018), for example, reports that 'immersing myself within the culture of a community in order to study it raised tensions in respect of distance and the maintenance of objectivity'. But ethnographers can—and do—use this paradox to enhance their research. For example, Jackson (1989: 135, cited in Rose 1990: 58) comments that:

> Many of my most valued insights into Kuranko social life have followed from comparable cultivation and imitation of practical skills: hoeing a farm, dancing (as one body), lighting a kerosene lamp properly, weaving a mat, consulting a diviner. To break the habit of using linear communication model for understanding bodily praxis, it is necessary to adopt a methodological strategy of joining in without ulterior motive and literally putting oneself in the place of other persons; inhabiting their world. Participation thus becomes an end in itself rather than a means of gathering closely observed data which will be subject to interpretation elsewhere after the event.

If you genuinely participate you will, in effect, *observe*. Equally, observation can readily be construed as participation, in the sense that the observer 'constructs' the observed. Here we might invoke myriad studies of surveillance or, indeed, the *observer effect* in physics. Participation and observation, it seems, are not mutually exclusive; for our purposes at least, participation (when conceptualized as an end in itself) is effective 'observation'. By concurrently participating *and* observing; by internalizing 'exotic' cultures *while at the same time* maintaining professional distance, the ethnographer thus has a unique opportunity.

2. The familiarization paradox. Expertise is typically understood by virtue of familiarity with a subject area. As scholars, perhaps above all else, we are expected to be *familiar*. In ethnography, it is rarely this straightforward. Silverman (2007) points out that ethnography actively seeks out both the mundane in the remarkable and the remarkable in the mundane. Another way to approach this is to either render the 'exotic' familiar (i.e. to familiarize ourselves with an alien culture to understand it from that perspective), or to make the familiar 'exotic' (i.e. to '*de*familiarise' ourselves with our existing culture in order to gain a fresh perspective). Bell (1999: 21) comments of this process in my native field: '[Some] organizational ethnography involves a process of defamiliarization, through which concepts like "strategy" and "human resource management", are made strange'. The notion of deliberately defamiliarizing oneself is, of course, paradoxical, but Hammersley and Atkinson (2007: 9) argue that it is necessary 'in an effort to make explicit the presuppositions he or she takes for granted as a culture member'. This paradox of familiarization is likely part of the broader concern academic ethnographers experience in terms of expertise. As academic ethnographers we are simultaneously expected to be experts (as befits the expectations of our students or subjects) while each of us is, at times, doubtful of our own abilities, not least in terms of *in*experience. The notion of *imposter syndrome* therefore takes on an interesting guise under the vicissitudes of ethnography. Do all ethnographers suffer perpetually from imposter syndrome? To complicate matters further, Hammersley and Atkinson (1983: 84–85, as cited in Holliday, 1995: 28) have suggested that, in many ways a favourable role for a participant observer to adopt in the early stages of fieldwork is as a 'socially acceptable incompetent'. Rather than presenting oneself as an expert, which may have the corollary effect of condescension, deliberately presenting oneself as foolish may well be more effective. It is probably part of the reason that ethnographers can't help but lie (Fine & Shulman, 2009: 193). However, as Vine (2010: 646) has commented, 'this thoroughly disheartening thought is alleviated, at least in part, with the hope that fibs too can be creative': the ethnographer's falsehoods create ethnographic realities.

3. *The insider–outsider paradox.* For Rose (1990: 10), ethnography represents a 'democratic epistemology' in the sense that 'the thinking of the ethnographer and those studied inhabit the same historical moment'. Atkinson and Hammersley (1994: 256) explain that

> prolonged immersion in 'the field' and the emphasis on participant observation commit the ethnographer to a shared social world. He or she has become a 'stranger' or 'marginal native' in order to embark upon a process of cultural learning that is predicated on a degree of 'surrender' to 'the Other'. The epistemology of participant observation rests on the principle of interaction and the 'reciprocity of perspectives' between social actors. The rhetoric is thus egalitarian: observer and observed as inhabitants of a shared social and cultural field, their respective cultures different but equal, and capable of mutual recognition by virtue of a shared humanity.

Most students of ethnography will be familiar with this 'egalitarian' approach. But we have a problem. In approaching ethnography this way, do we unwittingly prevent ourselves from obtaining an external perspective?

Atkinson and Hammersley go on to acknowledge that the classic texts of ethnography often inscribed a distinction between the Author and the Other as a means of securing this external perspective. So which approach is better? To 'talk the talk' of egalitarian rhetoric (in the interests of securing insider status), or to preserve outsider status with the perspective advantages that may bring but risk accusations of superiority? You're damned if you do and you're damned if you don't. Furthermore, for those already considered insiders in one sense or another (by the virtue of skin colour, perhaps, or some other shared demographic), Ganga and Scott (2006: 1) identify another complication: '[T]o a large extent, interviewing within one's own "cultural" community—as an insider—affords the researcher a degree of social proximity that, paradoxically, increases awareness amongst both researcher and participant of the social divisions that exist between them.' Of organizational ethnography, in particular, Holliday (1995: 26) suggests that 'The process of managing one's identity as a researcher—and the more complex schizophrenic identity of researcher-cum-employee—is itself very stressful, involving continual renegotiation.' This demonstrates how the researcher is both insider and outsider simultaneously, and echoes the 'professionally-induced schizophrenia' described by Mascarenhas-Keyes (1987: 180). And how uncanny a resemblance does this have to life more generally! Most of us will be accustomed to the experience of the first few months in a new job with a new employer. This schizophrenic positionality is thoroughly familiar. But, even beyond that immersion period, though not necessarily by name, many of us will be aware of the 'pronoun test'. For Rousseau (1998) the pronoun test is acutely relevant to conceptualizations of identity: Do employees refer to the organization for which they work (or are a member) as 'we' or 'us', or as 'they' or 'them'? Or to what degree do participants use both, at different times, depending on how they might feel about the organization? Certainly, my own experience of working for the University of Suffolk alternates between a desire to belong and a desire to distance. Holliday (ibid.) continues:

> Initial entry to the field can involve 'learning on the job' to be done during the period of fieldwork. Thus, it is possible to be both insider and outsider as a not yet fully fledged member of the organisation. The initial focus of fieldwork is concentrated around learning how to do the task, leaving little room for reflection. Later, when the job is learnt and a position within the firm consolidated, it is possible to take a more detached view of the study setting.

What could be more effective, then? Without even trying, an ethnographer is securing multiple perspectives of her setting simply by virtue of the learning process. Indeed, this interpretation need not be restricted to the context of work. We could easily substitute the business for a wider family, community, school, social club, a place of worship—or even a gang.

During my doctoral research (see Vine, 2011) at the intentional community—or commune—known as the Findhorn Foundation, in Scotland, I got the impression that I was perceived by my subjects as a 'mainstreamer' in their 'alternative' community. To some extent, this was probably self-consciousness. But what was I to make of the situation? I had read extensively on ethnography and although aware of the diverse approaches within the method, I certainly knew one thing: I didn't want to emulate the colonial tradition of cultural superiority. But I faced a problem. So conscious was I to secure insider status that I began to denigrate mainstreamer culture and I did so with 'born again' vigour. I engaged in what might be described as *ethnomasochism*. Worse still, I didn't really believe what I was saying, at least not without qualification (which I withheld). I was, in effect, engaging in the egalitarian rhetoric Hammersley and Atkinson describe. At the time I felt dreadful. But in the years that have passed since, I have accepted this. I see it less as deceptive and more as representative of real life. When introduced to new people in *any* situation, we rarely take issue with their beliefs. We search instead for common ground and, in so doing, inevitably compromise—and subconsciously re-evaluate—our own beliefs. My conduct at Findhorn was no different. In order to secure insider status, I had no choice but to *Other* the outsider. This felt like a natural strategy. The outsider (and her ritual denigration) was essential to secure insider status. The two were intertwined. Notably, Cooper and Law (1995) draw on the work of Starobinski to argue that there is a false distinction between inside and outside:

> *inside and out*side are not separate places; they refer to a correlative structure in which 'complicity is mixed with antagonism... No outside would be conceivable without an inside fending it off, resisting it, "reacting" to it'.
>
> *(Starobinski, 1975: 342, cited in Cooper & Law, 1995: 244)*

4. *The honesty paradox.* The term is not used, but Gans (1962) in Bryman and Bell (2011: 124) reveals a paradox when exploring the ethics of ethnography: 'the researcher must be dishonest to get honest data'. Indeed, Denzin (1968) cited in the same volume, argues for an 'anything goes' stance as long as it does not harm participants or damage the discipline. More recently, during the ethnography stream at the 2014 European Group of Organizational Studies conference I made a note of the words presenters used to describe their experiences of conducting ethnography. In addition to those with which we are by now quite accustomed, these words included *aggressive, betrayal,* and *deceptive*. This seems to be a world away from the descriptions brokered in the often brief sections on ethnography in

research methods textbooks. Related to this is the question as to whether ethnography ought to be covert or overt. While the 'observer effect' implies that overt ethnography will most likely modify subjects' behaviour (see, e.g. Barnes, 2018,) covert ethnography presents ethical problems. Inevitably, since the ethnographer is all too human (see *The all too human paradox*, below), she will most likely do a bit of both. However, crucially, this in no way represents a departure from real life since we present ourselves differently in accordance with circumstances; our behaviour is contingent on our environs. My own experience at Findhorn is again intructive. Given the highly emotive and contingent experience in a New Age community, the solicitation of permission to use a voice recorder was not only impractical but—notably—would have been extremely insensitive. I therefore did use a voice recorder, but kept it concealed in a pocket. When you are immersed in the field for weeks on end, there are times when the researcher's capacity for recall is bound to be compromised. I was, at various times, tired, frustrated, or confused. The voice recorder was essential to assist in the collection of relevant data. I acted dishonestly to acquire honest data. Of photographic documentation, too, how often does an ethnographer go through the process of securing formal permission to photograph her subjects? To do so would render the process ungainly, bureaucratic and—by implication—create 'dishonest' representations of those photographed. A dishonest strategy is essential if we are to generate truer photographic data. Tellingly, in their ethnography study of Glastonbury, Prince and Riches (2000: xi) suggest that their camera was used principally in situations whereby its use 'could pass for tourist snaps'.

5. The all-too-human paradox. I return, once again, to my data from Findhorn; in this instance, the 'hot tub' scene (see Vine, 2018c). The circumstances of the environs were not especially relevant to the point I was trying to make at the time (in respect of one of my participants—Sofie's— work life), but I decided to leave in the detail, conscious that I would reflect upon it in later publications. Sofie was an attractive woman and similar in age to myself. In spite of the professional expectations of academic research, I will not overlook the fact that I was physically attracted to her. We were alone in the hot tub and were both naked, as was conventional at Findhorn. The simple fact of the matter is that bathing nude in a hot tub was an erotic experience. However, at the time, I did not report this in my field notes. Why not? Perhaps it wasn't strictly relevant to my research endeavours. Perhaps, as a doctoral student, I felt compelled to maintain some sort of ill-defined and unspoken scholarly respectability. But in respect of intellectual insight, what a wasted opportunity! How many of us can claim to have gone through our many years of education, for example, without ever having an all-consuming crush on a teacher or classmate? How many of us have not felt considerable discomfort in respect of medical procedures which in some way invade our sense of the erotic? How many of us can say that our attraction to a colleague at work has not affected (for better or for worse) our ability to do our job? Such experience is intrinsic to the very fabric of our social lives and so as ethnographers to ignore it, or—worse still—repress it, is only going to compromise that insight.

During that same visit to Findhorn, I overslept one morning. I wanted to reflect on this as part of my research (notably that I was for the first time completely relaxed), but my supervisor commented to me back on campus that such a 'confession' was tantamount to sloppy ethnography and would imply to the reader a 'disinterested researcher'. It would paint me as 'lazy', he said, and that would not do. I yielded to his authority. In some respects I regret this because on a personal note it demonstrated that I felt at ease with life in the community. Surely, as ethnographers we have a responsibility to convey experiences beyond the parameters of what they might imply on a surface or 'respectability' level?

6. *The certainty paradox.* One of the recurring themes ethnography presents is that of existential uncertainty. Indeed, for several of the authors in our 2018 edited collection, *Ethnographic Research Methods: Anxiety, Identity and Self* (see Vine et al., 2018), the concept of uncertainty was a preoccupation for our contributors. In an early draft of his chapter, by way of a preface to his own experiences transitioning from a positivist researcher to an ethnographer and the sense of existential doubt this elicits, Barnes (2018), for example, opened with a quote from Rilke's *Letters to a young poet*: 'Have patience with everything that remains unsolved in your heart... live in the question.' This is pertinent. Historically, our attitude to paradox has been as in inconvenience; our approach is very much focused on how best to resolve or dissolve the paradox. But is this necessary or indeed desirable? Most of us will be familiar with the philosophical truisms that underpin these experiences: 'the only thing we can be certain of is uncertainty'; 'the only constant is change', and so on. In turn, these find an analytical lineage dating back to Heraclitus of Ephesus's observation that 'you cannot step into the same river twice'.

But what, if anything, is the ethnographer to make of this? The certainty (or lack thereof) reported in that book was more practical than existential. Strudwick (2018), for example, expressed concern that in her native discipline of radiography there was a danger that ethnographic research may be seen as 'un-scientific', and 'lacking rigour'. She utters the following questions: How much should I ask? How much should I participate? Should I simply observe? There is, of course, no straight answer.

Notably, several of the authors in that volume tackled the concept of liminality. These ethnographic experiences at the liminal state seem to imply on the part of most, if not all, a sense of both fear and fascination as two sides of the same coin. For Dale and Burrell (2011: 113), architectural ruins are emblematic of this peculiar coupling:

> Fear comes from the significance that ruins hold for the integrity of our own world whilst the fascination with ruins lies in their liminal status between organization and disorganization, architecture and dust, order and chaos, humanity and nature. They materialize tensions in temporality and spatiality, survival and decay.

Fear and fascination inevitably disorientate. Holliday (1995: 21) comments thus:

> ethnography allows the researcher to drift and formulate ideas in the research setting, and to explore uncharted ground. While at times this may feel like losing one's way, it in fact produces a far more dynamic and processual view of the research setting. Further it shows clearly how research itself is processual, and that in this way issues which may not have been thought of at the outset emerge through the fieldwork, and can rise to prominence.

It is a common concern among early career ethnographers that they feel as though they are losing their way. But, once again, this is exactly what life is like: ethnographic methods thus encapsulate verisimilitude. A little further on, Holliday (1995: 30) reflects on the 'chaotic nature of my experiences', and in so doing attempts to normalise the sense of confusion that academic research illicits. Such a rendering reflects in its entirety the picture of organizational life famously painted in *The Nature of Managerial Work,* by Henry Mintzberg in 1973. Management is not about command, control, and coordination, as convention would have it. On the contrary, management is about muddling through, getting interrupted, and keeping your head above water. Uncertainty propels inquiry. It is the backbone of intellectual endeavour. But just try declaring that on your next ethics application form!

7. *The plagiarism paradox.* We live in a world where plagiarism is scorned and yet, in research—particularly ethnography—it is the dangers of *inverse* plagiarism that are the more arresting. For Fine and Shulman (2009: 185):

> [Ethnographers] engage in the inverse of plagiarism, giving credit to those undeserving, at least not for those precise words. To recall the exact words of a conversation, especially if one is not trained in shorthand is impossible [or indeed if you are not using a voice recorder; see *The honesty paradox*]. This is particularly applicable with those who maintain the illusion of 'active' or 'complete membership' by not taking notes within the limits of the public situation.

In this sense, paradoxically, the more 'genuine' your ethnography, the less likely you are to accurately represent your subjects since your note-recording capacity is inhibited by immersion. Perhaps, therefore, and given the scholarly tradition of 'accuracy' in respect of sources, inverse plagiarism is inevitable. However, and once again, it need not detract from the strength of the ethnography. Inverse plagiarism is another inevitability of everyday lives (when embellishing stories in the interests of effect, for example). An inspiring book, a provocative film, an engaging lecture; each will likely involve inverse plagiarism, hyperbole, and embellishment. A dull one most likely will not.

8. *The linguistic construction paradox.* For Humphries and Watson (2009: 40), 'ethnography is writing'. More specifically, ethnographic writing is a highly reflexive form of reportage. As Liamputtong (2009: 42) reminds us, 'Through conversation… individuals have an opportunity to know others, learn about their feelings, experiences and the world in which they live. So if we wish to learn how people see their world, we need to talk with people'. However, given the centrality of writing to ethnography, the biases associated with linguistic construction affect ethnography more, perhaps, than any other research method. In this sense, then, every word the ethnographer transcribes and every word she uses as part of her interpretation, both enhances our understanding of a phenomenon *and* creates further bias. In this way, Best (2018) confesses to her readers: 'I've shaped you. I'm shaping you now.'

Vocabulary, too, is relevant. My own experience at Findhorn revealed a divisive vocabulary. To outsiders, Findhorn was most definitely a 'commune'. To insiders, the word commune was never used; 'community' was preferred. How was I to describe Findhorn? Which term would I use, or would I use a different term altogether? The academic literature had long abandoned commune in favour of intentional community, but this is in no way neutral. In abandoning the term 'commune' the discourse says, quite firmly, that it wishes to dissociate itself from those who regard such collectives derogatorily. This is clearly about identity. I felt that the use of 'intentional community' would prove rather ungainly throughout the entire narrative and so, ultimately, settled on 'community'. However, intentionally or not, this elicited an allegiance. It carved out an identity, a political position, and I wasn't entirely comfortable about this. It is much the same in respect of the relatively recent move by the academy to distance itself from the terms 'prostitute' (in favour of sex worker) or 'gypsy' (in favour of traveller). The terms 'sex worker' and 'traveller' are no less biased that their counterparts (prostitute and gypsy); they merely represent a shift in political position (or, more accurately, a shift in the labelling of such positions). Boggis's research in that volume reveals something interesting in respect of disability, too. Boggis (2018) explores Oliver's observation that for some 'the term "people with disabilities" should be used in preference to "disabled people" because this prioritizes people rather than disability' (1983: 261). However, for others, it seems, 'disabled people' is the preferred terminology of those within the disabled movement because it makes a statement: they are not 'people with disabilities', but people who are disabled or disadvantaged by society's responses to their differences.

9. *The autoethnographic paradox*. Autoethnography is an ethnography of the self. Most ethnographic research involves an autoethnographic component, at least to the extent that immersing oneself in the field will inevitably impress upon the researcher and influence them in ways they hadn't anticipated. And reflecting on this influence is, itself, a form of research. As Weir and Clarke (2018) argue, there is unquestionably an authenticity of knowing oneself. To this end, they defend autoethnography against its critics (specifically, Delamont, 2007). However, one might also argue—and persuasively so— that the worst person to ask about me is me. This is, of course, part of the reason dating websites such as *mysinglefriend.com* have been so successful. Rather than engage in the uncomfortably narcissistic exercise of marketing yourself to potential partners, the task is ostensibly delegated to a friend. However, this is—I think—slightly different to the argument regarding the purported inability to 'fight familiarity' proffered by Delamont (2007). It is about perspective, yes, but it's not that the autoethnographic perspective is *wrong*; it's just different. It's no less valid. There is a wonderful tension here. It's foolish to denigrate the tradition on the basis of an inability to fight subjectivity since it is that same subjectivity that enables the distinctive perspective in the first place. Notably, for Jeffcut (1991: 13, cited in Holliday 1995: 22). '...the objective of [ethnographic] interpretation is to bring us into touch with the lives of strangers, [and] one of those strangers is inevitably ourself'.

Here, then, we can invoke a *paradox of self-revelation*. In recent years, and especially in the more progressive qualitative methods, we have witnessed a call for increased use of the first person pronoun. This purportedly represents a more candid approach both to research and to writing. It helps address the mistakes of earlier research that naively assumed the researcher could maintain objective distance from her data. We are, it seems, inextricably a part of our data. However, it is worth stressing that the first person pronoun accords—unreflexively—centrality to the 'individual'. And, saliently, the concept of individual is a distinctly modern invention. In a certain sense, the individual did not exist in traditional cultures, and individuality was not revered as it is today. In this sense, use of the first person pronoun reflects a specific linguistic tradition and bias in which the concept of the individual is lent primacy over the collective. And this of course is a value judgement. Nietzsche [1886] (1989: 92) makes a further pertinent observation: 'Talking about oneself can also be a means to conceal oneself.'

The experience of autoethnography will likely be unsettling for generations of researchers to come. But this doesn't invalidate it; on the contrary, it underscores its vitality. The autoethnographer is not an objective scribe. Rather, what's revealing about autoethnography is the sense of change and transformation; tension and contradiction. For Learmonth and Humphreys (2012), for example,

> Throughout our adult lives we have been haunted by a sense of doubleness—a feeling of dislocation, of being in the wrong place, of playing a role... Presenting ourselves as objects of research, we show how, for us, contemporary academic identity is problematic in that it necessarily involves being (at least) 'both' Jekyll and Hyde.

Finally, there's the perennial accusations of narcissism. Narcissism was explored in autoethnography as early as William Whyte's infamous *Street Corner Society,* first published in 1943. And, yes, writing about oneself *is* narcissistic. That is inescapable. But, once again, therein lies its significance.

> As [we've] said several times, autoethnography should be celebrated and appreciated as the genre of doubt. Unlike traditional social science, which usually comes across as an exclamation point (!), autoethnography emphasizes the question mark (?). Doubt and awe should remain in our stories.
>
> *(Bochner & Ellis, 2016: 246)*

Towards an intersubjective research agenda

Ethnographic approaches rarely fall prey to the problems we've identified in respect of cause-and-effect, not least because a sense of critical reflexivity is coded into the method. Following the presentation of her autoethnographic story about working at a for-profit university, for example, Best (2018: 167) confesses: 'Everything I've presented is in a linear fashion—when no story is really linear—it's chaos...'. Only the very simplest of stories would adhere to the expectations of linearity. Are 'stories' in the natural sciences any different? No. In *Paradoxes of Progress,* Stent (1978: 148) writes:

> Provided that the questions one asks of Nature are not too deep, satisfactory answers can usually be found. Difficulties arise only when... the questions become too deep and the answers that must be given to these questions are no longer fully consonant with rational thought.

Where analysis remains shallow, cause-and-effect ontologies (or 'stories') tend to operate effectively; it is where we dig a little deeper that paradox emerges. As a result, we become fearful of deeper analysis.

However, and in spite of what we've said about truth, objectivity, and causality, we live in a world where there is a bias towards analytical simplicity, or 'elegance' (as has become the popular term). We are frequently told that simplistic explanations are the most effective (a corollary of the principle of parsimony, popularly known as *Occam's razor*). Certainly, most positivist/ quantitative research strives for simplicity. However, here lies a fundamental problem because our world is far from simple. 'Successful'—by which we really mean 'popular'—explanations are rarely accurate. Turning once again to my native discipline of organization and management studies, theoretical models tend to come in the form of *2x2* typologies. Examples include Porter's Generic Competitive Strategy Framework (Porter, 1985), the Boston matrix (Stern & Deimler, 2006), and even Burrell & Morgan's (1979) sociological paradigms for organizational analysis. Why is this? Is there some underlying elegance to the universe that favours such a configuration? It's unlikely. A more probable explanation for the prevalence of *2x2* typologies is that they are simple. Furthermore, although typologies may purport to reflect, in practice they tend to *reinforce*; typologies are a way of organizing. They are inevitably associated foremost with positivist/quantitative methodologies. By actively resisting a temptation to 'typologise', and instead pursuing research sensitive to a grounded theoretical approach, effective ethnography can move beyond these concerns.

Let's look at this another way. Ethnography might legitimately be described as the *method acting* of academic research. Method acting traces its origins to Konstantin Stanislavski's philosophy, a philosophy which was part of the theatrical realist movement based on the idea that good acting is a reflection of truth, mediated through the actor. For Shakespeare, of course, all the world's a stage and we are 'merely' actors. And—certainly—the methods by which social actors construct everyday life are vital:

> Such actors are viewed as engaged in constructing and reconstructing social realities through generating and using meanings to make events sensible. A dramaturgical metaphor is often employed; actors must manage appearances and constantly ad lib essentially vague social roles in an emergent stream of existential being and awareness. A basic assumption is that social reality is not merely a stable entity but passively entered and apprehended, but one which requires actors (members) to work at accomplishing this 'reality for all practical purposes'.
>
> *(Gephart, 1978: 556)*

'Real' life is, paradoxically, an act. For Deloria (1969: 146), 'irony and satire provide much keener insights into a group's collective psyche and values than do years of [conventional] research'. Ultimately, of course, human behaviour is based upon meanings that people attribute to and bring to situations, and that behaviour is not 'caused' in any mechanical way, but is continually constructed and reconstructed on the basis of people's interpretations of the situations they are in.

(Punch, 2014: 126)

Scientists cannot be external to their experiments. Molecular biologist, Gunther Stent (1978: 226) deliberately shifts our attention from the objective to the intersubjective:

> an individual's moral judgements arise by a transformational process operating on an innate ethical deep structure. But despite their subjective source, his [sic] moral judgements are not seen as arbitrary or completely idiosyncratic by others, because the innate ethical deep structure is a universal which all humans share.

Crucially, intersubjective insight is the bread and butter of ethnography. Crang and Cook (2007: 37), for example, argue that 'to talk about participant observation should not be to separate its "subjective" and "objective" components, but to talk about it as a means of developing intersubjective understandings between the researcher and the researched'. 'Ethnography is neither subjective nor objective. It is *interpretive*, mediating two worlds through a third' (Agar, 1986: 19, emphasis added). Similarly, we might also avoid the binary pull of either inductive or deductive techniques, but instead consider abductive approaches. An empirical focus on intersubjectivity also enables ethnography to generate understanding in respect of *process* rather than *result* (see Cooper & Law, 1995: 238). And this is why ethnography has a unique responsibility. Ethnography is non-finite; it is live; it is dynamic; it unfolds; it is 'flying by the seat of your pants' (Van Maanen, 1988: 120). It is forever 'in process'.

> Whether we like it or not, researchers remain human beings complete with the usual assembly of feelings, failings and moods. All of these things influence how we feel and what is going on. Our consciousness is always the medium through which research occurs; there is no method or technique of doing research other than through the medium of the researcher.
>
> *(Stanley & Wise, 1993: 157)*

Supposedly objective research seeks to distance the researcher from her experiment or study. However, the 'reality' is that this mediation is likely the only thing 'true' about the research. Herein lies the paradox.

As we are beginning to recognize, paradox is pervasive: from the cinematography of David Lynch, through the physics of relativity, to the pursuit for world peace. Paradox exists *between* disciplines too. Although usually considered in binary opposition, both science and religion presuppose a cause-and-effect ontology. They are frequently invoked to justify one another. Isaac Newton, for example, held that absolute space and absolute time are constituted by the omniscience and omnipotence of God, as his 'Sensorium' (Powers, 1982: 31). However, that paradox is pervasive means ethnographers must proceed with extreme caution. Though—ironically— we have demonstrated that ethnography often has the better claim to objectivity, there is no room for complacency or self-righteousness. For Yanow (2010: 1400):

> ethnography entails a complex interchange between the researcher's prior conceptual boxes and the field data generated—and one can only hope, from an interpretative methodological perspective, that the data are not being force fitted into those conceptual boxes but rather that the shape and content of the boxes are being allowed to develop into a bottom-up fashion in light of those generated, non 'given' data.

And this is crucial. The sensitivity built into the ethnographic enterprise does not guarantee it will be deployed. One concern is that while positivists may be blissfully ignorant of the biases underpinning their frameworks, interpretivists—who are not—may be using these to their personal advantage. In this sense, then, and as a paradox, it does of course work the other way too! And as Atkinson and Hammersley (1994: 253) imply, positivism may actually be more sensitive to participant wellbeing than interpretivism:

> It is suggested that by its very nature anthropology (and the point can be extended without distortion to ethnographic work in general) involves 'representation' of others even when it does not explicitly claim to speak for or on behalf of them.

Its clear advantages notwithstanding, ethnography is not a panacea to the world's ills.

Postlude

The discussions advanced in this chapter have, I hope, persuaded you of two things. First—and most important—the foundations of knowledge themselves are characterized by paradox. Second, and unlike almost all other methodological frames, subjective-ethnographic research actively embraces complexity and contradiction. It is in this spirit, then, that we are able to approach the topics of the following three chapters (ethics in Chapter 7, pleasure in Chapter 8, and agency in Chapter 9) not as philosophers, but as ethnographers. Although we take vital cues from philosophy in this latter part of the book, we place less emphasis on abstract reason, and more on experiential reflection.

PART II

The Pedagogical Potential for Paradox

7

PEDAGOGICAL LOGIC I

Paradox Thwarts Moral Closure

In the preceding chapters, we documented the pervasiveness of paradox across four principal domains of life: *art*, *society*, *organization*, and *nature*. We then saw how paradox characterized the very metaphysics of knowledge; that is *ontology*. In this latter part of the book we build upon the understanding of the pervasiveness of paradox developed in that earlier part of the book to consciously and deliberately manipulate the field in new directions. To this end, we advance three principal 'logics' of paradox. The first logic, and the focus on this chapter, is summarized as follows: *paradox thwarts moral or ideological closure*. And it does so irrespective of how apparently desirable, just or seductive a particular position may initially appear. We courted questions of ethics in earlier chapters but these now become our guiding concern. In distinguishing this discussion from purest philosophical tomes which typically grapple with ethics in a disembodied intellectual sense, our focus here is of course on the lived experience of ethics. In this spirit, Bochner and Ellis argue that ethical dilemmas necessitate navigation rather than abstract solution:

> [O]ur ethical decisions involve struggle and uncertainty. That's what makes them dilemmas. There are no perfect answers. Sometimes you just have to put your struggle and uncertainty on the pages and invite readers to enter your consciousness as you grapple with writing ethically. Revealing that struggle too is a contribution. [But] ...don't get too bogged down in unsolvable ethical dilemmas.
>
> *(Bochner & Ellis, 2016: 153)*

DOI: 10.4324/9781003203339-9

The chapter begins with an exploration of the relationship between paradox and ethics by recourse to the aphorism 'might makes right'. We then turn our attention to more specific paradoxes including 'the paradox of binary morality', 'the paradox of free will', 'the paradox of selflessness', and 'the paradox of conflict'. Restating the observation that without paradox a life-affirming calculus would be sufficient to determine direction, we conclude this particular chapter by suggesting that paradox can help animate, justify and legitimize the contentious concepts of both consciousness and agency. In so doing, we pre-empt the penultimate and concluding chapters of this book.

Might makes right

For Thrasymachus in Plato's *Republic*, 'justice is nothing else than the interest of the stronger'. This may well be the earliest documented precursor to the rhythmic aphorism, 'might makes right'. For my liberal readers brought up in the West, this is a bloody difficult pill to swallow. Women's rights, gender plurality and tolerance of divergent lifestyles *is* right, they shout. In practice, however, they are right only if these values are what you have grown accustomed to. The West—and its cultural predispositions—is our default. But how 'right' is it? Is it any more or less right than the conservative Christianity most liberals so vehemently oppose (or vice versa)? Consider, for example, liberal attitudes towards gender. Where—exactly—do we position ourselves in response to the cartoon below?

FIGURE 7.1   Malcolm Evans' *Cruel Culture.*

This cartoon is one I use regularly in class with my ethics students precisely because it is unsettling for both those with liberal predispositions and those of a more conservative bent. Let us assume that most readers of this book, when push comes to shove, harbour liberal attitudes. Who do you—as liberals—side with: the bikini babe or the devout Muslim? Or do you choose *not* to take sides, and if so, does this undermine your sense of ethical integrity? Or do you reject both castings? There is no straightforward response. The cartoon invokes considerations of spatial moral relativity; that is, the suggestion that what is right in one part of the world (or culture), isn't necessarily right in another. More interesting, perhaps, is what we can refer to as temporal moral relativity. As Nietzsche notes: 'What a time experiences as evil is usually an untimely echo of what was formerly experienced as good—the atavism of a more ancient ideal' (Nietzsche, 1886: s149; 1989: 90). Similarly, 'All good things were formally bad things; every original sin has turned into an original virtue' (Nietzsche, 1887: III, 9; 1989: 113). What Nietzsche is hinting at here is the cyclical nature of the ethical Zeitgeist. I have lots of fun with my undergraduates exploring this idea. I ask them: What attitudes of yesteryear (say, a generation or a century ago) do you find abhorrent today? Inevitably, this proffers a torrent of eager contributions. In recent years, my students have drawn upon the *Me Too* and *Black Lives Matter* campaigns to illustrate their arguments. In short, they are bubbling with ideas about how today's attitudes are so much more enlightened than yesterday's.

But I then ask them to speculate on how people a hundred years from now (or even a generation from now) might look back on what we do or how we act *today* and express alarm. This tends to attract more hesitation among the students. But surely we've figured out all the injustices, they think. Not so. Yesteryear, we were completely unaware about how our then attitudes would be perceived today. 'Every generation', wrote 1980s band *Mike & The Mechanics*, 'blames the one before'. Eventually, a few hands go up. But the offerings are pretty meagre. Most simply extrapolate, and, say, for example, 'I think a generation from now nobody will eat meat', or 'packaging will be fully recyclable'. Hardly revelation. I urge them to *think*. As we noted in the chapter on society, the writers of the hit single *Do They Know It's Christmas?* had only the very best intentions in mind, and yet a generation later the lyrics are now viewed as patronizing. Similarly, a generation from now, the *Black Lives Matter* movement may well be regarded as problematic, perhaps because it reflects—and reinforces—a predisposition to categorize people by colour. However well-intentioned it may be today, in the future it may be perceived as peculiar, or even damaging. In a generation from now, we may regard people as simply—well—*people*. No longer will skin colour be considered a determining—or even noteworthy—demographic. This is especially likely if we have, by then, detected life on planets other than our own and hence secured a fresh means of Othering (which—paradoxically—would more than likely forge a strong 'earthling' identity). As Moffett (2019: 4111) notes

> One possible means of attaining global unity might be to shift people's perception of who is an outsider—a point Ronald Reagan made often: 'I occasionally think how quickly our differences worldwide would vanish', he remarked in an address to the United Nations, 'if we were facing an alien threat from outside this world'. Popular science fiction tales like The War of the Worlds depict all of humankind pulling together against a common enemy.

Serendipity provided me with another way of exploring the possibility of about-turns in respect of moral position while writing up this book. In September 2022, my 3-year-old daughter's school marked 'Talk Like a Pirate Day' which, I understand, is now an international event. We received an email from the school inviting all students to turn up 'dressed as pirates' on the day in question. The expectation was, of course, that pupils turn up in a traditional West Country pirate costume. But is this problematic? Is it racist? Does it assume an imperial dominance? Would a more realistic rendering of a contemporary pirate—i.e. Somalian/Horn of Africa—be more appropriate? Or would *that* be racist? We did of course play it safe, and dress Sophie as a West Country pirate. But the point is our decision was dictated *entirely* by our reading of public opinion, rather than some sort of sublime transcendent condition of what is right or wrong. Indeed, a generation from now, for such an event the 'traditional' costume of the West Country pirate may well be considered both outdated and offensive. This example illustrates that deeply held assumptions are not just the preserve of racists, but are also at the heart of what's considered politically or morally correct.

Some have begun to acknowledge a greater sense of nuance with regards to ethics. This—I think—is due in no small part to Harry Potter author J.K. Rowling's stance regarding transgender rights vis-à-vis women's rights. For Potter, an ardent feminist, women's rights ought not to be extended to transgender women originally born as men. Thorny questions are raised when we recognize that both women's rights *and* transgender rights are considered liberal predispositions. Perhaps Isaac Asimov's character Salvor Hardin had it right when he uttered the following: 'Never let your sense of morals prevent you from doing what is right!' (Asimov, 1951: 141). In the final analysis, the liberal predispositions many of us hold so dear (feminism, multiculturalism, LGBTQ+, and so on), are—at source—manifestations of a Western hegemony: 'might makes right'. This, of course, is precisely why the likes of Russia and China, each of which harbour quite different—more orthodox—attitudes, exhibit such anti-West sentiment. It is also why those in the West find it so difficult to understand *them*. There is, it seems, a fundamental tension at the heart of any ethical endeavour.

Binary morality

We are each implicit in the co-construction of a world that thinks— primarily—in right and wrong, good and bad. Why and how exactly did we create such a world? It seems we are taught to think this way from an early age. For those of my readers who grew up in a culture informed by Christian values, you will no doubt be familiar with the *Tree of knowledge of good and evil* in the Garden of Eden (colloquially known as the *Story of Adam and Eve*). Did this posited binary relationship between good and evil lay the foundations for our pervasive—but clearly flawed—carving up of the world into 'goodies' and 'baddies', tropes frequently echoed in populist storytelling? Does either 'goodie' or 'baddie' actually exist? For sure, demarcating life into good and bad categories can make things easier for us, even if such as casting is existentially imprecise. But—let's be clear—good would make no sense without bad; God couldn't exist (if indeed, she does) without the Devil. And we certainly wouldn't be treated to the delights of blockbuster movies (irrespective of whether they are spawned from Hollywood, Bollywood, Hallyuwood, or Nollywood), since the pervasive traits of good and bad are so vital to their narratives. Good and bad are irrevocably interrelated. Notably, a more arresting examination of the Christian faith reveals a pervasive paradox which hinges on this binary problem.

> Early Christian philosophers were confronted with the baffling paradox inherent in most monotheistic religions, namely that they embrace the transcendental belief in a one-and-only, all-powerful, righteous, benign God, despite the obvious fact that the world He created abounds in evil.
>
> *(Stent, 2002: 59)*

This became known as theodicy; the vindication of God in view of evil. Attempts to resolve the theodicy paradox, Stent says, involve the re-examination of the concept of evil. What appears to be evil when seen in isolation or in too limited a context actually turns out to be a necessary element in the perception of the good when the world is viewed as a whole. This is because evil provides a contrasting background that makes the good shine more brightly. 'According to [theologian] Augustine, a world that contains as many different kinds of entities as are possible—good as well as bad—expresses more adequately His creativity than a world that contains only the highest type of created beings' (Stent, 2002: 65). For my money, however, this amounts not to a resolution of the paradox, but as a means of inferring constructively from it.

Let's now turn our attention to a number of applications in respect of binary ethics, and how—ultimately—they too reveal a sense of paradox. We have already engaged with some of these tensions in Chapter 3. However, here our analytical focus is driven by the moral dilemma at stake, rather than the broader ramifications on social conduct. In any event, and as Bochner and Ellis (2016: 45–46) remind us there is overlap here because the social sciences were originally intended as a sort of moral guidebook. To this end, let us consider some dilemmas revealed in respect of ethics vis-à-vis disability, ethics vis-à-vis minority analysis, and poverty and redistribution.

In recent years, two stories by the BBC revealed a greater-than-usual sense of nuance with regard to disability and race. In 2016, the BBC ran a biographical piece on South African, Sarah Baartman (see BBC, 2016b), famed for her appearance in Victorian-era freak shows in which she flaunted her large bottom and thighs. What was especially fascinating about this article is that while—and in line with expectation—it highlights the manner in which such parading is, in the words of the article, 'the epitome of colonial exploitation, racism, ridicule and commodification of black people', it also reveals more analytical subtlety. It notes, for example, that Baartman's fame provided for her a lifestyle she could scarcely have imagined back home in South Africa. More significantly, still, the article invokes an interesting point of comparison:

> In 2014, the cover of Paper magazine showed reality television star Kim Kardashian balancing a champagne glass on her protruding bottom. Some critics complained the image was reminiscent of contemporary drawings of Baartman. The Kardashian photo referenced a 1976 image by the same photographer—Jean-Paul Goude—which showed black model Carolina Beaumont naked and in a similar pose.

What is so revealing here, I think, is that while each of us more than likely feels a sense of shame at the purported exploitation of Baartman, do we feel similarly in respect of Kardashian? Possibly not because Kardashian is regarded as the proverbial spoilt brat. Of course, some may argue that Kardashian is herself a victim; in her case of an exploitative male-dominated culture. But to advance such an argument places us on shaky ground vis-à-vis agency, as we will see in Chapter 9. Ultimately, ethical judgement intended to 'protect the vulnerable' is brokered and monopolized by the privileged; it is patronizing. Later, in 2021, the BBC published a piece called 'You are the modern day Elephant Man' (BBC, 2021b) in which the author documents his own evolving attitudes to freak shows. The freak show is considered exploitative but at the same time it creates for its participants a sense of belonging and identity. Indeed, it is likely the perception of exploitation came from guilt-ridden privileged individuals (I'm thinking here of the 'Critical

Consensus'; see Vine, 2021). For the author of that article, he noted of one of his interviewees:

> I spoke to Black Scorpion—who also has Ectrodactyly—a man who is very much the heart and soul of the [freak show known as] 999 Eyes. He described how performing in freak shows had changed his life. Growing up, he felt like an outsider who didn't have a voice but the freak show gave him both a place to belong and a voice to tell his story.

The paradox of free will

As students of ethics very quickly come to realize, any meaningful discussion of what is right or good is contingent on a broader deliberation about the freedom of the will. This is of course because we are, in part at least, other-determined; that is, our actions are determined by our genotype (*nature*), the environment in which we are immersed (*nurture*), or some undisclosed combination of the two (*nature and nurture*). At this point, the thorny question of accountability rears its head. It is perhaps unsurprising, then, that for the late—and celebrated—semiologist, Umberto Eco, 'There is no thought more terrible, especially for the philosopher, than that of free will' (Eco, 1995: 479). The banal question, then, that we each ask ourselves at some point in our life is whether or not we have free will. Now, this age-old philosophical conundrum is so clichéd that I considered shirking it altogether in this book. But to do so would have amounted to a serious omission.

Early on in *Beyond Good and Evil*, Nietzsche draws attention to the duality associated with the will, and argues that we concurrently command and obey ourselves. In this sense, any abstract notion of free will completely misses the point. Instead, Nietzsche invokes the paradoxical qualities of the question, and spits the following witticism:

> It is certainly not the least charm of a theory that it is refutable... It seems that the hundred-times-refuted theory of a 'free will' owes to its persistence to this charm alone; again and again someone comes along who feels he is strong enough to refute it.
>
> *(Nietzsche, 1886: s18; 1989: 24–25)*

To challenge the theory of free will therefore requires, paradoxically, a strong will. Biologist Gunther Stent has explored—in extraordinary detail—paradoxes inherent to free will and readers interested in this particular branch of our thesis would do well to consult that text in full. However, for the purposes of our coverage, I summarize the key points. Somewhat surprisingly, perhaps, Stent begins with the bible, specifically the story of Adam and Eve and notes that while God expressly forbids Adam and Eve to reach for the tree's fruit, they do so anyhow and in so doing illicitly achieve a moral standing. Crucially:

> It was God, of course, who empowered them to defy Him in the first place, by having created them in His image, and endowed them with non-natural free will. Thus He had personally seen to it that, unlike their fellow animals in the Garden, Adam and Eve were capable of committing sin. Adam and Eve's awareness of their freely willed, sinful disobedience resulted in their shame and guilt and expulsion from Eden.
>
> *(Stent, 2002: 39)*

In this way, the price we pay for free will is culpability. Biblical allegory aside, the bulk of Stent's thesis is very much focussed on the philosophy of Immanuel Kant, and especially Kant's epistemic dualism. In the mid-eighteenth century, Stent says, Immanuel Kant presented a dualist solution to the mind–body problem that was significantly different from any that had previously been put forward. 'Kant's solution, to which we will refer as "epistemic dualism"... disentangled the seemingly intractable antinomy of free will and determinism' (Stent, 2002: 155). Kant was remarkably prescient with his overarching epistemological conjecture that reason inevitably falls into contradiction with itself whenever it ventures beyond experience and tries to think about the intelligible world as a whole (ibid.: 201). It is in reflecting on Kant's epistemic dualism, then, that we can observe paradoxical relations between pure theoretical reason (with its value-free, natural categories, such as space, time, causality, and object) and pure practical reason (with its value-laden, non-natural categories, such as good and evil, sacredness, free will, and personhood) (Stent, 2002: 237). The two spheres of reason remain, fundamentally, incommensurate relative to one another. To be human thus means 'to live as a dualist in *both* realms of the intelligible world and struggle with the paradoxes that arise from their incompatibility' (ibid.: 253, emphasis added). We have no choice then, other than 'to come to terms as best as we can with our paradoxical mental endowment' (ibid.: 166).

Nietzsche and Stent aside, we find a different interpretation of the paradox related to free will in the work of psychiatrist, Kenneth Pelletier. Pelletier points to the interesting relationship between free will and Heisenberg's Uncertainty Principle. He explains that early in the development of quantum mechanical theory it was recognized that the Heisenberg Uncertainty Principle (which we examined in Chapter 5) had a direct bearing on the philosophical problem of free will. Danish physicist Niels Bohr suggested that certain key points in the regulatory mechanisms of the brain might be so sensitive and delicately balanced that they should properly be regarded as quantum mechanical in nature—or 'nondeterministic'—and therefore could be considered to be the physical mechanisms of an individual's free will (Pelletier, 1982: 119). For some, then, the uncertainty principle is proof (of sorts) that free will *does exist*. However, in the very same text from which Pelletier's observations are drawn, we're treated to a candid—albeit insightful—dialogue between American philosopher Ken Wilber and the editors, which urges more restraint.

[Wilber]: Maybe we could say that the Heisenberg uncertainty principle represents all that is left of God's radical freedom on the physical plane. But the point is that if you try to understand the cosmos in reverse direction, from atoms up, you are stuck trying to account for free will, for creativity, for choice, for anything other than a largely deterministic cosmos. The fact is, even with its little bit of Heisenberg indeterminacy, the physical universe is much more deterministic than level two, biological beings. Any good physicist will tell you where Jupiter will be located a decade from now, barring disaster, but no biologist can tell you where a dog will move two minutes from now. So... by looking to illuminate the lower by the higher, and not vice versa, could make creativity the general principle, and then understand determinism as a partial restriction or reduction of primary creativity. [...]

[Revision Journal]: That's extraordinary, because I've seen so many attempts by new-age thinkers to derive human will from electron indeterminacy, or to say that human volition is free because of the indeterminate wave nature of its subcellular components, or some such.

[Wilber]: Yes, it appears the thing to do. It's a reflex thing to do—finally, after decades of saying the physical universe is deterministic and therefore human choice is an illusion, you find a little indeterminacy in the physical realm and you go nuts. It's only natural you then try to explain human freedom and even God's freedom as a blow-up of the lowest order. You get so exited you forget you have just pulled the reductionist feat of the century; God is that big electron in the sky. The intentions are so good, but the philosophy so detrimental. And imagine this: there are plenty of physicists who feel that the physical realm is purely deterministic—Einstein, for one—and that future research may disclose subatomic variables that are purely causal.

(Wilber, 1982b: 263–264)

Stratton (2022) expresses this back-to-front rationale in lay terms: since people are made of atoms it is assumed that we too are indeterminate and hence this is said to validate the theory of free will. But this is an extraordinary leap of faith and strikes me as another example of the fallacy of composition, which we originally invoked in Chapter 3.

In any event, it is necessary to hone in on the peculiarities of freedom. Philosopher Gareth Matthews, for example, invokes the Stoic doctrine that 'those and only those are free who know that they are not free', as his overarching example of paradox (see Sorensen, 2003: 6). This in turn invokes the 'fear of freedom' discourse, which is marbled through contemporary Western thought, and is especially prevalent in the work of the existentialists. The anxiety which it elicits is seemingly irresolvable. But existentialism is of limited value in addressing thorny questions of ethics. If free will is an illusion, does this mean that anything goes? What might this imply in respect of ethics? Fortunately, the Ancient Greeks nipped in the bud any sniff of a get out of jail free card.

> In ancient Greece, there was a popular story about the founder of Stoicism, Zeno of Citium (not to be confused with Zeno of Elea). He beat his slave for stealing. The slave, something of a philosopher himself, protested: 'But it was fated that I should steal'. 'And that I should beat you', retorted Zeno.
>
> *(Sorensen, 2003: 127)*

This anecdote never fails to bring a smile to even the most discerning of my philosophically inclined students. Sorensen goes on to note that if there is genuine conflict between determinism and freewill, then it is not clear that either can triumph: Whenever we deliberate, he continues, we presuppose that we are free to choose between genuine alternatives.

> If you are persuaded that only one outcome is possible, then you cannot try to decide which outcome to bring about. Since we cannot stop deliberating, we cannot share the belief that we are free. There is no choice about whether to believe in free choice.
>
> *(ibid.: 128)*

Even a cursory reading, then, of the countless dusty tomes that examine the paradox between determinism and voluntarism strengthens our resolve that the elicited tension is immanent to life. A purely deterministic universe would be profoundly inhospitable. But—similarly—a purely voluntarist universe would elicit anomic pandemonium.

The paradox of selflessness

We can approach paradox vis-à-vis selflessness in at least two senses. First, and as 1990s band, Catatonia, remind us: *selflessness stinks of fallacy*; that is, we are, by default, selfish. Second, selflessness in the short term is likely part of a long-term strategy of selfishness (winning friends, say, or securing a pass for the Pearly Gates). Nietzsche imparts some pertinent thoughts again, this time in *Ecce Homo*:

> Morally speaking: neighbour love, living for others, and other things can become a protective measure for preserving the hardest self-concern. This is the exception where, against my own wont and conviction, I side with the selfless drives: here they work in the service of self-love, of self-discipline.
>
> *(Nietzsche, 1888: III, s9; 1989: 254)*

However, here Nietzsche is using paradox to advance his particular belief system i.e. he uses it to support his conviction that we ought to be selfish. Our focus, however, is of course on drawing attention to the analytical potential of paradox, rather than using it to validate an ideological position. Arguably, a more effective way to examine the compelling dynamic between selflessness and paradox is to consider the broader concept of altruism. Is altruism all it has cracked up to be? Or is it, quite simply, a shrewd strategic orientation?

> Whatever it is called, the expression of altruism is not only an experience that is existentially satisfying. It is also, as [sociobiologist] Edmund Wilson describes, a requirement for the survival of one's culture. In fact, Wilson asserts that altruism is transferred genetically from generation to generation and that such transfer occurs because it has survival value. In more specific terms, cultures whose members express altruism in the form of forgiveness and grace survive. Cultures that lack the capacity for altruistic forgiveness and grace die.
>
> *(Harvey, 1988: 71)*

Similarly, Caulkin (2016) argues that a chief—and fundamental—tension at the heart of business is that the most profitable companies are those that are not profit-focussed. All this begs a more pertinent question, and as Einstein famously quipped: 'If people are good only because they fear punishment, and hope for reward, then we are a sorry lot indeed'. Unsurprisingly, Nietzsche is more damning:

> There is too much charm and sugar in these feelings of 'for others', 'not for myself', for us not to need to become doubly suspicious at this point and to ask: 'are these not perhaps—seductions?" That they please—those who have them and those who enjoy their fruits, and also the mere spectator—this does not yet constitute an argument in their favour but rather invites caution. So let us be cautious.
>
> *(Nietzsche, 1886: s33; 1989: 45)*

Abstract musings are all well and good, but a more robust reflection on experience is warranted. To this end, we can examine the selflessness paradox in the context of economic redistribution. There is, of course, a predisposition among liberal thinkers to assume that a well-resourced and effective welfare state is a panacea. They might even go on to suggest that anybody who challenges this is a callous bastard. But—again—there is more to it than meets this ideological eye. In his compelling thesis on Christianity and morality, Abraham (2020) for example, writes the following in respect of the immorality of the welfare state. Abraham draws attention to an alternative view that long-term unemployment coupled with unconditional welfare payments leads to an erosion of morals. To this end, Abraham invokes the view of Catholic neoliberal theologian Michael Novak (1996) who regards the welfare state as a principal source of the decline of moral seriousness in society.

> Unconditional welfare payments, in this view, erode virtues such as personal responsibility and proper working habits among its recipients, as well as eroding values of kindness and decency manifested in voluntary charity. In Novak's view, the whole idea amounts to a contradiction of Christian anthropology, a basic understanding of human moral weakness.
>
> *(Abraham, 2020: 164)*

Is genuine kindness to be found, then, in calculated cruelty? At any rate, and as Freud reminds us in *Civilization and its discontents,* 'A love that does not discriminate seems to me to forfeit a part of its own value, by doing an injustice to its object...' (Freud [1930] (1991: 291).

The paradoxes of conflict

In the opening pages of *Homo Deus,* Harari (2017) suggests that war (together with plague and famine) is obsolete. I disagree and worry that Harari is in grave danger of 'doing a Fukuyama'. (In *The End of History and the Last Man* (1992), writer Francis Fukuyama declared that liberal democracy marked the end of history as a triumphant finale and dominant world ideology. This position lost all traction less than a decade later, when anti-Western religious fundamentalists flew airliners into the World Trade Centre). In any case, and as we saw in the opening passage of this book, sociologist George Simmel [1922] (1955) regards conflict is fundamental to human relations. *Si vis pacem, para bellum,* as the Latin adage goes: 'If you want peace, prepare for war'. War is routinely presented as undesirable corollary of an otherwise irresolvable difference on the one hand, but as a uniting force on the other. This is perhaps best captured by the familiar utterance, *war brings people together.*

And peace, too, is characterized by paradox. Theorists of peace dating back to the political scientist Hans Morgenthau (1948) suggest that peace is realizable if no one nation (and hence way of life) has power over any other, and yet the evidence appears to suggest quite the opposite. *Pax Brittanica,* for example, described the period of relative peace during which Britain enjoyed unrivalled international military might. At the time of writing, the conflict in Ukraine is unfolding rapidly. Viewed from either Western or Russian perspectives, we'd unlikely be at war if a single global power had overall control. It's foul-tasting food for thought.

Although he did not conceptualize them explicitly as paradoxes, it is to Moffett's (2019) work to which we are indebted for both identifying and making sense of paradoxes related to conflict and peace. We might begin by asking whether or not conflict is necessary. Moffett grapples with this question and in so doing invokes a discussion of Voltaire. 'It is lamentable', wrote Voltaire, 'that to be a good patriot one must become the enemy of the rest of mankind' (ibid.: 253). Further on, Moffett hints at related paradoxes. He draws on sociologist William Sumner's work, in particular. 'To Sumner', he notes, 'external war and internal peace play out a horrid game of interdependence. Any competition and conflict with outsiders redirect people's attention from their competition and conflicts with each other and toward their identity as a group' (ibid.: 259). And perhaps most remarkable of all, he offers the following sobering conclusion:

> Considering the state of affairs we see across species when competition is intense, and the human response to competition and clashes of identity with foreign powers, it seems fair to assume that equanimity with the neighbors will be a perennial struggle.
>
> *(ibid.: 264)*

Indeed, Moffett regards the concept of harmony as inherently problematic. He argues that harmony between societies can ironically bring about violence across a region by establishing a more dangerous opponent for those left out of the entente: 'One enemy replaces another' (ibid.: 277), he quips. Moffett goes on to ask his readers the following question: *How do we avoid conflict when resources and opportunities dry up?* He responds by arguing that peace is fostered by enhanced intercourse between countries. Nations thus draw ever more on talents and resources from beyond their borders. Ideally, he says, this interconnectedness and interdependence should see nations through periods of shortfall, at times when what tranquillity exists between the societies of other animals tends to collapse.

Avoiding violence when the potential social and material gains from war are high takes more than good intentions, however; it requires cultivating, and recognizing, the greater payoff, over the long term, of peace over conflict—even among hated adversaries.... In no other species do societies coordinate to preserve peace.

(Moffett, 2019: 277–278)

This is pertinent to our broader enquiry as it allows us to reflect on one of the key paradoxes we observed in respect of both economics and politics. In particular, it enables us to defend the social virtues of capitalism (or, simply, trade) against its Marxist critics. The point is, of course, that trade helps preserve peace between nations. At the crux of the paradox is the implication that, ostensibly at least, the most socially minded of economic policies—i.e. Marxism—is, in effect, the most likely to yield conflict. Moffett goes on to consider the historical context and concludes that societies encompassing the conjoined bands of hunter-gatherers through to the great empires, never freely relinquish their sovereignties to build a still greater society. 'Aggressive acquisitions of both people and their lands, and not willing mergers, brought different societies into one fold. Greek philosopher Heraclitus was right to proclaim war to be the father of all things' (ibid.: 330). We have, therefore, unearthed a *fundamental* paradox. 'War made the state, and the state made war', sociologist Charles Tilly (1981) aptly observed. There have been no true pacifist states (ibid.: 348). War is, it seems, imperative for identity. Moffett (2019: 402) echoes this sentiment in reminding his readers that 'friction with outsiders draws a society together'. War is an articulation of our need to *Other*, our craving for an outgroup, here illustrated by recourse to a snippet of history:

For centuries, the Pacific island of Futuna, a low chunk of volcanic rock, at 46 square kilometres in size, offered space and resources for just two chiefdoms—Sigave and Alo. These societies, claiming opposite ends of the island, were in almost constant conflict, pausing only briefly... for island-wide ceremonies featuring a psychoactive drink made from a shrub native to the western Pacific. One wonders if this enabled their people to tolerate each other for the day. I can only imagine their spear-throwing clashes were a primary motivator in their lives, the Arab-Israeli conflict in microscosm. One might expect that in such a confined space, and over the course of so much time, one chiefdom would have conquered the other. That this never happened might bear on the human craving for an outgroup, if not outright opponent. Could Alo have continued on without Sigave—a society in vacuum? Would it, alone in the world, even be what we could call a society? [...] [C]alling a group a society—and recognizing any markers that identify the members as a society—makes sense only when more than one society exists. The implication is that the compulsion to be part of a society must be matched by the imperative to identify an outgroup—Sigave for Alo and vice versa, or at least 'others' vaguely rendered, as the barbarians were for the Roman Empire and Chinese dynasties—if only as a standard for comparison and a source of gossip, if not denigration. In this sense Futuna's chiefdoms, as simple and similar as they may be by our standards, exemplify human nature stripped to its heart.

(ibid.: 403, 404)

Finally, and beyond this fundamental paradox we've charted in respect of conflict, we discern several derivative paradoxes as well. These are the paradox of stability and war, war as a channel for lost enchantment, war as ethical mediator, and the usefulness of evil men. Of the *paradox of stability and war*, economist Hyman Minsky notes that 'Stability breeds instability. The more stable things become and the longer things are stable, the more unstable they will be when the crisis hits'. Of *war as channel for lost enchantment*, drawing on the wisdom of fantasist J.R.R. Tolkien, Curry (2012) comments that enchantment is as necessary for the health and complete functioning of the human as is sunlight for physical life. By implication, then, it follows that sanitized, stable modernist life in effect withholds something we cannot live well for long without. Thus the more consistent and thoroughgoing modernism is, the greater its vulnerability to a return of the repressed as enchantments that are inadmissible, hence preferably unconscious, and therefore uncriticizable and even more-than-usually dangerous. In this sense secularism strengthens the resolve of religious fundamentalists and their penchant for violence. The past two decades of global geopolitical activity provide ample evidence of precisely this. It is to Hegel that we attribute a casting of conflict as an ethico-organizational barometer. Indeed, Hegel (1946: 324) defended war:

War is not to be regarded as an absolute evil and as a purely external accident, which itself has some accidental cause, be it injustice, the passions of nations or the holders of power, or, in short, something or other which ought not to be.

War, Hegel insists, is

the state of affairs which deals in earnest with the vanity of temporal goods and concerns… War has the higher significance that by its agency… the ethical health of peoples is preserved in their indifference to the stabilization of finite institutions; just as the blowing of the winds preserves the sea from the foulness which would be the result of a prolonged calm, so also corruption in nations would be the product of prolonged, let alone 'perpetual' peace (*ibid.*).

We will, however, leave the last word to Nietzsche. For the controversial philosopher, 'evil men' have extraordinary utility:

> [O]ne has hitherto never doubted or hesitated in the slightest degree in supposing 'the good man' to be of greater value than 'the evil man', of greater value in the sense of furthering the advancement and prosperity of men in general... But what if the reverse were true? What if a symptom of regression were inherent in the 'good', likewise a danger, a seduction, a poison, a narcotic, through which the present was possibly living at the expense of the future? Perhaps more comfortably, less dangerously, but at the same time in a meaner style, more basely? So that precisely morality would be to blame if the highest power and splendour actually possible to the type man was never in fact attained? So that precisely morality was the danger of dangers?
>
> *(Nietzsche, 1887: preface s6; 1989: 20)*

Postlude

In this chapter, we have considered some extraordinarily thorny paradoxes: that ethics is founded on violence (i.e. 'might makes right'); that binary morality overlooks complexity; that free will is problematic in terms of exercising ethical judgement; and that conflict is imperative to productive human relations. Collectively, these observations contribute to a broader view that paradox works to thwart moral closure; that is, it ensures we are kept on our ethical toes. Paradox thus sustains an imperative and all-too-human sense of moral spirit, adventure, and innovation.

8

PEDAGOGICAL LOGIC II

Paradox Elicits Egalitarian Inertia

This chapter advances our second logic of paradox; that is, that *paradox elicits an egalitarian inertia*. Put simply, the mediating influences of paradox help even out lived experience in terms of pain and pleasure. It does this in two ways. First, it evens out lived experiences between fortunate and less fortunate human lives, or 'the haves' and 'the have nots' (i.e. interpersonally). Second, it evens out lived experience over the course of an individual's lifetime (i.e. intrapersonally).

'It's a bitter sweet symphony, that's life' droned 1990s Britpop act, *The Verve*. A frustratingly beguiling tune, it was overplayed in student union bars across Britain and probably beyond. Its headline lyric, however, was hardly a revelation. Perhaps more so than any other, the paradox that underlies the bittersweet dynamic between pain and pleasure is one most of us can identify. For many of us it is subconsciously—yet deeply—frustrating. Must perpetual pleasure (or happiness) be forever elusive? Frankly—yes. If it wasn't, humankind would succumb much more readily to blazing decadence. The very idea of 'being spoilt' is, of course, akin to having too much of a 'good' thing. We routinely label our kids with this term. The choice of word—spoiled—is revealing; it suggests that, intuitively, we acknowledge a problem with a linear logic. While gifting children toys or sweet treats makes them happy, at least fleetingly, too much creates problems; it *spoils*. In a very general sense, this chapter marshals evidence that runs contrary to both the pleasure principle (the seeking of pleasure and avoidance of pain) and the concept of jouissance (the suggestion that the pleasure principle itself can be transgressed). Notably, it is in discussions of pleasure and happiness that we can truly begin to get to grips with the existential pertinence of paradox;

DOI: 10.4324/9781003203339-10

unlike its manifestation in, say, physics or even economics, the notions of pleasure, pain, happiness, and sadness are highly accessible to all. What we are tasked with in this chapter, then, is not so much to demonstrate that the pleasure principle and the concept of jouissance are flawed (this should by now be self-evident), but to carve out *a new dynamics of pleasure*; that is to lend serious thought to how our experiences of pleasure can be understood and 'patterned'. It is to this end, then, that our posited second logic of paradox gains traction.

This chapter is structured as follows. In the first part of this chapter we explore key scholarly contributions in respect of *'The pleasure and pain game'*. As part of this discussion we also touch upon several derivative tensions. These include the paradox of aesthetics, the love–hate relationship, and sado-masochism. We then shift focus to examine how the relativizing tendencies associated with the paradoxes of pleasure contribute to the aforementioned evening out of experience. This second subsection is called *Pleasure, relativity and the egalitarian evening out of experience*. In the latter part of the chapter we then consider the pedagogical potential presented by the pleasure–pain paradox. To this end we marshal direction, first, *Towards a constructive approach to pain*. Second, we advance *Towards a new dynamics of pleasure*.

The pleasure and pain game

Vonnegut [1969] (2000: 88) seizes the paradox at the very crux of our lived experience. Part way through *Slaughterhouse 5* the author presents a sketch of a tombstone bearing a provocative—and now infamous—declaration (see Figure 8.1). The pleasure–pain paradox is one of the best-known and yet it seems we rarely ever make provision for it in the formal machinations of everyday life. This is rather baffling. The paradox has multiple manifestations (and, indeed, permutations), too.

We began this book by hinting that systematic examination of the pleasure–pain paradox yields pedagogical insight. The example cited was going for a jog in the rain (the wet run being the undesirable counterpart to the endorphin release, as preferable to—say—the hangover which of course constitutes the undesirable counterpart to a hedonistic night of heavy drinking). The science fiction novelist, Peter F. Hamilton's character in *Judas Unchained*, Dr Friland, recognizes this: 'You always resort to physical activity when confronted with a vexing problem... It allows your subconscious to review possibilities' (2005: 131). I rather like that. On balance, then, the pain/pleasure coupling inherent to the run in the rain accompanied by the endorphin release and sense of accomplishment compares favourably to the pleasure/pain coupling inherent to the night of heavy drinking accompanied by the inevitable hangover. Notably, in 2018, satirical newspaper *The Onion* ran a story with the heading: 'God admits

FIGURE 8.1 Vonnegut (1969).

there was probably a better way of giving humans taste of heavenly bliss than opioids'. No shit.

Narcotics aside, what about good old-fashioned fun? For one of German psychoanalyst Karen Horney's subjects in the mid-twentieth century: 'Ambition and satisfaction is all about doing a good job, having lots of fun, fun in a sort of gruelling way...' (cited in Pahl 1995: 89). Even fun, it seems, is tainted by paradox. In a similar vein, Robinson and Zarate (2006: 48) note in their assessment of Kierkegaard that 'A life that is restricted to enjoyment and pleasure ends in despair, regardless of all the clever strategies the aesthete employs to fight off boredom.' And, as you might expect, Nietzsche chimes in on the pleasure–pain paradox; this time in terms of what he describes as 'ascetic love', that is abstinence from sensual pleasures:

> Read from a distant star, the majuscule script of our earthly existence would perhaps lead to the conclusion that the earth was a distinctively ascetic planet, a nook of disgruntled, arrogant, and offensive creatures filled with a profound disgust at themselves, at the earth, at all life, who

inflict as much pain on themselves as they possibly can out of pleasure in inflicting pain—which is probably their only pleasure. For consider how regularly and universally the ascetic priest appears in almost every age; he belongs to no one race; he prospers everywhere; he emerges from every class of society. Nor does he breed and propagate his mood of valuation through heredity: the opposite is the case—broadly speaking, a profound instinct rather forbids him to propagate. It must be the necessity of the first order that again and again promotes the growth and prosperity of this life-inimical species—it must indeed be in the interest of life itself that such a self-contradictory type does not die out. For an ascetic life is a self-contradiction: here rules a ressentiment without equal, that of an insatiable instinct and power-will that wants to become master not over something in life but over life itself, over its most profound, powerful, and basic conditions [...] All this is paradoxical; we stand before a discord that wants to be discordant, that enjoys itself in this suffering and even grows more self-confident and triumphant the more its own presupposition, its physiological capacity for life, decreases.

(Nietzsche, 1887: III/11; 1989: 117–118)

In some respects it is nothing short of gobsmacking that those considered most noble (i.e. the priests) are the least likely to procreate. But the example of organized religion is a little out of date. Consider an example closer to home. Who procreates most prolifically: the 'high-achieving' middle classes or the 'low prospect' underclasses?

The paradox of aesthetics. In Chapter 2, we explored tensions in the arts and noted several paradoxes associated with beauty. Unsurprisingly, these paradoxes transcend the arts. In recent years, for example, my native field—management and organization studies—has become preoccupied with imperfection. In 2018, the principal theme at the annual *Standing Conference on Organizational Symbolism* (SCOS) was 'Wabi-sabi (侘寂): Imperfection, incompleteness and impermanence in organizational life'. It was billed as follows:

Wabi-sabi is an approach to life based on accepting the transience and imperfection of the world. As a Japanese aesthetic derived from Buddhism, wabi-sabi embraces the wisdom that comes from perceiving beauty in impermanence and incompleteness. What might such advocacy of the harmony found in the flawed, faulty, and weathered have to do with formal organisations, obsessed as they seemingly are with continually striving for perfection? The very ideal of perfection, as an antithesis of wabi-sabi, is embedded in managerial efforts as diverse as striving for continuous improvement, setting 'stretch' targets, managing the performance of ideal employees, promoting organizational cultures of excellence, and even the romanticized perfect bodies of employees. Is it then the case that the managerial aesthetic of organizations is the antinomy of wabi-sabi? The idea for this conference is to explore how the wabi-sabi aesthetic can offer a counterpoint to the forms of idealization that dominate so much of managerial and organisational thinking. This is an exploration of how ideas from an ancient Eastern tradition might fruitfully be brought to bear on organisational issues, challenges and problems, especially as they are dominated by Western intellectual habits and foibles. Wabi-sabi as a theme explores the imperfect idea of a dividing crack between 'the East' and 'the West' that we hope conference participants will illuminate with the sort of effervescent creativity and fluid thinking that have characterised SCOS conferences in the past.

(Standing Conference on Organizational Symbolism, 2018)

The conference webpage also quoted the late Canadian singer-songwriter Leonard Cohen: '*Ring the bells that still can ring/Forget your perfect offering/ There is a crack, a crack in everything/That's how the light gets in.*' That year the conference attracted some extraordinary papers. The theme of imperfection vis-à-vis the East–West split could not have been more prescient given the tyranny currently meted on the battlefields in Ukraine, and the growing antagonism between the United States and China, both despite the apparently mediating effects of the free market.

Of course, and as you might imagine, SCOS is quite a niche affair, typically attracting just 70 or so quirky delegates. However, there are signs that interest in imperfection is growing beyond these pioneers. This year—2022—the *European Group of Organization Studies* (EGOS) conference is billed as *The Beauty of Imperfection;* and unlike SCOS, EGOS routinely attracts delegate numbers in their thousands.

The love–hate relationship. Catullus was a Roman poet. In one of his works, *Catullus 85*, he declares the following: 'I hate and I love. Why I do this, perhaps you ask. I know not, but I feel it happening and I am tortured.' With these words, he has been credited with introducing the concept of the love–hate relationship to Western minds. The tension is an enduring and familiar motif. It is all-too-often those closest to us (those we love) that we seem so capable of hating, too. For Catullus, it was his lover, Lesbia. For Old Salamano in Camus's *The Stranger*, it was his dog. For me, I suspect the relationship I had with my late mother was similarly characterized. In typical Larkinesque style, I blamed my dear mum for most of my own foibles, but wept hysterically at her passing. Your parents. They fuck you up.

Sado-masochism. It is of course to Sigmund Freud that the popular understanding of sado-masochism must be credited. But perhaps even more so than Freud, Nietzsche had a fanatical obsession with the peculiar dynamic between pleasure and pain. Ultimately, it seems, pleasure and pain are rarely—if ever—opposites. First off, we can—and frequently do—take pleasure in another's pain. There is no direct word for this phenomenon in English, but the Ancient Greeks had *epicaricacy*, and of course the Germans have *schadenfreude*. In *Genealogy of Morals* Nietzsche explores the notion of suffering as recompense for wrongdoing.

> To what extent can suffering balance debts? To the extent that to make suffer was in the highest degree pleasurable, to the extent that the injured party exchanged for the loss he had sustained, including the displeasure caused by the loss, an extraordinary counterbalancing pleasure: that of making suffer—a genuine festival, something which, as aforesaid, was prized the more violently it contrasted with the rank and social standing of the creditor. [We might also ponder the] degree to which cruelty constituted the great festival pleasure of more primitive men and was indeed an ingredient of almost every one of their pleasures.
>
> *(Nietzsche, 1887: II/6; 1989: 65–66)*

In the case of 'suffering [as a means of] balancing debts', the pain is apparently 'farmed out' to another. It is on this very principle that Ursula Le Guin's (1976) short story, *The Ones Who Walk Away from Omelas*, is premised. The imprisoned child in the story is a kind of scapegoat to which the citizens of Omelas outsource the correlative negatives to pleasure and happiness. The pain and misery this child experiences is in Le Guin's own words the price the citizens pay to be kept 'permanently happy'. But more pertinent to our understanding of paradox, pain inflicted on oneself can be desirable, too. In *Thus Spake Zarathustra*, Nietzsche (1883–1885: XXIV; 1997: 83) says 'Creating—that is the great salvation from suffering, and life's alleviation. But for the creator to appear, suffering itself is needed, and much transformation'. Moreover, in *The Will to Power*, Nietzsche argues that drive is borne of dissatisfaction. He insists that every drive that desires to be satisfied expresses its dissatisfaction with the present state of things. Accordingly he prompts us to consider whether this represents the underpinnings of eternal dissatisfaction itself. Nonetheless, Nietzsche and others have gone so far to suggest that there is beauty in suffering. In *Beyond Good and Evil*, he notes:

> [O]ur thrill is the thrill of the infinite, the unmeasured. Like a rider on a steed that flies forward, we drop the reins before the infinite, we modern men, like semi-barbarians—and reach our bliss only where we are most in danger... You want, if possible—and there is no more insane 'if possible'— to abolish suffering. And we? It really seems that we would rather have it higher and worse than ever... Well-being as you understand it—that is

no goal, that seems to us a state… that soon makes man ridiculous and contemptible—and that makes his destruction desirable.

(Nietzsche, 1886: ss224–225; 1989: 153)

Similarly, methodologists Bochner and Ellis (2016) tease out some of the nuance that is elicited when suffering and happiness are examined side by side. Many people, they say, read autoethnographic stories as overly tragic or sad. This suggests that we need a deeper grasp of the connection between suffering and happiness.

Unfortunately, the way some stories get told (or read) creates the impression that tragedy and happiness are opposites. But happiness is at stake in every story of suffering. Indeed, the possibility of happiness in the presence of suffering is central to the whole project of autoethnography.

(ibid.: 69–70)

Quite rightly, they contend that a predictable life would be dull:

Stability, order, control—these are the words that [conventional] social science speaks. Ambiguity, chance, accidents—these are the terms that life echoes. Suppose we achieved the stability, order, and control we seek—what then? No variance—no differences—no chance—no fun—no adventure—no vulnerability—no deniability—no flirtation—no love.

(ibid.: 206)

As we have seen, then, the pain–pleasure paradox has numerous, multifaceted manifestations. Such is its pervasiveness, it is from the pleasure–pain paradox that we can begin to derive some interesting practical corollaries. In the evaluation of the paradoxes relevant to discussions of pleasure and happiness we can take important cues to enhance our understanding of why ours is a universe characterized by complexity and contradiction. To this end, we turn now to explore the relativity of happiness as an egalitarian mechanism through which experience is evened out, constructive approaches to pain, and the manner in which we might attempt to determine a sense of self-abstinence in a bid to more effectively surf the dynamics associated with paradox.

Pleasure, relativity, and the egalitarian evening out of experience

We often feel a sense of envy when presented with another's happiness. Bauman, for example, paints an inversely proportional transference of pleasure:

With all varieties of human habitat on the planet open to visits and scrutiny, every human being's or human group's success is likely to be perceived as another annoying and exasperating case of my own deprivation and so to add to the warehouse of my grievances. Everybody's success feels like my defeat.

(Bauman, 2017: 99, 100)

We have here a sort of quantity theory of happiness and it is something to which we can all relate. However, there is a whole lot more to the dynamics of pleasure. In *Civilization and its discontents*, Freud [1930] (1991) makes some astute—and revealing—observations in respect of experiential relativity. He notes that despite the extraordinary advances in the sciences and in their technical application over the past few generations, this newly won power over space and time and subjugation of the forces of nature has not increased the amount of pleasurable satisfaction which we might expect from life. It has not, he insists, made us happier. This leads Freud to ask us a pertinent question:

[I]s there, then, no positive gain in pleasure?... [H]ere the voice of pessimistic criticism makes itself heard and warns us that most... satisfactions follow the model of the 'cheap enjoyment' extolled in the anecdote—the enjoyment of putting a bare leg from under the bedclothes on a cold winter night and drawing it in again. If there had been no railway to conquer distances, my child would never have left his native town and I should need no telephone to hear his voice; if travelling across the ocean by ship had not been introduced, my friend would not have embarked on his sea-voyage and I should not need a cable to relieve my anxiety about him. ...It seems certain that we do not feel comfortable in our present-day civilization, but it is very difficult to form an opinion whether and in what degree men of an earlier age felt happier and what part their cultural conditions played in the subject matter.

(ibid.: 276–277)

An accessible corollary is our experience of television sets. Now in my 40s, I distinctly recall the television sets of the 1980s. These were bulky cathode ray tube designs, originally black and white and then later in colour. In the 1990s, the market introduced us to widescreen televisions. In the 2000s, we had flatscreens, and then shortly after this High Definition (HD) and smart television technology. Over the course of my lifetime, the standard television set has evolved from a black and white 14-inch screen, to a 50-inch 4K ultra HD unit. But has my enjoyment of television as a medium of entertainment increased in accord with this technological trajectory? No. In fact, I have found television less appealing over the years. Of course, one might protest and say: yes, but you've got older. Kids love telly; adults don't! There may be some truth in this but such an argument presupposes that we can plonk the enjoyment of television (as variable) in a temporal vacuum untainted by the passage of time. And—once again—to do so would be to make the mistake of applying a traditional ontology to experiential matters.

It was possibly from Freud that American rock band, *They Might Be Giants*, sought inspiration for their extraordinary lyric: 'No one in the world ever gets what they want and that is beautiful'. A more familiar—if less poetic—aphorism is: *Money cannot buy you happiness*. If it could, then the proposed underlying existential mechanism for evening out experience that we are proposing here would be flawed. Stafford (2013) argues that happiness is a complex, nebulous state that is fed by transient simple pleasures, as well as the more sustained rewards of activities that only make sense from a perspective of years or decades. Nebulous. Yes. And not least because it is subject to what is often described as hedonic relativism or hedonic adaptation (see, e.g. Brickmann & Campbell, 1971). Sorensen (2003: 14), meanwhile, reproduces the words of Herodotus: '… I know of no man whom continual good fortune did not bring in the end to evil, and utter destruction…'. Unsurprisingly, perhaps, hedonic adaptation crops up repeatedly in existentialist literature. We briefly touched upon Camus's *The Outsider* in Chapter 2 and do so again here. For Camus's protagonist, Meursault, '…one life was as good as another and… I wasn't at all dissatisfied with mine here'. Even when incarcerated, Meursault reminds us the salience of relativity:

> I suddenly realized how closed in I was by my prison walls. But that only lasted a few months. After that, I thought like a prisoner. I'd look forward to my daily walk in the courtyard or to my lawyer's visits. And I managed quite well the rest of the time. I often thought in those days that even if I'd been made to live in a hollow tree trunk, with nothing to do but look up at the bit of sky overhead, I'd gradually have got used to it. I'd have looked forward to seeing birds fly past of clouds run together just as here I looked forward to seeing my lawyer's curious ties and just as, in another world, I used to wait for Saturdays to embrace Marie's body.
>
> *(Camus, [1942] 2000: 75)*

In this way, then, paradox thus helps 'even out' experience in life, between the 'haves' (in this case, 'the free') and the 'have nots' (in this case, 'the incarcerated'). Of this broader idea, Freud passes the following comments:

> What we call happiness in the strictest sense comes from the (preferably sudden) satisfaction of needs which have been damned up to a high degree, and it is from its nature only possible as an episodic phenomenon. When any situation that is desired by the pleasure principle is prolonged, it only produces a feeling of mild contentment. We are so made that we can derive intense enjoyment only from a contrast and very little from a state of things. Thus our possibilities of happiness are already restricted

by our constitution. Unhappiness is much less difficult to experience. We are threatened with suffering from three directions: from our own body, which is doomed to decay and dissolution and which cannot do without pain and anxiety as warning signals; from the external world which may rage against us with overwhelming and merciless forces of destruction; and finally from relations with other men. The suffering which comes from this last source is perhaps more painful to us than any other.

(Freud, [1930] 1991: 264)

This is potent psychoanalysis and lends salient context to the concept of hedonic adaptation. It enables us to better understand the point made in the opening chapter regarding Schkade and Kahneman's (1998) finding that despite stereotyped preconceptions of the relationship between sunshine and happiness, Californians (who live in a sunny climate) and Midwesterners (who don't) report no difference in levels of happiness. Our task, then, is to take Freud's observation about the nature of how we experience happiness, fully theorize it by recourse to paradox, and place it in a broader experiential context. A page later, and there is our strongest hint yet that Freud recognizes the prevalence of paradox in respect of feelings of contentment:

An unrestricted satisfaction of every need presents itself as the most enticing method of conducting one's life, but it means putting enjoyment before caution, and soon brings its own punishment. [...]In the last analysis, all suffering is nothing else than sensation; it only exists in so far as we feel it, and we only feel it in consequence of certain ways in which our organism is regulated.

Freud, [1930] (1991: 265)

In any event, happiness is—it would seem—a rather perverse form of bet hedging. 'Just as a cautious businessman [sic] avoids tying up all capital in one concern, so, perhaps, world wisdom will advise us not to look for the whole of our satisfaction from a single aspiration' (ibid.: 272).

Moving beyond the musings of Nietzsche and Freud, French philosopher Gilles Deleuze is more exacting in his analysis. For Deleuze, a principal problem arises when we deliberately attempt to reproduce a pleasure. In *Difference and repetition,* Deleuze [1968] (2004: 4) argues that try as we might, each time we attempt to repeat a past pleasure, 'we throw ourselves into a demonic and already damned exercise which can only end in despair or boredom'. Once again we here bear witness to the mediating effects of paradox: repetition is destined to fail in these circumstances because paradox constitutes a form of egalitarian inertia to even out experience. It is, dare we suggest, a law (of sorts). Henry Sidgwick comments on such frustration after a discussion of self-love in *The Method of Ethics:* the pursuit of pleasure, he insists, is not necessarily self-defeating and futile. The problem, rather, is this:

> [T]he principle of Egoistic Hedonism, when applied with a due knowledge of the laws of human nature, is practically self-limiting; i.e., that a rational method of attaining the end at which it aims requires that we should to some extent put it out of sight and not directly aim at it.
>
> *(Sidgwick, 2001: 3)*

The American politician William J. Bennett (2022; online), puts it in terms palatable to the meme generation:

> Happiness is like a cat. If you coax it or call it, it will avoid you; it will never come. But if you pay no attention to it and go about your business, you'll find it rubbing against your legs and jumping into your lap.

Towards a constructive approach to pain

In the opening chapter of this book, we presented an example of how we might—potentially at least—use the arguments presented in this thesis to advance a more enhanced 'lifecraft', in this case a more constructive approach to the experience of pain. The provisional example outlined was to compare favourably the run on the rainy morning to the hangover following a night of excess. We turn now to explore this principle in more detail. In the beautifully crafted *Waterlog*, writer Roger Deakin exalts the delights of cold water swimming as the perfect preface to a hot bath:

> What with [endorphins], cold sensors, adrenalin, thyroxine and the hyperthalamus, the body has a hundred ways of protecting itself from the cold... [and] [w]hat greater pleasure than to come out of the sea glowing from your swim and then gently raise the temperature of your hands and feet by trickling the hot tap as you gently soak?' [Your bath] is the ante-room of the hammam to which you now proceed, opening the hot tap, letting rip with a scalding waterfall that reduces visibility to zero and raises the bath to new levels of pleasure. You lie and soak your chilled chops, feeling the warmth, the softness, the intoxication of guiltless indulgence permeating every cell, floating your toes up towards the steamy ceiling with sounds of dinner underway somewhere below.
>
> *(Deakin, 1999: 235–236)*

'Guiltless indulgence'. With these two simple words Deakin thus invokes the virtues of delayed gratification. Rather shrewdly, Marsden (2002: 12, original emphasis) notes the following in reflecting on Nietzsche's *The Gay Science*: 'If the art of transfiguration *is* philosophy it would seem that it is by redirecting the affects, making even the most painful experiences *productive*, that we know a new happiness...'. Marsden's 'productive pain' is analogous to Deakin's 'guiltless indulgence'. But for my money, action hero Arnold Schwarzenegger puts it best: 'No pain, no gain'. For Arnie, it was about muscle mass. But his quip is actually more far-reaching than that. Nietzsche insists that pain is something different from pleasure, not it's opposite (ibid.: 69). Furthermore, Nietzsche urges us to develop a *gratitude* for suffering. Nietzsche makes it clear, says Marsden (2002: 107–108) that sickness is not something to be stoically endured but actively affirmed as a positive force: 'one should not only beat it, one should love it: Amor fati. That is my inner nature' (ibid.). Understood this way, sickness becomes a vital form of creativity. Hence, of course, Nietzsche's now infamous utterance that whatever doesn't kill you makes you stronger.

> Wantan self-destruction becomes so inextricably bound up with desire that the boundaries between pleasure and pain become hopelessly blurred as each takes on the appearance of the other, reflecting back its features.
>
> *(ibid.: 136)*

In seeking out a constructive approach to pain we are thus compelled to exercise a sense of judicious moderation vis-à-vis our desires so as to preclude the possibility of them becoming self-destructive. An ability to moderate is, of course, what is lost in the case of individuals suffering from various pathologies; everything from alcoholism to video gaming. It is at this point that we might once again invoke the paradox of unintended consequences, which we first touched on in Chapter 3.

> We can even use a simple domestic example to illustrate the general tendency in social life for means to defeat the ends that they were meant to serve. Imagine members of a family arranging a holiday that will enable them to take a rest. But the means of getting that rest—getting away from work, booking tickets, arranging lodging for the cat, cancelling the milk, obtaining foreign currency, getting injections, packing bags, travelling to the airport, finding the hotel at the end of a long journey and so on and so on, lead the family to feel more exhausted after the holiday than it was before it... The means adopted to meet certain ends have completely undermined the achieving of those ends.
>
> *(Watson, 2006: 67)*

While Watson's overriding objective here is to critique bureaucracy as a mechanism by which means slowly subvert ends, I am more interested in the fact that relaxation (on holiday) only really makes sense if the arrangement of the holiday—and getting there—is at least a bit stressful; that stress enables a wonderful contrast as the family *does* begin to relax when they are sat gulping cocktails by the pool. Is holidaying—which involves organization and travel/stress—a *constructive* form of pain? In effect we impose upon ourselves a sense of abstinence in a bid to maximize pleasure.

From cultivating a constructive approach to pain, we conclude this subsection with a brief consideration of what I describe as 'engineering denial'. Many of us live in a world of abundance. We've not known hunger, poverty, or acute violence. In our post-scarcity society must we now engineer (self) denial if we are to maximize pleasure/utility? Must we self-tyrannize? Nietzsche, once again, this time from *Human, All-too-human*:

> There is a defiance of oneself among whose most sublimate expressions some forms of asceticism belong. For certain human beings have such a great need to exercise their force and lust to rule that... they finally have recourse to tyrannizing certain parts of their own nature, as it were sections or stages of themselves....
>
> *(Nietzsche, 1878: s137; 1984: 95)*

Ultimately, it seems, the paradox of pleasure is imperative for advance. Without it we would have long ago reached a level of contentment that meant we needed to do no more and *homo sapiens* would stagnate. For Davey (1997: xxiii): '...this tension becomes the definitive expression of our existential predicament: such suffering is an inevitable fact of our being and not an objection to it!' Most pointedly, and in a more prosaic sense, Nietzsche reminds us that pain has an important practical purpose; it is vital for recall.

> Man could never do without blood, torture, and sacrifices when he felt the need to create a memory for himself; the most dreadful sacrifices and pledges (sacrifices of the first-born among them), the most repulsive mutilations (castration, for example), the cruelest rites of all the religious cults (and all religions are at the deepest level systems of cruelty)—all this has its origin in the instinct that realized that pain is the most powerful aid to mnemonics.
>
> *(Nietzsche, 1887: II s3; 1989: 61)*

Towards a new dynamics of pleasure

By recourse to the mechanics of paradox, pleasure implies an insatiability. As Horney (1991: 30, cited in Pahl, 1995: 90) puts it:

> like any other compulsive drive, the search for glory has the quality of insatiability...There may be a glow of elation over the favourable reception

of some work done, over a victory won, over any sign of recognition or admiration—but it does not last.

(1991: 30)

For Curry, too, enchantment—like pleasure—cannot be experienced perpetually. Enchantment, he says, is impermanent and hence by necessity must be considered in the plural, but herein of course lies its value. The possibility of enchantment always remains open, that is, in principle at least, it could happen again:

> Whether the most satisfying meal, the most beautiful music, the most glorious sex, the most wonderful walk in the countryside—these being some of the commonest 'concrete' dimensions of enchantment—there is no one (or One), complete and ultimate experience of enchantment that puts an end to them all. It therefore cannot be completely or permanently captured, either, even promissorily. [...] It follows that any attempt at a programmatic use of enchantment necessarily coverts it into something else, no matter how similar that may appear to be, and its handlers want it to be, to the original. Let me repeat: enchantment cannot be used, no matter how good or progressive the cause, because any attempt to do so, being will-driven and instrumental, is already disenchanting.
>
> *(Curry, 2012: 78, 79)*

Enchantment cannot be disenchanted and remain itself, and delight can never be definitively separated from delusion. True scepticism, Curry insists, is scrupulously even-handed and reflexive. It, therefore, has nothing to do with the dogmatic scientism of recent years that calls itself sceptical but never doubts its own truth (ibid.: 81, 84). What both Horney and Curry point to, then, is the ephemeral nature of pleasure. We cannot simply indulge and expect to reap the rewards. It is probably for this very reason that, for most of us, our lives are underpinned by 5:2 split that seemingly reflects an intuitive sense of division between pain and pleasure. This, of course, is what we know and experience as the working week. Nietzsche comments on this, thus: 'Industrious races find it very troublesome to endure leisure; it was a masterpiece of English instinct to make the Sabbath so holy and so boring that the English begin unconsciously to lust again for their work—and week-day' (Nietzsche, 1886: s189; 1989: 102). Nietzsche's rapier wit aside, this invokes an acute understanding we might associate with the dynamics of pleasure. In truth, and such is the nature of the paradox to which it remains subject, a formula for happiness must forever remain elusive. Even those who look to *love* as a means of transcendence soon come unstuck. Love it seems is itself plagued by the pleasure–pain paradox: '...love paradoxically accords both intense pleasure and intense pain, it is both pure and scandalous, and while it can liberate the human spirit, it can also be devastating or, at the least, constraining' (Cunha et al., 2016: 17). In order to cultivate a fresh dynamics of pleasure, then, we are compelled to engage with the experiential wisdom imparted by others. In *Man's Search for Meaning*, Viktor Frankl, for example, notes that happiness cannot be pursued. Rather, he insists, it must ensue, and it only does so as the unintended corollary of one's personal dedication to a cause greater than oneself: 'Pleasure is, and must remain, a side-effect or by-product, and is destroyed and spoiled to the degree to which it is made a goal in itself' (Frankl, [1946] 2004: 12). We build on this rationale—that is, how pleasure might be approached most efficaciously—in the concluding chapter of this book.

Postlude

Towards the end of *Paradoxes of Peace*, and in reflecting on a particularly challenging period in his life, Mosley (2009: 157) asks himself the following question: 'But what was my own success or failure at dealing with paradoxes at this time?' This is the point of our current treatise, and an overriding objective for our concluding chapter: our effectiveness in dealing with paradox is a key determinant of our happiness. Ultimately, it seems, it is probably in reflecting on the pain-pleasure paradox that a discernible sense of sagacity begins to emerge.

9
PEDAGOGICAL LOGIC III
Paradox Augments Understanding of Agency

This chapter advances our third logic of paradox. This final logic is summarized as follows: *paradox augments our understanding of human consciousness and agency*. To this end, while a world characterized by linear cause-and-effect could viably be tenanted by non-conscious beings operating in accordance with algorithmic reflexes, one characterized by paradox necessitates conscious agents to navigate the complexities that world elicits.

This chapter is structured as follows. Initially, we outline the concept of agency, drawing attention to the manner in which it can be distinguished from free will. We then take this opportunity to explore some of the paradoxes inherent to the concept of agency, before turning our attention to the related concept of consciousness. Here we marshal arguments that consciousness emerged precisely because it enables us to operate in a world underpinned by paradoxical complexity. Finally, and by way of putting this hypothesis to the test, the latter part of the chapter then considers the potential for artificial intelligence (AI) to reproduce this ability. We speculate, in particular, on whether or not machine consciousness could navigate the paradoxes that life elicits.

Agency

As ardent fans of Martin Scorsese's *Taxi Driver* (1976) will know, for antihero Travis Bickle, 'There never has been any choice for me. My whole life is pointed in one direction. I see that now.' For Bickle, then, it is definitive. He is other-directed. But do we all lay claim to the same? The perpetual tension between what are technically described as 'agency' and 'structure' constitutes one of the most fundamental paradoxes. While some have used

DOI: 10.4324/9781003203339-11

the term agency in exceptional cases to describe the behaviour of non-human actors such as, for example, corporations (see Mansell et al., 2019), the term agency is generally reserved for describing a *person's* capacity for autonomous action. Conversely, structure denotes the environment in which those persons are immersed, and the determining influence this environment has on their actions. It remains unclear which of the two factors prevails, if indeed one can be said to prevail at all. While philosophers—particularly ethicists—tend to speak in terms of 'voluntarism' (or 'free will') vis-à-vis 'determinism', sociologists prefer to speak in terms of agency vis-à-vis structure. If nothing else, the latter coupling shifts the analytical focus from moral considerations to broader social concerns. It is a debate with which the field of sociology has preoccupied itself since its inception, albeit not necessarily using the vocabulary of paradox. Attempts to transcend the paradox have been advanced by numerous contributors and under several guises. For Elias (1939) this went by the name of 'figuration' (a rather oblique attempt to bridge the subject–object divide); for Berger and Luckmann (1966), 'institutionalization' (the suggestion that humans create institutions—which in turn influence human behaviour—to apparently make up for our relative lack of instinct when compared to other animals); for followers of Foucault (1977, 1978), 'post-structuralism' (a conscious departure from pre-existing—and static—definitions that ostensibly constrain behaviour), and for Giddens (1984), 'structuration' (an attempt to re-train our focus on the intercourse *between* agency and structure).

In his excellent book, *Individualism, Holism and The Central Dilemma of Sociological Theory,* Jiří Šubrt (2019) advances an insightful discussion of the relationship between agency and structure, documenting its historical emergence. He notes that the introduction of the term figuration is one of Elias's theoretical innovations with which he sought to bridge the traditional conceptual polarization that set the subject in opposition to the object. Insightful examples of figuration include a teacher and students in a classroom, a doctor and patients in a therapeutic group, or guests in a pub seated at a table reserved for regulars (ibid.: 88). For Elias, there is extraordinary vitality to the dynamic between subject and object. This is of course why it is so challenging to deliver a lecture or presentation to an empty (or even a poorly attended) room. Such events are co-constructed; the audience is critical to the co-creation of the ambiance. As many a rock star has commented—often glibly—*it's the fans that make it happen!* In terms of paradox, the crucial point here is people mistakenly assume it is most nerve-racking to present in front of a packed auditorium; in reality, it is quite the reverse. Presenting at a poorly attended event is more often than not a disorienting, soul-crushing experience. Elias's sociology of figuration was widely discussed and hopes were placed in this approach as a means of transcending the agency/structure debate. However, as time has passed, we can see that it has not made much progress and it is now of principal interest to only a small circle of scholars. 'It appears that even Elias himself, who was very aware of and wrote extensively on the conflict between individualism and holism, was unable to overcome it with figuration' (ibid.: 89). In any event, my chief concern here is that the word 'overcome' is comparable to 'solve', which is of course the approach that many paradox theorists have taken (mistakenly in my view). Šubrt sees greater potential in latter approaches:

> [T]he constructivist conception of Berger and Luckmann (1966) and Giddens' (1984) structuration theory, seem to be more helpful and inspirational. Common to both these approaches is the idea that the creators of these structures—and also of institutions—are acting individuals. By their actions these individuals first of all create structural rules, and through subsequent actions show respect for and subordinate themselves to them.
>
> *(ibid.: 120)*

Here then the peculiar dynamic between agency and structure is brought to the fore. An accessible way of illustrating this dynamic in our daily lives, and one I use with my own students, is the behaviour inherent to keeping a diary. For Samuel Pepys this was of course a paper-based journal, and some diary-keepers continue in this tradition today. Increasingly, however, others have shifted to online blog-type alternatives enabled by social media. Either way, in writing entries in a diary, we simultaneously document *and* interpret our actions. The very act of writing (ostensibly agentic) serves to create a document (ostensibly structural). As such, the practice of rendering our thoughts and reflections to paper—either literally or metaphorically—involves the processing of those thoughts and reflections; it is thus a form of 'documentation' as a verb (both agentic and structural). For those readers schooled in psychology, you will no doubt be aware that this is of course a crucial part of the purpose and effect of what has become known as the 'therapeutic letter' i.e. a letter which is penned but never actually posted. The point is that it is the writing of the letter that allows us to both organize and process our thoughts. The fact that the letter doesn't actually get posted or read by the intended participant is immaterial.

The relationship between structure and agency is certainly complex but it is in no way impossible to disentangle if we accept—as many an undergraduate philosophy student will have done—*it's a bit of both*. It really is. It could not be otherwise. To this end, the agentic human being not only co-creates the paradoxical world she inhabits, but requires the self-same agency to operate effectively within it.

Consciousness

Beyond enquiries trained on the complex dynamic between agency and structure, a more arresting question from our point of view is: Why agency at all? And prior even to this: Why consciousness? Notwithstanding the sizable (and oftentimes platitudinous) philosophical discourse that is dedicated to tackling these sorts of conundrum, I am confident that a keener understanding—and *experience*—of paradox can afford significant traction in addressing such questions. And from there, of course, scholarly work in respect of paradox has the potential to contribute to our understanding of agency and structure, and inform our conceptualization of free will. It is thus to a discussion of the manner in which paradox might help illuminate the perplexing concept of consciousness that we now turn to.

For the bewildered reader of Nietzsche, it becomes apparent that if life was linear and reducible to some form of calculus, consciousness would be entirely unnecessary. Marsden (2002: 150) reminds us that

> Nietzsche never tires of insisting that the body is a constellation of commanding and commanded impulses, that 'consciousness' is the means through which non-conscious activity is interpreted as 'knowledge' but perversely, according to impulses which are less strong than those for which they speak.

This is particularly pertinent in the context of ethnographic endeavours because—and as we saw in Chapter 6—ethnography places experience at the very centre of its empirical enterprise, and experience is unequivocally contingent on the concept of consciousness. Arguably the best philosophers are [macro] autoethnographers *par excellence*. For Barbour (2000: 52) 'Structure in itself, no matter how intricate and ordered, cannot explain how it can be self-aware. Consciousness is the ultimate mystery'. Yes—but paradox sheds a gentle light on its logic. Cue Dostoevsky [1864] (1972: 31):

> Come on, gentlemen, why shouldn't we get rid of all this calm reasonableness with one kick, just so to send all these logarithms to the devil and be able to live our own lives at our own sweet will?' [...] If the formula for all our desires and whims is someday discovered—I mean what they depend on, and what laws they result from, how they are disseminated, what sort of good they aspire to in a particular instance, and so on—a real mathematical formula, that is, then it is possible that man will at once cease to want anything, indeed I suppose it is possible he will cease to exist. Well, what's the point of wishing by numbers? Furthermore, he will at once turn from a man into a barrel-organ sprig or something of the sort; for what is a man without desires, without will, but a sprig in the cylinder of a barrel organ?

> *(ibid.: 34)*

So far, so good. But next comes the magic. The Russian bard drills down into the dynamic between paradox and consciousness:

> And why are you so firmly and triumphantly certain that only what is normal and positive—in short, only well-being—is good for man? After all, perhaps prosperity isn't the only thing that pleases mankind, perhaps he is just as attracted to suffering. Perhaps suffering is just as good for him as prosperity.... I am certain that man will never deny himself destruction and chaos. Suffering—after all, that is the sole cause of consciousness.
>
> *(ibid.: 41)*

There are of course echoes here of Nietzsche's celebration of suffering. But for my money, Dostoevsky takes this one step further. Suffering, says Dostoevsky, is the sole cause of *consciousness*. This is notably distinct from Nietzsche's assessment, for whom suffering is simply desirable. In truth, I'm not entirely sure I agree with Dostoevsky, but I'm pretty sure his assessment had detected a hitherto overlooked—and subtle—existential aroma. Bakhtin (1984: 279) reflects on Dostoevsky's approach and understanding of consciousness across his broader canon, and notes the following:

> [For Dostoevsky's major protagonists, including] Raskolnikov, Sonya, Myshkin, Stavrogin, Ivan and Dmitry Karamazov, the profound consciousness of their own unfinalizability and indeterminancy is realized in very complex ways, by ideological thought, crime, or heroic deed. A man never coincides with himself. One cannot apply to him the formula of identity A = A. In Dostoevsky's artistic thinking, the genuine life of the personality takes place at the point of non-coincidence between a man and himself, at his point of departure beyond the limits of all that he is as a material being, a being that can be spied on, defined, predicted apart from its own will, 'at second hand'. The genuine life of the personality is made available only through a dialogic penetration of that personality, during which it freely and reciprocally reveals itself.

Although Bakhtin doesn't explore Dostoevsky's conceptualization of consciousness in terms of paradox, it is—I think—revealing that he uses the words 'unfinalizability' and 'indeterminancy' to describe the nature of the human condition and the characters' consciousness thereof.

Beyond Nietzsche and Dostoevsky, we can also take inspiration from the work of Schopenhauer. In her wonderfully lucid exploration of ecstasy and rapture, Jill Marsden (2002: 62) passes some provocative comments in respect of Schopenhauer's philosophy. She asks, first of all, whether or not truth is consistent with the human condition:

In what is tantamount to the claim that one must abdicate from the human condition in order to attain knowledge of fundamental reality, Schopenhauer singles out aestheticism and aesthetic activity as privileged corporeal conduits to the 'truth' of pre-individual desire.

Perhaps, then, to appreciate the role and purpose of paradox, we must transcend our all-too-human predisposition to make (linear) sense of the world. She continues: 'According to Schopenhauer, the genius is fated to suffer from an "abnormal" proclivity for perceiving the world objectively' (ibid.: 96). Here, however, we are dangerously close to getting ourselves into an epistemological tangle. On the one hand, contemporary academics chastise those of their colleagues who continue to slave doggedly to a positivist master, and yet—and as we saw in Chapter 6—it may actually be the subjective methods that yield our best hopes for objectivity. The real genius, then, is the one who can realize a sense of intellectual transcendence; that is objectivity *via* subjectivity.

A hypothetical world without paradox could feasibly be inhabited by non-conscious life in which straightforward linear cause-and-effect reflexes maintain existential bearing. Put another way, in a world without paradox, life could technically be reduced to a predetermined calculus (and the concept of *being* would become meaningless). For Nietzsche, God would get bored of determinism:

> [T]he course of a completely deterministic world would have been predictable for the gods and they would have quickly grown weary of it—reason enough for those friends of the gods, the philosophers, not to inflict such a deterministic world on their gods!
>
> *(Nietzsche, 1887: II/s7; 1989: 69)*

In a similar vein, Wirth comments thus in his preface to Mannheim's *Ideology and Utopia*:

> Reason, consciousness and conscience characteristically occur in situations marked by conflict. Professor Mannheim, therefore, is in accord with that growing number of modern thinkers who, instead of positing a pure intellect, are concerned with the actual social conditions in which intelligence and thought emerge. If, as seems to be true, we are not merely conditioned by the events that go on in our world but are at the same time an instrument for shaping them, it follows that the ends of action are never fully stable and determined until the act is finished or is so completely relegated to automatic routines that it no longer requires consciousness and attention.
>
> *(Wirth, 1936: xxii)*

In accordance with this line of thought, there can be little doubt that consciousness exists precisely because we live in a world characterized by paradox. Consciousness, it seems, provides for us a tool and sense of agency that enables us to navigate complexity. But what now? This interim conclusion inevitably poses an interesting question vis-à-vis AI, and it is to this question that we now turn.

Paradox and AI

In the 1940s and 1950s, mathematician and polymath John von Neuman recognized that computers would become very important, 'but he also began to realize that one must understand clearly how real-life situations are different from computer situations, exactly because they do not have the precise solutions that chess or engineering calculations do' (Bronowski, 1976: 433). Cochrane (2016) suggests that astute research may one day enable us to formulate a picture of 'AI sociology'. This is a tantalizing prospect for a social scientist. Of course, scholarly investigations in respect of android epistemology (see e.g. Ford et al., 1995) are not new. However, like Cochrane, I get the feeling that we are beginning to take these questions more seriously. And paradox is especially relevant here. As we have seen, a world characterized by paradox requires of its inhabitants an ability to maintain contradictory positions and beliefs; it necessitates existential manoeuvring, ongoing ontological re-adjustment and an ability to maintain some semblance of balance. These, it would seem, are possible only by recourse to conscious agency. Inevitably, this position has implications for the prospects of AI. Can we seriously envisage a world in which AI is able to transcend cause-and-effect reflexes and mimic the existential manoeuvring required to survive autonomously in a world characterized by paradox? I'm not sure that we can. Discussions of AI, particularly in respect of android epistemology or machine consciousness, will inevitably have to ask whether AI premised on silicon-based technologies could cope in a world riddled with paradox, irrespective of how sophisticated the programming behind its constituent algorithms had become. In a distinctly pre-feminist vernacular, Ruzicke (1973: 1, cited in Pahl, 1995: 91–92) makes some noteworthy remarks:

> [I]in an age when men [sic] are making computers that rival and even surpass some capabilities of the human being, a converse development is also taking place. Men are themselves becoming more like computers. Many aspects of a person's functioning in today's business and professional work can be more effectively performed if he can function more like a programmed computer. Thus, the more success a man achieves in his attempt to function objectively, mechanically and predictably, the more he comes to resemble a computer. When he becomes too successful in

his attempts to remake his personality in the image of a computer, he does so at the expense of losing his individuality on the way. [Those] who suffer most from this loss are those who rely on him for emotional, human interaction—especially his wife and children. And yet, in the rare movements when he allows himself to be something other than the image he so painstakingly tries to maintain, he perhaps feels the loss most acutely of all. He is not happy.

Ruzicke's observations may well be accurate, but they overlook a much more interesting consideration, and one which dystopian science fiction has grappled with for decades: the (potentially terrifying) possibility of machine consciousness. If, however, we take inspiration from our thesis in respect of paradox, this need not concern us. *Moravec's paradox,* for example, is the observation by AI and robotics researchers that, contrary what we might imagine, reasoning (which people typically find challenging) requires very little computation, whereas sensorimotor and perception skills (which come to people naturally) require enormous computational resources. This is certainly interesting, but it misses an even more acute observation. That is, an existence characterized by the sort of complexity presented by paradox is going to prove extraordinarily difficult to model. In fact, I would venture so far as to suggest that it cannot be accurately modelled. I say this not as a glib defence of the sanctity of the human condition. Take Einstein's point about common sense—*how exactly can we model the idea that common sense is a set of prejudices?* The difficulty associated with holding two or more contradictory ideas in human behaviour is labelled cognitive dissonance; as human beings we must each learn to cope with life's inherent contradictions. Will machines be able to do likewise? I'm not convinced that they will. A useful proxy—and visual aid—for this argument is the Uncanny Valley (see Figure 9.1).

The Uncanny Valley model suggests that in a world of android aesthetics, those representations of human form that exhibit poor human likeness rarely threaten us. Nor are we threatened by those whose likeness is indistinguishable from our own. The troubling zone is where they are close—but distinguishable—from the human form. This of course is analogous to the trend we saw in Chapter 2 in our discussion of art and complementary colours. It's also worth stressing that the very act of attempting to model human behaviour will—by virtue of the observer effect—adversely affect it. Yet another paradox. Paradox might thus be described—*paradoxically*—as a vague 'rule' of sociology.

Postlude

Our brief sojourn in the world of AI enables us to make a formidable proposition. The concepts of agency and—specifically—consciousness

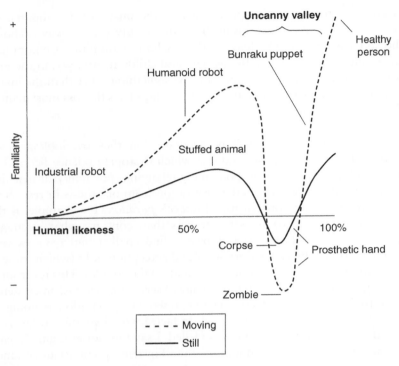

FIGURE 9.1   The Uncanny Valley.

Source: Androidscience.com, 2005.

have evolved precisely because we live in a world characterized by paradox. Despite the ongoing—and hugely controversial—efforts to create sentient machines, the one hurdle that remains (and will possibly remain in perpetuity) is that the complexity associated with paradox is of a sort which simply doesn't gel with silicone. If what we are proposing is accurate, paradox is what makes the existential concept of 'being' unique. Historically, our epistemological bias towards a conventional linear logic has primed us to attempt to solve paradoxes. An alternative approach is to examine the patterns—both systemic and existential—produced by paradoxes in a bid to understand better how they shape our lives, the focus of our concluding chapter.

10

CONCLUSION

In the 1960s, logician Willard Van Orman Quine observed that 'more than once in history, the discovery of paradox has been the occasion for major reconstruction at the foundations of thought' (cited in Goldstein, 1996: 300). While I wholeheartedly agree that these discoveries ought to have served the catalytic function Quine describes, I remain unconvinced that this has happened. Unlike Quine, what I see is a stubborn and dogged faith in linear logic. In any event, if these 'major reconstructions' have had any traction at all, it has been both modest and peculiar to discipline.

Now is the time to take paradox seriously as a distinct logic that shapes the fabric of our lives. Irrespective of scholarly discipline or empirical focus, our experience and understanding of the world around us is constrained by paradox. But—and this is all-too-often overlooked—it is also *nourished* by paradox. Paradox animates life as we know it. If I have succeeded in what I set out to do, I will have demonstrated that paradox is far from exceptional; rather, it is a decree that undergirds our very existence. It is hoped, therefore, that we are able to offer another casting of the ways in which we understand our thought processes (to Quine's point), and indeed live our lives. But a word of caution. Barbour (2000: 229) reminds us that while a theory may be able to tell us why one thing rather than another is created and experienced, 'no theory can ever explain why anything is—that is the supreme mystery'. It is certainly tempting to claim that paradox exists precisely because it makes life remarkable. But such an utterance would both violate Barbour's warning, and undermine the purpose of paradox advanced in this thesis. In any event, and as Kierkegaard (cited in Stent, 2002: 1) justifiably notes: 'in the end, every truth is true only up to a certain degree. Once it transcends that degree, [it] meets its negation and turns into a falsehood'). Indeed, it

DOI: 10.4324/9781003203339-12

seems any abstract notion of theory is itself subject to temporal relativity. Consequently, the efficacy of 'today's theory' is limited to 'today's problems' Bronowski (1976: 140). As far as anyone can tell, the prosaic problems the world presents, for which linear logic is equipped to deal with, have already been addressed. Now, it seems, we must concentrate our cognitive faculties elsewhere. As we have seen over the course of this study, many—perhaps even most—of today's substantial problems are in some important sense related to our hitherto limited abilities to navigate paradox. Now is the time the shake up the professoriate.

In the first part of the book we examined the pervasiveness of paradox. We saw how paradox manifests itself within all academic disciplines, and across these disciplines, too. What is more, we saw how paradox manipulates the ontological, epistemological and methodological foundations these disciplines are built upon. In short, we advanced the case that paradox undergirds our shared *sensorium*, irrespective of whether that reality is consider socially constructed or—in some purported sense—objective. In the latter part of the book, we then discerned three distinct logics of paradox. First, we noted, paradox wards off moral closure. Second, it helps even out subjective experience. Finally, we ventured to suggest that it can help reconceptualize our understanding of both consciousness and agency.

In this concluding chapter, then, we ask: Are these paradoxes surface manifestations of deeper contradictions that go to the very heart of human existence? If so, do they therefore contribute to defining—or constraining— the human condition? This chapter thus represents the first tentative steps towards a metatheory of paradox. To this end—and once again—Nietzsche's philosophy represents a useful point of departure:

> for all those well-constituted, joyful mortals who are far from regarding their unstable equilibrium between animal and angel as necessarily an argument against existence—the subtlest and brightest among them have even found it in... one more stimulus to life. It is precisely such 'contradictions' that seduce one to existence.
>
> *(Nietzsche [1887, III/2]; 1989: 99)*

For Nietzsche, then, human existence is unequivocally contingent on contradiction.

This chapter is divided as follows. We begin by identifying those paradoxes which transcend discipline, before going on to describe the manner in which paradox is *patterned*. As part of this discussion, and building on precedent found in the work of Kant, Nietzsche, and Marsden, we take metaphorical inspiration from the mechanics of music to make sense of the manner in which the dynamics of paradox reveal a sense of pattern. We then explore possibilities for developing a rigorous 'epistemology of balance' to help navigate the paradoxes life presents, before exploring the ways in which paradox can enhance education. Finally, we ask ourselves whether we must completely abandon attempts to solve paradoxes, before imparting our closing remarks.

Pervasive paradoxes

Further distillation of the material examined in this book reveals multiple *pervasive paradoxes*. Presentation of the paradoxes in this way inevitably invites comparison to Buddha's Avyakrta (imponderable questions) or Kant's antinomies. Both Buddha and Kant identified key underlying tensions that frame our world. In each case, four specific tensions were identified (see Figures 10.1 and 10.2).

Evidently, there is a significant overlap between these two sets of tensions. And—notably—over the course of this thesis we too have identified paradoxes that correspond to the sets advanced by Buddha and Kant. These are: the paradoxes relating to space–time (Chapter 6), composition (Chapters 3 and 7), free will (Chapter 7), and belief (Chapter 5). Of course, these might all be grouped under the banner of complexity. We might even be so bold to refer to this collection of tensions as a *complexity paradox*. In a very trite sense, everything is subject to this paradox. As we have seen, psychology, for example, teaches us that our nature (that is, what is instinctive) must be repressed in order for civilization to flourish. Similarly, in science, entropy (that is, disorder) is natural, but must be arrested in the form of 'organization' for life to flourish.

More pertinently, however, and unlike the catalogues advanced by Buddha or Kant, our discussion of paradox is not intended to constitute a framework. In any event, though certainly comparable to both Buddha's and Kant's respective observations, the pervasive tensions we delineate here are cast in the vocabulary of paradox—rather than 'imponderable questions' or 'antinomies'—and expand beyond the limits that either Buddha or Kant set. And, notably, it is only beyond those rudimentary tensions that we get a true sense of the pervasiveness of paradox. To this end, the following

---

1 Does the world have both a beginning and an end in time, or only one or the other, or neither?
2 Is the world finite in space, or is it infinite?
3 Are body and soul one and the same thing, or are they different things?
4 Is there a Perfect Being who can know things as they really are and is immortal?

FIGURE 10.1 Buddha's Four Imponderables.

1 Space and time:
  Thesis: The world has a beginning in time, and is also limited as regards space.
  Anti-thesis: The world has no beginning, and no limits in space; it is infinite as regards both time and space.
2 Atomism:
  Thesis: Every composite substance in the world is made up of simple parts, and nothing anywhere exists save the simple or what is composed of the simple.
  Anti-thesis: No composite thing in the world is made up of simple parts, and there nowhere exists in the world anything simple.
3 Spontaneity and causal determinism:
  Thesis: Causality in accordance with laws of nature is not the only causality from which the appearances of the world can one and all be derived. To explain these appearances it is necessary to assume that there is also another causality, that of spontaneity.
  Anti-thesis: There is no spontaneity; everything in the world takes place solely in accordance with laws of nature.
4 A necessary deity:
  Thesis: There belongs to the world, either as its part or as its cause, a being that is absolutely necessary.
  Anti-thesis: An absolutely necessary being nowhere exists in the world, nor does it exist outside the world as its cause.

FIGURE 10.2 Kant's Four Antinomies.

pervasive paradoxes are identified: the paradox of unintended consequences, the paradox of pleasure, the paradox of identity, the paradox of observation, the paradox of commitment, the paradox of competition, and a paradox of wellbeing. Each is outlined briefly, below.

The pervasive paradox of unintended consequences. The unintended consequences paradox transcends politics, economics, organization, medicine, and morality. In politics, Edmund Burke's observation that radical social action yields results far more problematic than intended is something that history illustrates all too often and yet few of us ever seem to cotton on: resistance strengthens the resolve of one's opponent. In economics, Adam Smith's observation that individual self-interest elicits social virtue is an outstanding derivative of the unintended consequences paradox. For organization theorists, this tension manifests itself most obviously in terms of bureaucracy; organizational problems are simultaneously created—but also ostensibly solved—by an appeal to greater proceduralization. On a very practical level, too, we noted also how all-encompassing operational methodologies—such as TQM—paradoxically create cultures in which mistakes are concealed and hence no longer provide the all-important opportunities for learning that they once did. Finally, in medicine, most—perhaps all—drugs have unintended consequences, more commonly described as side effects. The paradox of unintended consequences reminds us that attempts to meddle in complex systems such as the economy or the body create unforeseen and often undesirable outcomes (see e.g. Norton, 2008). Beware our own hubris; beware the folly that we are 'in control'. Perhaps most pertinently, the paradox of unintended consequences undergirds the first alternative logic we advanced (see Chapter 7). Here we recognized that considerations of morality in any of the categories we explored in that chapter (i.e. 'might makes right', binary morality, free will, selflessness or conflict) can be framed in terms of unintended consequences.

The pervasive paradox of pleasure. The pleasure paradox transcends psychology, economics, organization, and biochemistry. In psychology, it manifests most obviously in respect of sado-masochism. For economists, it is framed chiefly in terms of the documented tendency for the most successful entrepreneurs to have experienced deprivation in their formative years. In terms of organizational behaviour, we noted that the ostensibly benign pursuit of success is inherently self-limiting (Pahl's 1995 work in respect of what he describes as 'the nightmare of success' is especially relevant here). Beyond these social observations, the field of biochemistry yields a paradox of pleasure. We noted that psychotropic foods trained at addressing mental illness—specifically the drugs known as Selective Serotonin Reuptake Inhibitors—involve an exacerbation of the underling pathology prior to any prospect of improved mood. The broader mechanism that underpins the process of immunization (initial pain, prior to improved wellbeing) is similarly cast.

The pervasive paradox of identity: The paradox of identity transcends philosophy, psychology, sociology, organization, and politics. In psychology, the paradox of identity manifests itself most obviously through the recognition that our sense of self can only emerge vis-à-vis the other. In sociology, there are numerous articulations of this very tension: Elias's 'figuration', Berger and Luckmann's 'constructivism', Giddens' 'structuration', Foucault's 'post-structuralism', and—of course—the dualism that has become known as 'agency-structure'. All suggest that the structures—or institutions—which shape our behaviour (and with which we identify) are of course themselves created by agentic individuals. In philosophical terms, this is described as the tension between voluntarism and determinism (upon which we advance a paradox of free will). Empirically, this tension was illustrated most effectively in the field of psychology courtesy of Zimbardo's infamous Prison Experiment, during which he demonstrated unequivocally that role precedes behaviour and professed identity.

The pervasive paradox of observation: The observer's paradox apparently transcends all natural and social endeavours. While the observer's paradox is a phenomenon we associate most readily with physics (and is broadly conflated with Heisenberg's Uncertainty Principle), it is something all academic researchers—irrespective of discipline—ought to be conscious of. Arguably, it is something all of us must be conscious of. It has taken on a fundamental importance in discussions of epistemology as we researchers debate the degree to which our presence has an unconscious influence on the data yielded by our research. It is, I have been informed by linguist and phonologist Dr Jenny Amos, of especial relevance to the field of sociolinguistics: research subjects subconsciously modify the way they speak in the presence of the researcher, much as we each fine-tune our accent, range of vocabulary and intonation in respect of the present company.

The pervasive paradox of competition. The paradox of competition transcends economics, biology, and organization theory. In economics, competitors do not distance themselves from their competitors, as might be expected, but gravitate towards them in a process known as economic clustering. In microbiology, and—again—unexpectedly, we see extensive evidence of resource competition between bacteria in times of abundance, while we see cooperation in times of scarcity. 'Co-opitition' thus occurs in both biology and economics (Briggs & Peat, 1985). Finally, we also see evidence of a derivative tension between homophily (love of the same) and heterophily (love of the other) play out in discussions of both group behaviour in economic (organizational) contexts, and in terms of breeding in biological (genetic) contexts.

So what—if anything—can we glean from these pervasive paradoxes? Well, they each reflect—and reinforce—a worldview that is characterized by two important factors. First, it is a worldview which is *patterned* (but *not predictable*). Second, they reinforce the three unseen—and in all probability unknowable—alternative logics that we have broadly described as 'moral closure prevention' (paradox ensures a sense of moral dynamism; see Chapter 7), 'egalitarian inertia' (paradox helps even out the lived experience of all human beings; see Chapter 8), and 'emergent agency' (paradox necessitates conscious and agentic beings so as to navigate the complexities the world elicits; see Chapter 9).

The pattern of paradox

We can respond to the realization that we live in a world of paradox in one of several ways. The first potential response is simple: nihilism. This certainly appears to be Nietzsche's position when faced with a world of uncertainty. To the extent that nihilism is conflated with a fundamental suspicion of (or disbelief in) *all values*, this presents as a reasonable retort. But is the more prevalent understanding of nihilism (in the sense that it implies a belief system bereft of hope) relevant here? Let us *hope not*. The second potential response is that which has been taken historically: a concerted—if ultimately fruitless—endeavour to solve, resolve, or dissolve paradox. Over the course of this thesis, we have discounted the efficacy of this approach. A third response is proposed by Buddhists. A Buddhist view suggests that we must strive to transcend both suffering (pain) and craving (pleasure) by 'living in the moment'. At first glance, this is compelling. However, scratch a little deeper and it amounts to yet another desire, in this case a desire to transcend. In a functional sense, then, it is not especially different to capitalism (a desire for more), Marxism (a desire for equity), or any other worldview you care to consider. The insurmountable problem is that the substance of *any* experience, however desirable it may be in the first instance, will inevitably— and invariably—elicit its opposite. To this end, the desire for transcendence that Buddhism teaches is I suspect unrealizable. Despite the apparently universal respect Buddhism commands among ranks of progressive thinkers, I am by no means the only theorist to reject Buddhism on this basis (see, e.g. Bronowsk, 1976: 437). In any event, and reservations regarding the specifics of Buddhism aside, a sensitivity to paradox must not become yet another all-encompassing belief system. Responses one, two, and three are clearly problematic, and for this reason I advance a fourth: the development of a rigorous epistemology of balance. In plain language, this takes the form of an endeavour dedicated to exploring how best to intuit a truly efficacious sense of balance. Before tackling this challenge, however, we must first identify and make sense of the patterns inherent to our experience of paradox.

Schema (2018) suggests that '[w]e have a biological compulsion to pattern. It's what we humans do, what we want to do, what we can't stop ourselves doing'. In many respects, the concept of the archetype, Jungian or otherwise, represents a way of looking at life through the lens of pattern. Indeed, in the wake of findings by neuroscientists in respect of mirror neurons (brain cells that fire both when an animal performs a certain action and when that same animal observes the same action performed by another), Hogensen (2009) argues that archetypes reveal 'elementary action patterns' in human behaviour. Similarly, Wirth (1936: xix) argues that if there is to be any knowledge at all beyond the sensing of the unique and transitory events of the moment, we must open up the possibility of discovering general trends in both physical and social worlds. If nothing else, and in a manner analogous to what has been described in respect of archetypes, paradox is *patterned*. Like the Fibonacci sequence. Or the golden ratio. Or fractals. Or symmetry. Even birdsong can be interpreted by recourse to pattern (see e.g. Burridge & Kenney, 2016). Here, then, we seek inspiration from the work of mathematicians. Much as say, *Pi*, hints at an underlying pattern in our world I'm curious to ascertain whether or not there is an underlying (albeit not necessarily a mathematical) pattern in respect of the proliferation of paradox. Recognition of such a pattern would not so much enable us to live 'perfect lives' but it would at least enable us to figure out how best to navigate paradox. Some ostensibly banal questions can actually be rather instructive: to what degree should chocolate be blended into a cupcake (are chips of chocolate preferable to a more even dispersal of cocoa throughout the sponge)? How much—and what kind of—exercise should we do to elicit the desired endorphins in pursuance of pleasure? How much should we deny ourselves before indulging?

Heavyweight philosopher, Jill Marsden (2002: 56), whose work we built upon extensively in the latter part of our thesis, herself invokes a sense of pattern when exploring the dynamics between pleasure and pain in comparable terms: 'Pleasure and pain in the experience of the sublime appear to participate in an energetic dynamic of perpetual overcoming formally analogous to that observed in Nietzsche's account of the recursive libidinal reverberation of the Dionysian.' In a similar sense, but in this case trained more closely to the concerns of sociology, Šubrt (2019: 122) suggests that structuration theory demonstrates that 'patterns are repeatedly revived, reproduced and "played back" in the everyday behaviour of human beings'. And—finally—in the world of psychotherapy we find yet more precedent. Drawing on the work of Edgar Levenson (1976), Wilber (1982c: 12, original emphasis) concludes that 'the therapist does not succeed because he [sic] explains' [but because] he expands awareness of *patterning*'. To present paradox as a pattern that emerges across disciplines, we take inspiration first from Bohr's phrase: 'the conspiracy of nature', a phrase he used to describe nature's point blank refusal to yield its fundamental secrets.

> Bohr's [conclusions point] to a fiendish conspiracy of nature (or of God) to keep us from attaining an objective description of reality. She (or He) ties observer and object together so that, in the microcosmic realm of applicability of quantum mechanics, no sharp line that can be drawn in any experimental setup would demarcate where the 'observer' ends and the 'object' begins. Thus, according to Bohr, in the drama of existence, we play the dual role of actor and observer. It seems ironical, indeed bizarre, that a conclusion so subversive for the metaphysics of materialism should have been forced on us by twentieth-century physics.
>
> *(Stent, 2002: 251)*

Stent's examination of this conspiracy demonstrates that—and in addition to its prevalence in the world of physics—it also manifests itself in biology (ibid.: 256), chemistry (ibid.: 257), and psychology (ibid.: 258). Where Bohr observes what he describes as a fiendish conspiracy of nature in physics, biology, and psychology, I observe a pattern of paradox that it is observable not just in physics, chemistry, biology, and psychology, but in *any* field we care to consider. Let's turn again to an interpretation of Nietzschean thought, this time in respect of his concept of 'eternal recurrence':

> The tight analytic relationship between the concepts of suffering, becoming, willing and creating which [Nietzsche's work] achieves is enormously impressive... it also combines creativity with the doctrines of amor fati and the eternal recurrence. [...] Not only is everything that has gone before a necessary prelude to the moment of an individual's creative act, but also the meaningfulness of everything that has gone before hangs in the balance, awaiting affirmation or denial. Thus the destiny of the future depends upon what is decided in the world-historical vortex of the creative moment: 'Every moment beginnith existence, around every "Here" rolleth the ball "There". The middle is everywhere'.
>
> *(Davey, 1997: xxvi–xxvii)*

We turn now then to describe—and represent diagrammatically—how these paradoxes behave in accordance with a patterned logic. To this end, the pattern advanced is one that lays claim to three specific characteristics: (1) it is broadly U-shaped, represented most effectively by *the horseshoe*; (2) it is contradictory, represented most effectively by *the Mobius strip*; and (3) it is in a perpetual state of flux, represented most effectively by *the pendulum*.

The horseshoe: towards a U-shaped ontological pattern

In a conceptual track comparable to what Charles Handy (whose work we discussed in Chapter 4) describes as 'curvilinear logic', we can infer distinct experiential dynamics related to extremities in the paradoxes presented. They contribute to what we can describe as a 'U-shaped' ontology (see Figure 10.3). This can, of course, be gleaned most obviously from our discussion of ideological conviction. Readers will recall what has become known as the 'political horseshoe' from Chapter 3. The political horseshoe image is used to illustrate the observation that political conviction is not a continuum between the 'Political Left' and the 'Political Right'; rather, extremist positions on either side tend to resemble one another (hence the horseshoe shape). However, over the course of this thesis, we have detected this dynamic associated with extremities elsewhere, too. For example, recall our observations vis-à-vis complementary colours in Chapter 2. Recall the Veblen effect in economics or the dialectical shift between permissive and conservative political attitudes between generations in Chapter 3. Think about our relationship to control, as explored in Chapter 4. And—perhaps most prosaic of all—recall the horticultural paradox from Chapter 5, that is, the practice of cutting plants and trees back in order to encourage

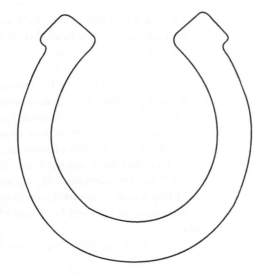

FIGURE 10.3   The Horseshoe as Representative of a U-Shaped Ontological Pattern.

growth. Finally, readers are encouraged to think about how many statistical distributions in graphical form resemble a comparable pattern. These all hint at an underlying U-shaped nature of being.

Inevitably, speculation along these lines requires, once again, reflection on the pertinence of conventional cause-and-effect. In recent decades there has been a burgeoning interest in alternatives to causal analytics. Pribram (1982: 34), for example, says: 'In the absence of space-time coordinates, the usual causality upon which most scientific explanation depends must also be suspended. Complementarities, synchronicities, symmetries, and dualities must be called upon as explanatory principles.' More generally, we can cite robust arguments for moving away from a dependence on linear logic. Drawing on Bergson's (1975; 1998) 'theory of knowledge', Styhre (2007: 175) presents the following observation:

'Changes without ceasing' and 'spontaneous movements' are not apprehended by mathematical calculation.... Organic creation, on the contrary, the evolutionary phenomenon which properly constitutes life, we cannot in any way subject to mathematical calculation. This is part of Bergon's 'theory of knowledge': intellectual thinking is incapable of understanding change, and since life and biological organisms are change, intellect is incapable of understanding processes of becoming, that is, life. Life is, for Bergson, the coming together of consciousness and matter. Consciousness and matter appear to us... as radically different forms of existence, even as antagonistic forms, which have to find a modus vivendi.

Matter is necessity, consciousness is freedom; but though diametrically opposed to one another, life has found a way of reconciling them. This is precisely what life is—freedom inserting itself within necessity, turning it to its profit. Life would be an impossibility were the determination of matter so absolute as to admit no relaxation.

This is persuasive stuff and begs the inevitable question: Should we dispense altogether with linear cause-and-effect and usher in a post-linear dynamics, built around the U-shape? No. For two reasons. First, and as we noted in Chapter 6, even if ultimately wrong, linear logic is an extremely useful approximation. Second, and while a sensitivity to curvilinear (or U-shaped) logic is vital, any attempt to place post-linear dynamics on a pedestal—to reify it—will more than likely precipitate its own undoing. It may therefore be most effective as a vocal 'backbencher'; an alternative voice.

The Mobius strip: towards an inverted ontological pattern

Beyond our contributions to what we have described as a U-shaped ontology, we can glean something else from the transdisciplinary paradoxes presented. They reveal an egalitarian inertia; a means—perhaps—of evening out both spatial and temporal experience. This inertia helps mitigate the most challenging of human frailties, such as injury (e.g. experiential relativity), wealth (e.g. the resource curse), and tyranny (e.g. manumission). While the U-shaped image helps illustrate the tendency for extremities to curve back onto themselves, the Mobius strip (see Figure 10.4) is an effective pedagogical tool for demonstrating how paradox can subvert—completely—one's intentions. It is an extremely effective didactic device for illustrating the manner in which paradox yields an egalitarian inertia; that is, it helps moderate subjective experience.

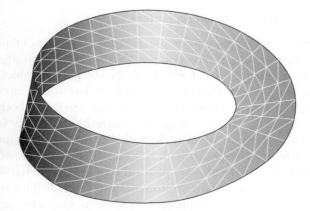

FIGURE 10.4 The Mobius Strip as Representative of an Inverted Ontology.

The most accessible means of making sense of this inverted ontology is, of course, courtesy of the pleasure-pain paradox, and particularly the concept of hedonic adaptation. We cited numerous empirical examples of precisely this, most of which hinge on the mediating effects of relativism i.e. the long-term effects of bereavement or a debilitating illness, your place of residence, or indeed the much longed for—but ultimately cursed—lottery win. In a similar vein, becoming a victim of one's success is one of the paradoxes that is best illustrated using the Mobius strip. This evening out of the experience was reported elsewhere, too. So, for example, in the worlds of literature (specifically existential literature; and particularly in the works of Camus), in economics (in terms of the intergenerational paradox), and—perhaps most pervasive of all—in respect of the transdisciplinary complexity paradox. As Marsden (2002: 126) reminds us: '[there exists a] fundamental tendency of life to squander its riches—a process that Bataille makes central in his own theory of non-productive expenditure'. Perhaps the most memorable example, however, is courtesy of Spartacus: 'When a free man dies, he loses the pleasure of life. A slave loses his pain. Death is the only freedom a slave knows. That's why he's not afraid of it.'

However, we need to be extremely careful about our position in respect of relativism, not least because it can invoke a semantic trap. For Stedman-Jones (1998: 125), for example, there is a paradoxical quality to the central proposition of relativism: 'it has a peculiar ring of absolutism about it. How can it be asserted so absolutely that all is relative?' As enthusiasts of Monty Python's *Life of Brian,* will be only too keen to quote:

> *Brian: 'You're all different'*
> *Mob: 'Yes, we're all different'*
> *Individual: 'I'm not.'*

The Pendulum: towards a dynamic ontological pattern

At its most rudimentary, the representation of paradox as a pendulum implies—quite simply—that there is a temporal, perpetual to-ing and fro-ing between opposite positions, positions which may be shaped by politics, ethics, physics, or some other designation. However, the analogy has still greater potential. For example, the distance from axis to ball will determine both its reach and speed. Notably, the ball moves quickly where kinetic energy is greatest which is at the lowest point; whereas the ball is at its slowest point at the extremities, after which it reverses its path (see Figure 10.5). Might we observe something similar in respect of, say, political swings? And what—exactly—happens when we increase the length from the axis to the ball (or in our political analogy, we cultivate the conditions for most extremist left- and right-wing parties)? Such questions fall outside the scope of this current project,

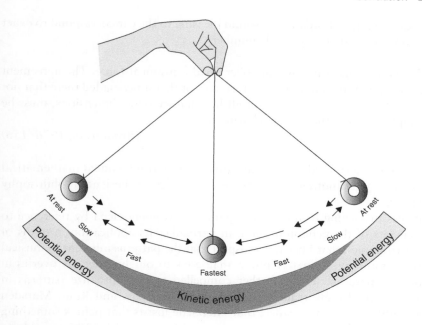

FIGURE 10.5   The Pendulum as Representative of a Dynamic Ontology.

but represent an interesting direction in which to pursue future research. Related to the pendulum, we can also invoke the analogy of the metronome, a mechanical device used by musicians. A metronome takes the form of an inverted pendulum. However, and unlike the uniform motion of a pendulum which keeps virtually the same time whether it swings in a large or a small arc (Bronowski & Mazlish, 1960: 120), a metronome is designed in such a way that a weighted slider can be adjusted to reflect the desired tempo; the closer the slider is to the pivot point, the faster the tempo. Oscillation frequency reflects tempo in music, but could also relate to the workings of bi-partisan democracy in politics, or the dialectical experience of pain and pleasure. For our purposes, of course, the slider on the metronome implies a degree of control. Assuming we can exercise some such control (and, as we saw in Chapter 4, we must exercise caution in making such assumptions), where, then, might we position the slider in respect of oscillations between extremities?

Conceptualizing the patterns of paradox in accordance with musical metaphor

The Ancient Greek philosopher Pythagoras of Samos is best known for his work in mathematics and, especially, geometry. However, Pythagoras made some interesting contributions to our understanding of music. He discovered, for example, that chords which sound pleasing to the ear correspond to exact divisions of the string by whole numbers.

> To the Pythagoreans that discovery had a mystical force. The agreement between nature and number was so cogent that it persuaded them that not only the sounds of nature, but all her characteristic dimensions, must be simple numbers that express harmonies.
>
> *(Bronowski, 1976: 156)*

Pythagoras interpreted music in accordance with transcendent mathematical principles; put another way, his was the first experiential philosophy of music.

It was in seeking to understand paradoxical phenomena by reference to movements of the pendulum (and, in particular, its application in terms of the metronome), that I began to suspect that the patterns inherent to musical composition may ultimately prove analogous to our broader discoveries in respect of paradox. I was further compelled to conceptualize patterns in musical terms by my reading of Marsden, Nietzsche, and Kant. Marsden (2002: 69) reminds her readers that Nietzsche insists that pain is something distinct from pleasure, not its opposite, and '...it may [thus] be possible to understand the pleasure in terms of overcoming a hindrance'. This, of course, is comparable to Ogden Nash's infamous suggestion that happiness is not freedom from discomfort but having an 'itch for every scratch'. To this end, we might reasonably conceptualize pattern-as-rhythm this way: itch/scratch/ itch/scratch/itch/scratch [...]. More generally, and following on from our brief discussions of Wagner and Schopenhauer earlier in the book, readers will recall that music is widely considered to be the only art form that *isn't* trained on representation; it thus holds extraordinary promise as a direct porthole to the soul, rather than merely its symbolic depiction. To the extent that music—and the rhythmic patterns it invokes—represents a manifestation of the character of life, it is of course wholly relevant to our musings in respect of paradox.

> [P]leasure is conditioned by a certain rhythmic sequence of smaller, unpleasurable stimuli: in this way a very rapid increase in the feeling of power, the feeling of pleasure, is achieved. This is the case, e.g. in tickling, also the sexual tickling in the act of coitus: in such a way we see displeasure active as an ingredient of pleasure. It seems a small hindrance is overcome and immediately followed again by another small hindrance that is again overcome—this game of resistance and victory arouses most strongly that total feeling of surplus, superfluous power that constitutes the essence of pleasure.
>
> *(Nietzsche, The Will to Power 699, cited in Marsden, 2002: 69–70)*

Eco's canon is comparably insightful in respect of the didactic potential of music. In *History of Beauty,* his invocation has a discernible Deleuzian flavour. Eco (2004: 83) explains that in the ninth century, Irish intellectual John Scotus Eriugena sought to understand the 'Beauty of Creation', and concluded that it was generated by the simultaneous playing of the 'same' and the 'different' to produce a harmony in which the voices, listened to in isolation, say nothing, but once merged into a single concert produce a natural sweetness. In this sense, then, the two 'sides' of any paradox only make sense when consciously and deliberately bound together. And this—of course—is precisely how we succeeded in distinguishing paradox from its synonyms in the introduction chapter.

The pattern of paradox: tempo, rhythm, and melody

For Deakin, author of *Waterlog,* there is a fundamental problem with decadence:

> That hot baths are now two a penny for many of us may not be such a boon as it seems. G. M. Trevelyan's housemaster at Harrow, Edward Bowen, an ascetic bachelor who once walked the eighty miles from Cambridge to Oxford within twenty-four hours, told him 'O boy, you oughtn't have a hot bath twice a week; you'll get like the later Romans'. T. H. White thought once a fortnight was probably about right, arguing that 'The true voluptuary wears sackcloth nearly all the time, so that when he does put on his sheer silk pants he can get full satisfaction out of rolling in the hay.
> *(Deakin, 1999: 236)*

According to White, then, a moment of indulgence once a fortnight was about right. But who is to say he is correct? Interestingly, for Nietzsche, in *Beyond Good and Evil,* the working week is configured on a specific pleasure/pain tempo, but in typically Nietzschean style, it is done in such a way that the experience of the pleasure is arranged such that it elicits an embrace of the return to pain: 'Industrious races find it very troublesome to endure leisure; it was a masterpiece of English instinct to make the Sabbath so holy and so boring that the English begin unconsciously to lust again for their work—and week-day' (Nietzsche, 1886: s189; 1989: 102).

But White's words got me thinking. Prior to their notorious descent into decadence, the Romans may well have been on to something in respect of the design of their infamous baths. Roman bathhouses typically included hot, cold, and tepid pools arranged in a specific configuration. The ideal, one is compelled to conclude, was for the bather to alternate between these. Perhaps, I wondered, we might glean some mathematical formula from these by reflecting on (a) their architectural design and (b) the time the bather would typically spend in each pool. This is of course esoteric stuff and—unsurprisingly—I was unable to find any relevant extant research by archaeologists or anybody else for that matter. However, all was not lost. During the closing stages of research for this book my wife turned 40. To celebrate her birthday, she expressed a desire to travel to Italy, specifically Naples. From the point of view of my research this was fortuitous, as it meant we'd be visiting Pompeii which is located a short distance from the city of Naples. After a couple of days dodging battered Fiats on the narrow streets of Naples (a small price to pay for enjoying the world's finest food), we took the train to Pompeii. Armed with nothing more than a smartphone and a scruffy guidebook, we set off to explore the remains of the baths in the ancient city. For readers who have visited Pompeii, they will no doubt recall that curation does not appear to be an Italian strongpoint. Happily, however, the signage adjacent to the baths included some useful instructions. Figure 10.6 is a representation of the layout, taken directly from this signage.

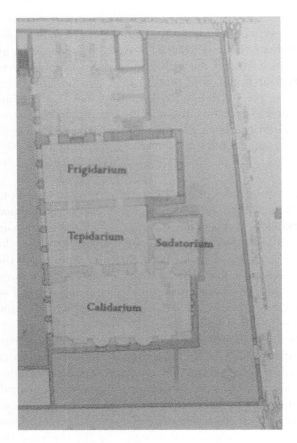

FIGURE 10.6 Plan of the Baths on Via Stabiana, Pompeii.

More or less equal space is put aside for cold, tepid, and hot baths implying, perhaps, that bathers would spend more or less the same amount of time in each. Beyond this, however, three much more interesting implications can be gleaned. First, the location of the entrance to the baths would suggest that it is the cold bath that bathers begin with (this implies pain before pleasure, rather than the other way round). Second, the access points *between* baths suggest that bathers would engage in a sort of cyclical rhythm, that is, begin in the cold, move through to the tepid, then the hot, then back to the tepid, then the cold, and so on. The fact that there are two access points between baths implies that there was likely an orderliness; a single access point would present congestion. Finally, that there is a 'sudatorium', in addition to the three baths implies—perhaps—the importance of variation in pleasure (noted earlier in terms of indulging in chocolate and other types of confectionary), that is, on occasion at least, bathers might plump for a hot steam bath rather than a warm water bath.

Of course, despite its potential, this interpretation is guesswork. But we should not overlook the fact that bathing in this respect is an activity that has stood the test of time. Think about high-end hotels—they reproduce this effect in the configuration of their own leisure complexes. Yes, they have saunas and Jacuzzis, but they also have cooler pools and (very cold) plunge pools. And, in a rather different context, consider Mary Schmich. Schmich penned the words that eventually became the infamous *Sunscreen Song*. In imparting her wisdom, she insisted that one must live in New York (but not for too long or else it will make you hard). Equally, one must live in California (but not for too long or else it will make you soft). Buoyed, then, by this detective work in Pompeii, we turn now to consider how these three aspects of music—rhythm, melody, and tempo—might help make further sense of the patterns paradox presents.

Rhythm and paradox. Enthusiasts of Jamaican dancehall and ragga music place an importance on rhythm (or 'riddim') over and above melody. It has a key bearing on our study of paradox, too. The example we used to illustrate the peculiar dynamic between pain and pleasure was as follows: Most of us can relate to a paradox of happiness when we think of drink or drugs (a high and then a low), or exercise (a low then a high). Should the beat (the high) precede the off-beat (the low), or vice versa? As I write these very words, I have my eye on the news and the BBC has just reported a rather interesting story, the headline of which is 'In the east, Ukraine braces to launch counter-attack':

Julia, a 35-year-old nursery school teacher, laughs when I ask her about living under [the Russian] threat. 'Imagine that war came to you and you had to pack up and leave your home in 24 hours,' she asks. 'You would, just like me, try to hang on to what you have spent your whole life making.'

Her sister Liliia stands nearby. On her wrist she has a tattoo—'dulcius ex asperis' it reads—Latin for 'sweetness follows hardship'.

Our illustration of the Pompeii bathhouse, above, would imply the same. For the Romans, then, the order was clear: pleasure must follow pain.

Melody and paradox. Melody is important, not least because—unlike beat and tempo—it captures the creative and agentic aspect of the human condition. But how—exactly—can we describe melody in relation to paradox? In his wonderful tome, *Man at Play: Nine Centuries of Pleasure Making,* John Armitage (1977: 67) reflects on Robert Burton's (1621) *The Anatomy of Melancholy* and notes, pertinently, that 'games (as a source of pleasure) should remain refreshments and not become a way of life as they were for so many gentlemen'. Of course, we've heard this argument in various forms numerous times now, and especially so in our discussion of the paradoxes inherent to the pursuit of pleasure. But what is so notable about Hermitage's utterance is his choice of vocabulary, particularly the word refreshment. How often and in what form might 'refreshment' take? One way to think about refreshment, and particularly the scheduling of refreshment intervals, is to think—metaphorically—in terms of music. Notably, an interval in music is not simply a break, but describes the difference in pitch between successive tones. If we place our faith in the metaphorical potential of music, then, this implies not only must we periodically take breaks (i.e. conventional intervals) but the demarked activities must themselves be different (i.e. different tones, the concatenation of which form a melody). To this end, it is *not* enough to—say—indulge in chocolate, then take an interim period of detoxification before re-indulging in that same chocolate. Rather, for the periods of indulgence, we must experiment with different types of chocolate; and perhaps even take it upon ourselves to sample a distinct confectionary altogether.

Tempo and paradox. What sort of tempo is appropriate for alternating between the extremities of a paradox? Fast to-ing and fro-ing, or a more leisurely pace? The 'science' behind the perfect pop song suggests a periodic flitting between a familiar beat and a more dynamic difference (or between verse and chorus). A change here occurs every 30 seconds or so. And, yet, and as noted in Chapter 9, for most of us the primary unit of temporal distinction is the working week. Most of us work for five days on and then have two days off. This temporal template appears to have stood the test of time. And, for gardeners who follow certain botanical/horticultural rules, you cut back plants and trees (to paradoxically encourage further growth) on an annual, or biannual basis. We are therefore presented with a very wide range of 'ideal' tempos.

In sum, then, it seems that while a temporal rule for paradox is difficult to discern since so many of life's experiences themselves vary in terms of tempo, we *can* make some generalizations vis-à-vis rhythm and melody. In terms of rhythm, it is clear that for most experiences pain must precede pleasure. In terms of melody, we are compelled to ensure just enough variation to our pleasures to maintain intrigue and to satisfy life's yearning for novelty without departing from what it is about the pleasure that appeals in the first place. Furthermore, it may be the case that some paradoxes (e.g. those associated with ideological conviction or pain and pleasure) are sensitive to tempo, while others might be more accurately understood by recourse to rhythm or melody (e.g. agency-structure).

Before we move on to explore the concept of balance, it is apposite to comment more broadly on the concept of pattern vis-à-vis paradox, and—pertinently—to set limitations on the degree to which we are justified in speculating on 'how to live'. Much as individuals *co-create* patterns of microbehaviour (in the form, say, of daily prayers, or alcoholism), so too—presumably—are patterns of macrosocial incidence such as the prevalence of the pattern we observe in respect of paradox. And just as serendipity plays a big part in determining whether our individual lives are 'patterned' by the Morning Prayer or by the daily abuse of alcohol, that our world is 'patterned' by paradox is probably chance. By this we mean paradox is not so much intrinsic to life in so far as it is part of life's 'unique recipe'; rather, things have simply evolved this way. Indeed, and once again drawing upon Robert Burton's canon, Armitage (1977: 68) says that while many have tried 'to make play into a recipe for life', this rarely—if ever—succeeds, 'for melancholy [inevitably] creeps in'. Speculating on 'how to live' is a specious enterprise. We cannot figure out a 'formula' for living an ideal life and this must be a caveat to my discussions in respect of intuiting an ideal approach to maximizing pleasure and/or balance. It was none less than Machiavelli who demonstrated that the ensemble of our social aspirations is paradoxical and so the belief that the correct, objectively valid solution to the question of how we should live can be discovered is itself, in principle, not true (see, e.g. Stent, 2002: 231). This is a salient concession not least because it enables us to distinguish 'pattern' from causality.

Paradox and the complexity of balance

True paradox is irresolvable. As Stent (2002) notes in respect of the paradox of moral responsibility, for example, the would-be resolvers of this paradox have included *behaviourists, immaterialists, libertarians, compatibilists, and physicists* but none of their proposed resolutions have withstood incisive philosophical critique. Our response to paradox is then to usher in a rigorous 'epistemology of balance' (and, as I have noted previously, while 'balance' is an extremely commonplace motif, the concept has not been given anything like the amount of intellectual interrogation it warrants; see Vine, 2021). Notably, countless contributors have championed the merits of balance: from Aristotle's *Golden Mean* to the ancient Chinese philosophical concept of *Yin and Yang*; and from Toffler's *Futurism* to Giddens' *Third Way*. Balance is it seems indubitable for theorists. However, and without exception, what these contributors fail to do is to explore—systematically— how balance might actually be realized. The concept has not been given anything like the amount of intellectual interrogation it warrants. How, exactly, might we go about leading 'balanced' lives? It is here, of course, that we might rekindle—but actively move beyond—the Aristotelian concept of the 'golden mean', a desirable middle position between two poles. Balance might also be achieved through genuinely multi—and trans-disciplinary pursuits. A good start, of course, is to establish clear dialogues between different scholarly traditions. A multi-disciplinary schedule of research might make us savvier human beings. We might learn to navigate paths between the extremes that constitute the poles of each paradox discussed here, and many more besides. We might learn how to strive for desirable ends without falling victim to countervailing forces. We might learn how to present arguments constructively, without succumbing to ideological or moral closure.

More specifically, we are compelled to ask ourselves some pertinent questions. Is balance best approached as an average, as an equation, as an equilibrium, as a compromise, as a sense of harmony, or as something else altogether? And if, say, as an average, then as mean, mode, or median? And if as an equation, who is responsible for determining the parameters for what will presumably involve sophisticated algebra? Or perhaps balance ought to be approached by recourse to Rawlsian reflective equilibrium. Might an approach that evokes an equilibrium (as opposed to an average or equation) afford—and perhaps even cultivate—a more *dynamic* understanding of balance? Understood this way, balance becomes less about plotting an agreed value and sticking to it, but recognizing instead that any plotted 'midpoint' can only ever be provisional as the multifarious influences to which it is subject evolve. This sort of fluid approach will in all probability better reflect the characteristics of the paradoxes we've encountered in this book. And—interestingly—with the exception of economics—the concept of equilibrium is underrepresented in the social sciences, an oversight we are urged to address.

For Dale and Burrell (2011: 120) the trick is to avoid privileging either/ or thinking and to embrace both/and approaches. Yes—this is undoubtedly true. However, and much like the aforementioned theorists, what Dale and Burrell do not comment on is how such balance is to be achieved. Balance must be deliberately *made complex* if we are to learn from it. Not only is 'balance' a crucial—but hitherto underrated—concept, but it warrants much more sophisticated examination and theorization. So how—*precisely*—might we approach the concept of balance? Let's consider some competing perspectives.

Moderation. Umberto Eco (2011: 270) declares that 'I would like a world ruled by moderation'. Regrettably, however, the novelist fails to flesh out what this might look like, or indeed what implications it might elicit. In a sociological vein, Durkheim's findings in respect of suicide rates, however, paint a more compelling defence of moderation. Durkheim's work built on a sophisticated understanding of our social attachment to the group to analyse suicide rates across different societies and regions. He found that suicide rates typically rise in settings where people become anomic, or detached from their social group. Normative social control, he suggested, is therefore a key mechanism for helping the individual remain attached to the social group. However, there is it seems to be an ideal level of normative control since Durkheim also found that suicide rates rise again in settings with too much social integration, where social control becomes oppressive (see Dobbin, 2013: 203). In Durkheim's case, then, moderation represents an effective approach to balance, at least in terms of mitigating suicide. And yet, for Dostoevsky (1972: 59, emphasis added), his troubled protagonist is '[e]ither a hero, or dirt, *there was nothing in between*'. This of course implies that an approach to balance premised on moderation is not necessarily right in all circumstances. And—famously—Oscar Wilde quipped: '[We must approach] everything in moderation, including of course moderation itself'. Balance, in this sense then, must never be final; it must always be fluid. Moderation implies ambiguity, and we tend not to endure ambiguity well. For one of Pahl's (1995: 87) interviewees, ambiguity was especially problematic: 'David is distressed because he cannot please me. He cannot control himself or be controlled by me and there is no place or peace between these extremes'. Clearly, for David, moderation is not—and *cannot be*—the answer. Similarly, for Tony Adams (2006: 721, cited in Bochner & Ellis, 2016: 71) moderation is of little help when agonizing over the moral choices presented to him as he reflects on the aftermath of coming out as a gay man to his father:

> I'm stuck between two canonical stories: one that says my father and I must always try to work things out to fulfil my responsibilities as son and another [that] tells me to let go, to realize that I 'can't chose my relatives,' and to view the relationship as a waste of time.

Such thoughts provide Tony with an all-or-nothing scenario; they proscribe the possibility of a moderate midpoint. Perhaps the most persuasive argument against moderation is one of the most familiar. Readers will no doubt be familiar with English Poet Alexandra Pope's proverb: 'A little learning is a dangerous thing; drink deep, or taste not the Pierian spring: there shallow draughts intoxicate the brain, and drinking largely sobers us again'. In other words: take all or nothing. I am reminded here of the sorely misguided devotee of the Daily Mail newspaper fastidiously reading yet another nasty piece of propaganda in their mistaken assumption that they are 'keeping up with current affairs'. Wisdom is to be desired, yes, but ignorance is bliss. It is the cognitive space in between the two, Pope suggests, where problems arise. Ultimately, we are compelled to concede that the balance-as-moderation thesis is flawed.

Compromise. If not moderation, how about compromise? A compromise offers us less a means by which we can moderate, but a distinct 'middle way' which actively draws on the merits of each counterposition. Tellingly, many of the great traditions have the idea of 'the way' at their very centre; the Chinese teaching of Taoism is named after tao, the Way, the Buddha's teaching is called 'The Middle Way', and Jesus Christ himself declares: 'I am the way' (Schumacher, 1977: 79). Brought up as a Catholic, I can confirm that Jesus's way was pretty definitive, but there is almost certainly a more discernible sense of balance to be found in the philosophy advanced by both Taoism and Buddhism. Notably, the 1990s ushered in a profound interest in compromise. Charles Handy (1994: 82), for example, urged us to engage with what he called the 'morality of compromise'. And towards the end of that decade, an approach to politics which hinged on compromise (and became known as 'Third Way' thinking; see, e.g. Giddens, 1998) began to make waves. Both American (under Clinton) and British (under Blair) governments were built on this rationale. What's interesting, of course, is that this 'compromised' roundtable approach to politics didn't last. Today, particularly in the United States (but increasingly in the United Kingdom as well), politics is more divisive than ever. To this end, third-way compromises have had a very short shelf life. In any event, there is no sense of an explicit interest in paradox in the concept of either compromise or 'middle' or 'third' way thinking. Furthermore, of this 'middle way', there is no determined engagement with pattern, pendulous temporality or Mobius strip-like inversion. And this is, of course, where advanced discussions of paradox differ from that associated with an arbitrary 'way'.

Harmony. If not compromise, then perhaps harmony? In *History of Beauty*, Umberto Eco invokes some pertinent insights from antiquity:

> Pythagoras and his immediate disciples thought that when two opposites are in contrast to each other, only one of them represents perfection: the odd number, the straight line, and the square are good and beautiful; the elements placed in opposition to them represent error, evil, and disharmony. Heraclitus was to propose a different solution: if the universe

contains opposites, elements that appear to be incompatible, like unity and multiplicity, love and hate, peace and war, calm and movement, harmony between these opposites cannot be realised by annulling one of them, but by leaving both to exist in a state of continuous tension.

(Eco, 2004: 72)

What's most interesting is that this comes not from Eastern but Western thinking. So, while Eastern mysticism (especially in the form of Yin and Yang) would prove to be hugely popular among progressive thinkers in the West in the latter part of the twentieth century and beyond, this sense of nuance is actually found in the Western canon too. And as we saw earlier in this chapter, discussions of harmony also invoke considerations of music. However, Moffett is among those who regards the concept of harmony as inherently problematic. In an anthropological context, he stresses that '[h]armony between societies can ironically bring about violence across a region, by establishing a more dangerous opponent for those left out of the entente. One enemy replaces another' (ibid.: 277). In this sense, at least, harmony can elicit unintended consequences.

Homeostasis. Perhaps, then, our approach to balance ought to be more akin to homeostasis. The concept of homeostasis derives, of course, from biology and describes any self-regulating process by which an organism tends towards the maintenance of stability while adjusting to conditions that are best for its survival. The Encyclopaedia Britannica (2022) puts it in plain terms: 'If homeostasis is successful, life continues; if it's unsuccessful, it results in a disaster or death of the organism'. Unlike moderation, then, homeostasis prompts a sense of dynamism. Here, we can invoke for the first time the notion of the 'balancing act'. Moffett, once again, provides an instructive example, this time drawing on considerations of identity:

[S]ocieties have to stay sufficiently distinct to preserve their members' sense of worth and meaning.... Herein lies the balancing act that has influenced the course of so much history. Commonalities are a plus—[but only] to a point. Too much interchange can be seen as a threat to people's unique identity. Perhaps compounding the problem, being alike can also backfire should societies find themselves desiring, and coming to blows, over the same scarce resources. [...] Individuals [must] strive to be enough like other members of their society to earn their respect yet at the same time seek to be different enough to feel special. A reasonable hypothesis is that in building relationships with their neighbours, societies similarly gravitate to this middle ground—an intense bonding that arises from the solace brought on by their similarities, and pride at their distinctiveness. To be a robust society, or a well-adjusted person, is to be the same and different.

> Even the most look-alike societies must preserve hallmark differences close
> to people's hearts.
>
> *(Moffett, 2019: 274)*

Optimal distinctiveness, then, involves a carefully curated balancing act. In
effect, this is a form of homeostasis. Finally, Šubrt (2019: 24) reminds us that
sociologist Talcott Parsons' discussion of balance was explicitly analogous to
the biological concept of homeostasis, and certainly to the extent that 'forces
that disrupt the order and balance of the social system are perceived as
pathological and [so] tend to be compared to malignant diseases'. However,
although the balance-as-homeostasis thesis provides us with an important
sense of dynamism, is it sufficient to guide our manoeuvrings in respect to
paradox? On the basis of how homeostasis has been described, it harbours
pre-programmed bias. In the case of biological systems, this is against
diseases. In the case of social systems, this is against disorder. Although these
may appear to be perfectly reasonable biases on which to base a broader
predisposition, where paradox represents our overarching analytical lens,
such biases remain fundamentally problematic.

Pendulous equilibrium. Unlike the approaches to balance we've considered
thus far—i.e. moderation, compromise, harmony, and homeostasis—the
concept of equilibrium admits to a significantly more pronounced sense
of dynamism, particularly if prefaced with the word pendulous. Moffett
celebrates the antagonism between political positions as a vital prerequisite
for effective balance:

> The fact is that a clash of perspectives within societies, although at times
> so extreme as to verge on the dysfunctional, may have always been integral
> to human survival. [...] Even though people with opposing perspectives
> might not see eye to eye, a society with too few or too many individuals at
> either end of the spectrum could be open to catastrophes. This promotion
> of behavioural diversity has parallels in unlikely animal species. Social
> spiders are most successful when their colonies contain both individuals
> that retreat from danger but fastidiously tend the nest, and bold ones that
> put more effort into defence against social parasites, which steal the colony's
> food; the colonies of certain ant species function most efficiently when
> they contain a similarly effective mix of personality types. For humans,
> the hazards of a population of overly committed to either nationalist
> or patriot extremes are manifest. Nationalists see the patriot's greater
> openness to weak borders and sharing across ethnicities as promoting
> social dependence and cheating, fears that reflect the competitive nature
> of groups present across species. Meanwhile, the prevalence of nationalists
> across societies, convinced their ways are right and prepared to fight for
> them, means the dangers that nationalists fear can indeed be realized.

Still, by readily espousing oppression and aggression, extreme nationalists bring to mind the historian Henry Adams's description of politics as a systematic organization of hatreds. Their outlook feeds on certain facets of psychology. It's intoxicating to fall in line against an enemy, at times at a whiff of trouble. For those swept up in a nationalist perspective, the swell of group emotions and awareness of common purpose gives life greater meaning. Not just morale, but mental health improves among civilians when nations face conflict.

(ibid.: 400–401)

Any sense of balance in respect of paradox, then, is subject to perpetual flux. Taking into consideration the numerous paradoxes we have grappled with over the course of this book, and the manner in which they contribute directly to the three alternative logics we've identified (in the sense that paradox (i) wards off moral closure, (ii) evens out subjective experience, and (ii) enhances our understanding of consciousness and agency), an approach to balance that accommodates such flux, principally—but not exclusively— in the form of pendulous swings is apposite. Alternative *static* approaches to balance (in accordance with a 'steady mean') lack the necessary dynamism to have sufficient traction. And given that ours is a world characterized by Heraclatic change (in which, of course, paradoxically *change is the only constant*), is it any surprise that our preferred approach to balance must itself accommodate significant—and dynamic—change? This conclusion applies across the numerous disciplinary contexts we've explored, but is illustrated most effectively in the realm of politics. I thus feel compelled to champion an ongoing tempestuous discourse between bleeding-heart liberals and rabid conservatives. Does anybody really want to live in a world colonised by a cadre of centrists?

Enhancing education through paradox

As readers will no doubt expect, there are fundamental tensions inherent to education. For example, one standard (and rarely challenged) assumption is that teaching is pivotal to learning. However, empirically this doesn't bear out. Teaching is, apparently, not much use for learners; it's principal benefit is for the teacher herself (sometimes referred to as *The Protégé Effect;* see e.g. Chase et al., 2009). Even Oscar Wilde (1894) quips that 'Education is an admirable thing, but it is well to remember from time to time that nothing that is worth learning can be taught'. Similarly, drawing on empirical data collected by Shealy et al. (1974) in respect of skiing, Salancik (1977: 22) suggests that instruction can cause more problems than it solves: '[There is] delusion in the epidemiology of ski accidents. [Shealy et al.] found that formal ski instruction resulted in a significant increase in accidents; the neophyte's assumption of improvement after lessons led him to put aside good judgement.' It would be ironic if we now took it upon ourselves to try to solve these tensions. Our task is instead to explore ways in which education might be enhanced by paradox. It seems likely, for example, that any sense of wisdom or self-actualization is only really achievable once we abandon our misplaced faith in linear logic. However, this ought not to suggest that an acute and all-consuming awareness of paradox must now be subsumed into the machinations of life. To do so would almost certainly devalue paradox. Rather it should be accepted and used as a pedagogical device to help understand the potential of (but limitations to) variation, difference and diversity. The Ancient Greeks, as Sorensen (2003) points out, deployed paradoxical anecdotes to help hone their debating skills. For example, 'Many witnesses to Zeno's *reduction ad absurdum* arguments believed he was showing off his debating skill. First Zeno would prove one side of the case and then, in a turnabout, prove the other side' (Sorensen, 2003: 47). More generally, there is it seems a considerable precedent for the pedagogical potential of paradox. For Hofmann (2001: 369) one of the 'important functions' of paradox is 'to arrest attention and provoke fresh thought'. This is perhaps more insightful than the author recognizes. Let us repeat that: *to provoke fresh thought.* Could it be, perhaps, that the emergent schematic of our lifeworld is directly contingent on paradox since without it we'd retreat into the comfort of certainty? There would be no need for *fresh thought.* Similarly, followers of Kierkegaard have argued that the paradox inherent to religion—specifically Christianity—was a fundamental justification for the Dane's faith:

> [W]hat Kierkegaard now holds is that Christianity need not be in the least bit afraid of philosophy because there is no connection between them. In fact, it is the difference between them which now occupies his mind. In 1839 he remarks that 'the paradox is above every system'; and in 1841 makes this cryptic entry 'the idea of philosophy is mediation—Christianity's is the paradox'. This is Søren Kierkegaard the anti-Hegelian we know so well. He perceived that the synthesis that Hegelianism offered really took too much for granted, and did not face up to the enormous qualitative difference between genuine faith and its speculative philosophy. The aim of the Hegelian philosophy was a synthesis, and its method the mediation of opposites.
>
> *(Thomas, 1957: 10–11)*

Notably, for Kierkegaard, Christianity embraces (or, at least, ought to embrace)—rather than seeks to mediate, solve, resolve, or dissolve—paradox. But a big problem remains. As academics we are all-too-often reticent to engage with paradox because to do so would in effect undermine our role as 'experts'. This, of course, is because 'expertise' invariably assumes a conventional logic. However, and aside from the lengths to which we have gone to demonstrate the transdisciplinary pervasiveness of paradox, we have—I hope—also debunked the concept of the conventional 'expert' (in terms of the familiarity paradox), earlier in this thesis. In his study of Kierkegaard's thought, Gates (1960) channels the Dane's philosophy and concludes that 'the thinker who is without paradox is like a lover without a passion—an inconsiderate fellow…', but perhaps closest to the bone—and hence most pertinent—he cautioned: 'take away the paradox from the thinker and you have the professor'. This was over 70 years ago and—regrettably—the academy remains largely unchanged.

So how exactly might we use paradox by way of pedagogical device? As a simple rule, educators must—I think—be prepared to avoid closure of any kind, and to direct their students to do likewise. Consider the paradox associated with identity. Academics the world over are fond of lending voice to marginalized groups. But how desirable is this? The pressures of identity politics, for example, seek to assert overt recognition of minority groups such as, for example, LGBTQ+. But, and as we saw in Chapter 3, to what extent does this actually further marginalize minorities from forming part of an integrated community? The point, of course, is *not* for the pedagogue to suggest that LGBTQ+ designations are destructive; rather the point is to suggest that any research that smacks of ideological closure should be viewed with suspicion, irrespective of how noble its ambitions initially appear.

What is paramount is the conscious—and concerted—rediscovery of abrasion. One of my current PhD students, Laura Messer, is a significant way through her doctoral research in which she is exploring academic identity in the neoliberal age. As part of this study, she has grappled with the concept of abrasion, that is the discomfort felt by individuals when encountering views which are in tension with their own (Cohen, 2019). For Cohen, this ought to be a defining academic principle, and one that is upheld in the two key academic domains: teaching and peer-review. The problem, of course, is that while we scholars flirt with abrasion in those academic domains Cohen mentions, in terms of the wider academic discourse (and this is especially true of the social sciences), it is—to all intents and purposes—absent. Liberal, progressive positions reign supreme in the academy. In my experience, too many academics are content to occupy an echo chamber where they simply read and regurgitate a common—principally progressive or 'liberal'—ideology. Will an awareness of paradox help address this? I sincerely hope so.

Must we now abandon pursuits dedicated to the resolution of paradox?

Over the course of the research for this book, and the numerous conversations I had with collaborators and highly decorated colleagues, without exception they assumed that my book would be geared towards resolving paradoxes. What other purpose might it have, they collectively pondered. Indeed, others have dedicated their faculties to precisely this. Rappaport (1981), as we saw in the introduction to this book, was unequivocal: our task must be to contribute to the resolution of paradoxes. Hofmann (2001), too, is guided by practical zeal and takes time to divide healthcare paradoxes into those which he argues can be resolved and those that can't. Sensible, you might think. However, on the basis of the arguments marshalled in this book, I urge Hofmann to re-examine his thesis. Of these 'resolvable' health care paradoxes, for example, he considers Barsky's research which reflects on the argument that 'the better the medical treatment gets, the less satisfied people are'. He continues:

> [T]he more we know [in this case about improved health], the more we know that we still don't know. Besides, health care constantly faces new challenges, such as resistant bacteria and AIDs. On the other hand, people's general knowledge about what health care can do increases their expectations. [The] media's focus on disease influence[s] people's healthcare demands. Furthermore, health has increasingly become synonymous with happiness (Nordenfelt, 1987), and we might interpret people's increasing illness as a result of a general dissatisfaction with life. Hence there might be reasons why we are concerned with our own health, even though we are healthier than before and health care is more proficient than ever. By altering these conditions the paradox can be solved.
>
> *(Hofmann, 2001: 372)*

By altering these conditions, Hofmann suggests, the paradox can be solved. Can it? Tellingly, Hofmann offers no further guidance about how these conditions might successfully be altered so as to achieve the promised solution. If the rationale advanced in the book you are reading prevails, any alteration to conditions (say, a public service campaign reminding the populace that they are healthier than their predecessors) will backfire. Such a message would almost certainly sow a seed of complacency and, in turn, initiate a decline in the general level of health! In this sense, then, a well-meaning campaign backfires. Either way we have paradox. Interestingly, later on in the same paper (though under the banner of antinomies rather than paradoxes), Hofmann concedes the following: 'even if one can resolve antinomies by shifting reference, perspective, or paradigm, this might create new ones' (ibid.: 379). There is no might about it. It *will* create new ones! As Sorensen (2003: 173) implies, paradox resolution is futile: 'introducing almost any apparatus to resolve paradoxes makes that tool the subject of other paradoxes'. Paradox is, it seems, autopoietic.

Nevertheless, despite *everything* that we have said in this book, it may be that an acute awareness of the pervasiveness of paradox will compel other scholars to search for ways forward that are, ostensibly at least, 'immune' from the mediating effects of paradox. Might an acute awareness of paradox one day enable scholars to identify 'glitches in the paradox matrix' where particular ends can be championed without fear of repercussions? So, for example, we have seen that ideological victory (much like any victory which is, in the final analysis, pyrrhic) ultimately yields its opposite. However, in the seemingly perpetual battle between liberal and conservative predispositions, it may be that liberals—who preach tolerance—could argue that ultimately they will always have the upper hand. In a conversation I had with a very conservative friend in the United States, I told him that I had just returned from a trip to Indonesia and suggested he take the time to visit the country as my experiences had been so positive. He explained that the problem many Americans have with Indonesia can be summarized in one word: Islam. I was a bit taken aback but responded by saying how that in my experience Indonesia's was a liberal—rather than a conservative—form of Islam and hence quite agreeable for those familiar with Western attitudes. It was entirely unintentional—a fluke, it you like—but this statement stopped my friend in his tracks. It dawned on both of us, that he (as a conservative) was likely to be more accommodating of disparate cultures that were liberal. Nothing more was said, and we very quickly changed the subject. On later reflection, I realized that while disparate *liberal* cultures will more than likely tolerate one another, the same cannot be said for disparate *conservative* cultures. I doubt very much there would be much common ground between, say, conservative Christians in Bible-belt America, and conservative Muslims in the Levant. However, liberals from America and liberals from the Middle East are much more likely to find common ground. In the final analysis, and irrespective of what we might say in terms of one or the other, is it the case that the propensity for coordination between disparate liberals (in comparison to disparate conservatives) means that liberal cultures will eventually triumph? In truth, probably not, and not least because Otherness—that is distinguishing ourselves favourably from other groups—appears to be intrinsic to the all-too-human processes of identity creation.

Another potential example of moving beyond paradox is the oft-cited statistic that no two democratic countries have ever been at war with one another, whereas the same clearly cannot be said of totalitarian countries. On the one hand my claims in respect of paradox suggest that democracy and totalitarianism occupy the extremes of the ideological system and—hence—participate in a paradoxical relationship. However, if democratic states (like liberal politics, identified above) are tolerant of one another, whereas totalitarian ones aren't, does this mean that democracy will eventually prevail? Again, the answer is probably no. Democracy is a far from perfect;

aside from anything else, it has a tendency to yield anaemic government, which—in turn—makes it difficult for that government to take genuinely impactful decisions. Contrariwise, although a totalitarian system lacks the representation and equity of its democratic counterparts, it does elicit a strong, decisive regime. Ultimately, our broader claims about paradox would suggest that each must remain in dynamic tension.

Closing thoughts

For a generation now, chaos theory has dominated advanced intellectual cross-disciplinary thinking. It has, of course, been remarkably fruitful. Indeed, today it would seem that *everything* can be interpreted by reference to chaos theory. However, chaos theory doesn't really depart from a cause-and-effect mentality; rather it suggests that systems are *so* complex (i.e. there are so many different overlapping chains of cause-and-effect within a given system) that we simply lack the computational power to make sense of them. It is therefore practically impossible to determine—or predict—outcomes. Although intellectually compelling, such a position is markedly different from paradox, the consideration of which reveals not so much that complexity is at play (although paradoxical phenomena are extremely, if not infinitely, complex) but that such experiences reveal an underlying ontological pattern/ predicament, the transcendence of which would violate a condition of our very existence. To outwit paradox would amount to a Faustian pact. Drawing on the work of Tranøy (1998), Hofmann (2001: 383) quite rightly poses the following question in the concluding section of his paper in which he explores paradox in healthcare: 'Maybe paradoxes are to live with... an inevitable and constitutive part of life? [...] Maybe they are both a limitation and an asset?' No question about it. And let us not forget that for Freud, struggle—an all-too-familiar manifestation of paradox—*is* life:

> [T]he meaning of the evolution of civilization is no longer obscure to us. It must present the struggle between Eros and Death, between the instinct of life and the instinct of destruction, as it works itself out in the human species. This struggle is what all life essentially consists of, and the evolution of civilization may therefore be simply described as the struggle for life of the human species. [This struggle characterises] the process of civilization which mankind undergoes but it was also brought into connection with the development of the individual... it was said to have revealed the secret of organic life in general.
>
> *(Freud, [1930] (1991): 314, 333)*

Regrettably, Freud did not live long enough to advance this particular aspect of his work. This is unfortunate because he was clearly onto something in suggesting that 'struggle' is the secret of organic life. In the event, I don't think he went far enough. It is paradox that underpins life, and of course paradox is a whole lot more than rudimentary *struggle*.

The big question at the back of my mind that remains—and perhaps yours as reader—is does our newfound recognition of the pervasiveness of paradox undermine our much cherished sense of what it means to *progress*? Does it mean that *progressivism* must forever remain unobtainable? Are we, simply, damned? No. I don't think it does. An acute recognition of the pervasiveness of paradox is itself a form of progress. To reiterate one final time, the point is *not* to solve, dissolve, or resolve paradoxes but to recognize that life *is* paradox. Any attempt to 'educate' ourselves out of paradox will invite existential ruin.

We bring this thesis to a close by suggesting that *paradoxically* paradox affords a relatively coherent means by which life can be interpreted. For Nietzsche (1887: II, 7; 1989: 67), there exists a persistent—and stubborn—'riddle of life'. In senselessly embracing linear cause-and-effect thinking, we ignore the dynamic tension that is inherent to the riddle of life. But beyond the sage words of Nietzsche, Freud, Einstein, and Kant, each of whom we have relied on extensively throughout this thesis, we conclude with the remarks of a relatively unknown—but formidable—scholar: German-American sociologist, Louis Wirth (1936: xxvii–xxviii):

> Despite the age-old effort to resolve the relationship between experience and reflection, fact and idea, belief and truth, the problem of the interconnection between being and knowing still stands as a challenge to the modern thinker. But it no longer is a problem that is the exclusive concern of the professional philosopher. It has become a central issue not merely in science, but in education and politics as well. [It is an] ancient enigma.

Not only does this enigma prevail nearly a century on from Wirth's elegiac utterance, but its ubiquity has become only more palpable. It is for us to learn to speak not to its disadvantage but to its consummate value.

REFERENCES

Abraham, I. (2020) 'Religion after work: Christianity, morality, and serious leisure', in Bell, E., Gog, S., Simionca, A., & Taylor, S. (eds.) *Spirituality, Organization and Neoliberalism* (pp. 149–170), Cheltenham: Edward Elgar.

Accorigi, A. (2011) 'Energy and climate policy; local production of renewable energy and resilience', *Case study presented to the University of Essex*, Colchester, UK.

Adams, T.E. (2006) Seeking father: Relationally reframing a troubled love story, *Qualitative Inquiry*, 12(4): 704–723.

Adger, W. (2000) 'Social and ecological resilience: Are they related'? *Progress in Human Geography*, 24(3): 347–364.

Adorjan, M., Christensen, T., Kelly, B., & Pawluch, D. (2012) 'Stockholm syndrome as vernacular resource', *Sociological Quarterly*, 53(3): 454–474. doi:10.1111/j.1533-8525.2012.01241.x. JSTOR 41679728. S2CID 141676449.

Agar, M. (1986) *Speaking of Ethnography* (Vol. 2), London: Sage.

Alvesson, M. & Deetz, S. (2000) *Doing Critical Management Research*, London: Sage.

Ando, V., Claridge, G., & Clark, K. (2014) 'Psychotic traits in comedians', *British Journal of Psychiatry*, 204(5): 341–345.

AndroidScience.com (2005) www.androidscience.com/theuncannyvalley/proceedings2005/uncannyvalley.html, accessed 15 July, 2022.

Anonymous. (1892, 23 October). No title. *Fliegende Blätter*.

Armitage, J. (1977) *Man at Play: Nine Centuries of Pleasure Making*, London: Frederick Warne.

Asimov, I. (1951) *Foundation*, New York: Gnome Press.

Atkinson, P. & Hammersley, M. (1994) 'Ethnography and participant observation', in Denzin, N. & Lincoln, Y. (eds.) *Handbook of Qualitative Methods* (pp. 248–261), London: Sage.

Atwood, M. (2003) *Oryx and Crake*, London: Bloomsbury.

Bakhtin, M. (1984) *Problems of Dostoyevsky's Poetics*, Minneapolis: University of Minnesota Press.

Barbour, J. (2000) *The End of Time*, London: Phoenix.

Barnes, S. (2018). Living with uncertainty: The ethnographer's burden. In: Vine, T., Clark, J., Richards, S., Weir, D. (eds.) *Ethnographic Research and Analysis* (pp. 113–125), Palgrave Macmillan, London. https://doi.org/10.1057/978-1-137-58555-4_7

Barnett, L. (1948) 'The Universe and Dr. Einstein', *Harper's Magazine*, Volume 196.

Barsky, A. (1988) 'The paradox of health', *New England Journal of Medicine*, 318, 414–418.

Bartle, J. (2015) 'New Analysis of British Social Attitudes Reveals Britain's 'Political Centre' Has Shifted Left Since 2010'. Retrieved 31 January, 2017, from www.nat cen.ac.uk/

Bastiat, F. [1850] (2010) *That Which Is Seen and That Which Is Not Seen: The Unintended Consequences of Government Spending*, CA: Createspace Independent Publishing Platform.

Bastow, S. & Martin, J. (2003) *Third Way Discourse*, Edinburgh: Edinburgh University Press. p. 2. ISBN 978-0748615612.

Bauman, Z. (1989) *Modernity and the Holocaust*, Polity: Cambridge.

Bauman, Z. (2017) *Retrotopia*, Cambridge: Polity Press.

BBC (2015a) 'Deradicalisation programme referrals on rise', www.bbc.co.uk/news/uk-34469331, accessed 10 December, 2022.

BBC (2015b) 'Terrifying time loop: The man trapped in constant déjà vu', http://m.bbc.co.uk/news/uk-30927102, accessed 11 December, 2022.

BBC (2016a) 'The significance of Sarah Baartman', www.bbc.co.uk/news/magazine-35240987, accessed 21 July, 2022.

BBC (2016b) 'Will LSD ever be accepted as mainstream treatment?', www.bbc.co.uk/news/magazine-36029723, accessed 11 December, 2022.

BBC (2020) 'The science of addiction: Do you always like the things you want?' www.bbc.co.uk/news/stories-55221825, accessed 11 December, 2022.

BBC (2021a) 'Edvard Munch wrote 'madman' graffiti on Scream painting, scans show', www.bbc.co.uk/news/entertainment-arts-56127530, accessed 11 December, 2022.

BBC (2021b) 'You are the modern day Elephant Man', www.bbc.co.uk/news/disabil ity-35325475, accessed 21 July, 2022.

Beardwell, I. & Holden, L. (1997) *Human Resource Management: A Contemporary Perspective*, London: Pitman.

Becker, H. (1967) 'Whose side are we on?', *Social Problems*, 14(3): 239–247.

Beckett, S. [1978] (2006) *Waiting for Godot*, London: Faber & Faber.

Bell, E. (1999) 'The negotiation of a working role in organizational ethnography', *International Journal of Social Research Methodology*, 2: 1, 17–37.

Bennett, W. (2022) www.goodreads.com/quotes/214763-happiness-is-like-a-cat-if-you-try-to-coax, accessed 24 November, 2022.

Benvenuto, S. (2000) 'Fashion: Georg Simmel', *Journal of Artificial Societies and Social Simulation*, 3(2).

Berger, P. & Luckmann, T. (1966) *The Social Construction of Reality: A Treatise in the Sociology of Knowledge*, New York: Anchor Books.

Bergson, H. [1920] (1975) *Mind-energy* [L'Énergie spirituelle, 1919]. McMillan.–a collection of essays and lectures.

Bergson, H. (1998) *Creative Evolution* (*L'Évolution créatrice*, 1907). Henry Holt and Company 1911, University Press of America 1983: ISBN 0-8191-3553-4,

Dover Publications 1998: ISBN 0-486-40036-0, Kessinger Publishing 2003: ISBN 0-7661-4732-0, Cosimo 2005: ISBN 1-59605-309-7.

Berlin, I. (1958) 'Two Concepts of Liberty': *An Inaugural Lecture delivered before the University of Oxford* (31 October 1958).

Best, K. (2018) 'Saying the unsayable: An autoethnography of working in a for-profit university', in Vine, T., Clark, J., Richards, S., & Weir, D. (eds.) *Ethnographic Research and Analysis: Anxiety, Identity and Self* (pp. 155–170), London: Palgrave Macmillan.

Biroc, J. (2008) 'The science and psychology of chaos theory', www.youtube.com/watch?app=desktop&v=ettre2Uz6bs, accessed 25 July 2022.

Bochner, A. & Ellis, C. (2016) *Evocative Autoethnography: Writing Lives and Telling Stories*, London: Routledge.

Boggis, A. (2018). Ethnographic practices of listening. In: Vine, T., Clark, J., Richards, S., Weir, D. (eds.) *Ethnographic Research and Analysis* (pp. 77–96), Palgrave Macmillan, London. https://doi.org/10.1057/978-1-137-58555-4_5

Boncori, I. (2018). The salience of emotions in (auto) ethnography: Towards an analytical framework. In: Vine, T., Clark, J., Richards, S., Weir, D. (eds.) *Ethnographic Research and Analysis*, Palgrave Macmillan, London. https://doi.org/10.1057/978-1-137-58555-4_11

Bowie, M. (1979) 'Jacques Lacan', in Sturrock, J. (ed.) *Structuralism and Since: From Levi-Strauss to Derrida*, Oxford: Oxford University Press.

Brickmann, P. & Campbell, D. (1971) 'Hedonic relativism and planning the good society', in M.H. Apley (ed.) *Adaptation Level Theory: A Symposium* (pp. 287–302), New York: Academic Press.

Briggs, J. & Peat, D. (1985) *Looking Glass Universe: The Emerging Science of Wholeness*, Glasgow: Fontana.

Brinkmann, S. (2016) *Diagnostic Cultures: A Cultural Approach to the Pathologization of Modern Life*. London: Routledge.

Bronowski, J. (1976) *The Ascent of Man*, London: British Broadcasting Corporation.

Bronowski, J. & Mazlish, B. (1960). *The Western Intellectual Tradition, From Leonardo to Hegel*, New York: Harper & Row.

Brooker, R. (2011) *Genetics: Analysis and Principles* (4th ed.). McGraw Hill Science. ISBN 978-0-07-352528-0.

Bryman, A. & Bell, E. (2011) *Business Research Methods*, Oxford: Oxford University Press.

Burkitt, I. (1999) *Bodies of Thought: Embodiment, Identity and Modernity*, London: Sage.

Burrell, G. & Morgan, G. (1979) *Sociological Paradigms and Organisational Analysis: Elements of the Sociology of Corporate Life*, London: Heinemann.

Burridge, J. & Kenney, S. (2016) 'Birdsong dialect patterns explained using magnetic domains', *Physical Review E*, 93(6): 062402.

Burton, R. [1621] (1989) *The Anatomy of Melancholy*, Oxford: Oxford University Press.

Cain, S. (2022) *Bittersweetness: How Sorrow and Longing Make Us Whole*, New York: Viking.

Calder, B. (1977) 'An attribution theory of leadership', in Staw, B. & Salancik, G. (eds.) *New Directions in Organizational Behaviour* (pp. 179–204), Chicago, IL: St Clair Press.

Camus, A. [1942] (2000) *The Outsider*, London: Penguin.

Capra, F. (1982) 'Chapter 9: The Tao of physics revisited: A conversation with Fritjof Capra (Conducted by Renee Weber)', in Wilber, K. (ed.) *The Holographic Paradigm and other paradoxes: Exploring the leading edge of science* (pp. 215–248), Boulder, Colorado: Shambhala.

Carey, J. (1999) *The Faber Book of Utopias*, London: Faber & Faber.

Carrette, J. (2007) *Religion and Critical Psychology: Religious Experience in the Knowledge Economy*, London: Routledge.

Carrette, J. & King, R. (2004). *Selling Spirituality: The Silent Takeover of Religion*. London: Routledge.

Caulkin, S. (2016) 'Companies with a purpose beyond profit tend to make more money', *Financial Times*, www.ft.com/content/b22933e0-b618-11e5-b147-e5e5b ba42e51, accessed 09 March, 2022.

Chandler, J. (2012) 'Work as dance', *Organization*, 19(6): 865–878.

Chaplin, S. (2006). 'The placebo response: An important part of treatment', *Prescriber*, 17(5): 16–22. doi:10.1002/psb.344. S2CID 72626022

Charlton, W. (1995) 'Apeiron', in Honderich, T. (ed.) *The Oxford Companion to Philosophy* (p. 41), Oxford: Oxford University Press.

Chase, C.C., Chin, D.B., Oppezzo, M.A., & Schwartz, D.L. (2009) 'Teachable agents and the protégé effect: Increasing the effort towards learning', *Journal of Science Education and Technology*, 18(4): 334–352.

Cheal, J. (2020) *Solving Impossible Problems: Working Through Tensions and Managing Paradox in Business* (2nd edn.), East Sussex: GWiz Publishing.

Christie, L. (2020) 'The evolution of monsters in children's literature', *Palgrave Communications*, 6, 41. https://doi.org/10.1057/s41599-020-0414-7

Chung, H. & Cheng, L. (2019). 'Coopetition and Firm Survival in a Cluster: Insights from the Population Ecology on the Yacht Industry in an Emerging Economy', 1957–2010, *Management and Organization Review*, 15(4), 837–856. doi:10.1017/mor.2018.60

Clegg, S., e Cunha, M. P., Munro, I., Rego, A., & de Sousa, M. (2016) 'Kafkaesque power and bureaucracy', *Journal of Political Power*, 9: 2 (157–181).

Clifton, J. (2011) 'Ecocultures: A case study of the Bajau in Indonesia', *Case study presented to the University of Essex*, Colchester, UK.

Cochrane, J. (2016) 'The Sociology of Things', University of Suffolk Research Blog: www.uos.ac.uk/content/sociology-things, accessed 11 December, 2022.

Cohen, A. (2014) 'Philosophy and history: The paradoxes of history', in *The Routledge Companion to Eighteenth Century Philosophy* (pp. 777–796), London: Routledge.

Cohen, A.J. (2019) Academic values and the possibility of an academic impartial spectator, *Society* (New Brunswick), 56(6): 555–558.

Coon, E., Quinonez, R., Moyer, V., & Schroeder, A. (2014) 'Overdiagnosis: How our compulsion for diagnosis may be harming children', *Pediatrics*, 134(5): 1013–1023.

Cooper, D. (Ed.) (1967) *Psychiatry and Anti-psychiatry*, London: Routledge.

Cooper, R. & Law, J. (1995) 'Organization: Distal and Proximal Views', *Research in the Sociology of Organizations: A Research Annual*, 13: 237, 274.

Crang, M. & Cook, I. (2007) *Doing Ethnographies*, London: Sage.

Cullen-Unsworth, L. & Wallace, M. (2011) 'Resilience and returning to country: Rainforest Aboriginal people of the Wet Tropics of Queensland, Australia', *Case study presented to the University of Essex*, Colchester, UK.

Cunha, M., Clegg, S., Costa, C., Leite, A., Rego, A., Simpson, A., de Sousa, M., & Sousa, M. (2016) 'Gemeinschaft in the midst of Gesellschaft? Love as an organizational virtue', *Journal of Management, Spiritualty and Religion*, 14(1): 3–21.

Curry, P. (2012) 'Enchantment and modernity', *PAN: Philosophy, Activism, Nature*, 9: 76–89.

Dale, K. & Burrell, G. (2011) 'Disturbing structure: Reading the ruins', *Culture and Organization*, 17(2): 107–121.

Dalí, S. ([1964] 1990) *The Diary of a Genius*, London: Hutchinson, translated by Richard Howard.

Davey, N. (1997) 'Introduction', in Nietzsche, F. (ed.) [1883–1885]. *Thus Spake Zarathustra*, Hertfordshire: Wordsworth Classics.

Deakin, R. (1999) *Waterlog: A Swimmer's Journey Through Britain*, London: Chatto & Windus. ISBN 0-7011-6652-5.

De Carolis, M. (2018) *The Anthropological Paradox*, London: Routledge.

de Castro, E. (2011) 'Zeno and the art of anthropology: Of Lies, Beliefs, Paradoxes, and Other Truths', *Common Knowledge*, 17(1): 128–145. doi:10.1215/0961754X-2010-045

Delamont, S. (2007) 'Arguments against Auto-Ethnography'. Paper presented at the British Educational Research Association Annual Conference', Institute of Education, University of London, 5–8 September, 2007.

Delbaere, K., Close, J., Brodaty, H., Sachdev, P., & Lord, S. (2010) 'Determinants of disparities between perceived and physiological risk of falling among elderly people: cohort study', *BMJ* 2010; 341: c4165. doi:10.1136/bmj.c4165

Deleuze, G. [1968] (2004) *Difference and Repetition*, London: Continuum.

Deloria, V. (1969) *Custer Died For Your Sins: An Indian Manifesto*, Norman: University of Oklahoma Press.

Denzin, N. & Lincoln, Y. (1994) 'Introduction: Entering the field of qualitative research', in Denzin, N. & Lincoln, Y. (eds.) *Handbook of Qualitative Research* (pp. 1–17), London: Sage.

Dibdin, M. (1994) *Dead Lagoon*, London: Faber & Faber.

Dickson, A. (1991) 'Editor's introduction', in Freud, S. [1930] (1991) 'Civilization and its discontents', in Volume 12. *Civilization, Society and Religion* (pp. 245–249), London: Penguin.

Dixon, K. (1980) *The Sociology of Belief: Fallacy and Foundation*, London: Routledge.

Dobbin, F. (2013) 'Chapter 9: How Durkheim's theory of meaning-making influenced organizational sociology', in Adler, P. (ed.) *The Oxford Handbook of Sociology and Organization Studies: Classical Foundations* (pp. 200–222), Oxford: Oxford University Press.

Dostoevsky, F. [1864] (1972) *Notes from the Underground/The Double*, London: Penguin Books.

Durkheim, E. [1893] (1984) *The Division of Labor in Society*. New York: Free Press.

Dychtwald, K. (1982) 'Chapter 6: Commentaries on the Holographic Theory' (Multiple Authors), in Wilber, K. (ed.) *The Holographic Paradigm and Other Paradoxes: Exploring the Leading Edge of Science*, Boulder, Colorado: Shambhala.

Eco, U. (1984) *The Name of the Rose*, CA: Harcourt.

Eco, U. (1995) *The Island of the Day Before*, London: Secker & Warburg.

Eco, U. (2001) *Five Moral Pieces*, San Diego, CA: Harcourt.

Eco, U. (2004) *History of Beauty*, New York: Rizzoli.

Eco, U. (2011) *The Prague Cemetery*, London: Random House.

Einspahr, J. (2010) 'The beginning that never was: Mediation and freedom in Rousseau's political thought', *Review of Politics*, 72(3): 437–461. doi:10.1017/S0034670510000318. S2CID 146668402

Einstein, A. & Infeld, L. (1938) *The Evolution of Physics: The Growth of Ideas from Early Concepts to Relativity and Quanta*, Cambridge: Cambridge University Press.

Elias, N. [1939] (1994) *The Civilising Process*, Oxford: Blackwell.

Encyclopaedia Britannica (2022) 'Homeostasis', www.britannica.com/science/homeostasis, accessed 12 December, 2022.

European Group of Organizational Studies (EGOS) (2014) Rotterdam; Subtheme 15: (SWG) Organizational Ethnography: The Theoretical Challenge.

Ewen, S. (1976) *Captains of Consciousness: Advertising and the Social Roots of Consumer Culture*, New York: Basic Books.

Featherstone, M., Robertson, R., & Lash, S. (1995) *Global Modernities*, London: Sage.

Fine, G. & Shulman, D. (2009) 'Lies from the field: Ethical issues in organizational ethnography', in Ybema, S., Yanow, D., Wels, H., & Kamsteeg, F. (eds.) *Organizational Ethnography: Studying the Complexities of Everyday Life* (pp. 177–195), London: Sage.

Ford, K., Glymore, C., & Hayes, P. (Eds.) (1995) *Thinking About Android Epistemology*, Menlo Park, CA: American Association for Artificial Intelligence.

Forster, E. [1909] (2011) *The Machine Stops*, London: Penguin.

Foucault, M. (1973) *The Birth of the Clinic: An Archaeology of Medical Perception*, London: Tavistock.

Foucault, M. (1977) *Discipline and Punish: The Birth of the Prison*, New York: Pantheon.

Foucault, M. (1978) *The History of Sexuality*, New York: Pantheon.

Fox, J. (2021) *Nature and Us: A History Through Art*, BBC (S. 1 Ep. 1, 42:50).

Frankl, V. [1946] (2004) *Man's Search for Meaning*. London: Penguin.

Freud, S. [1930] (1991) 'Civilization and its discontents', in *Volume 12. Civilization, Society and Religion* (pp. 251–340), London: Penguin.

Frost, J. & Brockmann, J. (2014) 'When qualitative productivity is equated with quantitative productivity: Scholars caught in a performance paradox', *Z Erziehungswiss (Suppl.)*, 17: 25–45.

Fukuyama, F. (1992) *The End of History and the Last Man*, New York: Free Press.

Ganga, D. & Scott, S. (2006) 'Cultural "insiders" and the issue of positionality in qualitative migration research: Moving "across" and moving "along" researcher-participant divides', *Forum: Qualitative Research*, 7(3): Article 7.

Gastin, J. (2017) 'Caught between happy and sad: The anatomy of a bittersweet ending', www.forefrontfestival.com/bittersweet-ending, accessed 25 July, 2022.

Gates, J. (1960) *The Life and Thought of Kierkegaard for Everyman*, Philadelphia: Westminster Press.

Gelsthorpe, L. (1992) 'Response to Martyn Hammersley's paper "On feminist methodology"', *Sociology*, 26(2): 213–21.

Gephart, R. (1978) 'Status degradation and organizational succession: An ethnomethodological approach', *Administrative Science Quarterly*, 4(23): 553–581.

Giddens, A. (1984) *The Constitution of Society: Outline of the Theory of Structuration*, Cambridge: Polity Press.

Giddens, A. (1994) *Beyond Left and Right: The Future of Radical Politics*, Cambridge: Polity Press.

Giddens, A. (1998). *The Third Way: The Renewal of Social Democracy*, Cambridge: Polity Press. ISBN 978-0745622675.

Goldstein, L. (1996) 'Reflexivity, Contradiction, Paradox and M.C. Escher', *Leonardo*, 29(4): 299–308.

Goswami, A. (2017) 'Krishna the god of paradox', www.dailypioneer.com/2017/sunday-edition/krishna-the-god-of-paradox.html, accessed 25 July, 2022.

Govan, M. (2006) 'Foreword', in Barron, S. & Draguet, M. (eds.) *Magritte and Contemporary Art: The Treachery of Images*, New York: Distributed Arts Publisher.

Graeber, D. (2016) *The Utopia of Rules: On Technology, Stupidity, and the Secret Joys of Bureaucracy*, London: Melville House.

Grayling, A. (1995) 'Dichotomy', in Honderich, T. (ed.) *The Oxford Companion to Philosophy*, Oxford: Oxford University Press.

Greenwood, M. & Nunn, P. (1994) *Paradox and Healing: A Book About Medicine, Mythology and Transformation*. Victoria, BC: Paradox.

Gregory, N. (2013) 'Broken Ground', *Dissertation (Creative Writing: Poetry)*, University of East Anglia, UK.

Grint, K. (2010) *Leadership: A Very Short Introduction*, Oxford: Oxford University Press.

Hamelink, C.J. (1994) *The Politics of World Communication*, London: Sage.

Hamilton, P. (2005) *Pandora's Star: Part One of the Commonwealth Series*, Oxford: Macmillan.

Hammersley, M. (1992) *What's Wrong with Ethnography? Methodological Explorations*, London: Routledge.

Hammersley, M. & Atkinson, P. (2007) *Ethnography: Principles in Practice* (3rd edn.), London: Routledge.

Handy, C. (1994) *The Empty Raincoat*, London: Random House.

Haney, C., Banks, W., & Zimbardo, P. (1973) 'A study of prisoners and guards in a simulated prison', *Naval Research Review*, 30: 4–17.

Harari, Y. (2014) *Sapiens: A Brief History of Humankind*, London: Vintage.

Harari, Y. (2017) *Homo Deus: A Brief History of Tomorrow*, London: Vintage.

Hardy, C. & Maguire, S. (2016) 'Organizing risk: Discourse, power, and "riskification"', *Academy of Management Review*, 41(1): 80–108. Retrieved from www.proquest.com/scholarly-journals/organizing-risk-discourse-power-riskification/docview/1753056485/se-

Harvey, J. (1988) *The Abilene Paradox and Other Meditations on Management*, Oxford: Maxwell Macmillan.

Hayashi, N. (2011) 'Environmental knowledge in motion and larger forces that hinder persevering hunters from coping with environmental change in north Greenland', *Case study presented to the University of Essex*, Colchester, UK.

Hegel, G. (1946) *The Philosophy of Right* (T. M. Knox, trans.) Oxford: Clarendon Press.

Heller, J. (1961) *Catch-22*, New York: Simon & Schuster.

Heras, A. & Vieta, M. (2020) 'Self-managed enterprise: Worker-recuperated cooperatives in Argentina and Latin America', in *The Handbook of Diverse Economies* (pp. 48–55). Cheltenham, UK and Northampton, MA: Edward Elgar Publishing.

Hill, W. (1915) 'My wife and my mother-in-law. They are both in this picture—find them', in *Puck*, v. 78, 6th November 1915, p. 11.

Hillson, D. (2003) *Effective Opportunity Management: Exploiting Positive Risk*, Boca Raton, Florida: CRC Press.

Hinnebusch, R. (2007) 'The US Invasion of Iraq: Explanations and Implications', *Critique: Critical Middle Eastern Studies*, 16(3): 209–228. doi:10.1080/10669920701616443. ISSN 1066-9922. S2CID 143931232.

Hirsch, P., Fiss, P., & Hoel-Green, A. (2013) 'Chapter 10: A Durkheimian Approach to Globalization', in Adler, P. (ed.) *The Oxford Handbook of Sociology and Organization Studies: Classical Foundations*, Oxford: Oxford University Press.

Hoffer, P. (2008) *The Historians' Paradox: The Study of History in Our Time*. New York: New York University Press.

Hofmann, B. (2001) 'The Paradox of Health Care', *Health Care Analysis*, 9, 369–386. https://doi.org/10.1023/A:1013854030699

Hogenson, G.B. (2009) 'Archetypes as action patterns', *Journal of Analytical Psychology*, 54(3): 325–337.

Holliday, R. (1995) *Investigating Small Firms: Nice Work?*, London: Routledge.

Homans, P. (1988) 'Psychology and popular culture: Psychological reflections on *M*A*S*H*', in Browne, R. & Fishwick, M. (eds.) *Symbiosis: Popular Culture and Other Fields* (pp. 108–127), Bowling Green, OH: Bowling Green State University Popular Press.

Horney, K. [1950] (1991) *Neurosis and Human Growth*, New York: W.W. Norton.

Howells, A. (2022) 'Restorying trauma: Child sexual abuse', in Vine, T. & Richards, S. (eds.) *Stories, Storytellers, and Storytelling* (pp. 217–238). Cham: Palgrave Macmillan. https://doi.org/10.1007/978-3-031-07234-5_10

Hühn, M.P. (2019) 'Adam Smith's Philosophy of Science: Economics as Moral Imagination'. *Journal of Business Ethics*, 155: 1–15. https://doi.org/10.1007/s10551-017-3548-9

Humphries, M. & Watson, T. (2009) 'Ethnographic practices: From "writing-up ethnographic research" to "writing ethnography"', in Ybema, S., Yanow, D., Wels, H., & Kamsteeg, F. (eds.) *Organizational Ethnography: Studying the Complexities of Everyday Life* (pp. 40–55), Sage: London.

Huntington, S. (1996) *The Clash of Civilizations and the Remaking of World Order*, New York: Simon & Schuster. ISBN 0-684-84441-9.

Husserl, E. [1936] (1970) *The Crisis of the European Sciences and Transcendental Phenomenology: An Introduction to Phenomenological, Philosophy*, IL: Northwestern University Press.

Huxley, A. [1931] (1969) *Brave New World*, London: Penguin.

Huxley, A. [1959] (2004) *Brave New World Revisited*, London: Vintage Classics.

Ibarra, H. (2015) 'The Authenticity Paradox', *Harvard Business Review*, 2015 (January–February edn.) https://hbr.org/2015/01/the-authenticity-paradox, accessed 23 May, 2022.

Ingold, T. (1992). 'Editorial', *Man (New Series)*, 27(4): 693–696.

Jackson, N. & Carter, P. (1985) 'The ergonomics of desire', *Personnel Review*, 14(3): 20–28.

Janis, Irving L. (1972) *Victims of Groupthink: A Psychological Study of Foreign-policy Decisions and Fiascoes*, Boston: Houghton, Mifflin. ISBN 0-395-14002-1.

Janus, S. (1975) 'The great comedians: Personality and other factors', *American Journal of Psychoanalysis*, 35(2): 169–174. doi:10.1007/bf01358189. ISSN 0002-9548. PMID 1190350. S2CID 20762581.

Jones, T. (1998) 'Interpretive social science and the "Native's point of view": A closer look', *Philosophy of the Social Sciences*, 28(1): 32–68.

Kallinikos, J. (2004) 'The social foundations of the bureaucratic order', *Organization* 11(1): 13–36.

Kaufman, D. (2013) 'Should Selena Gomez apologize for wearing a bindi at the MTV Movie Awards?', www.today.com/popculture/selena-gomez-causes-controversy-wearing-bindi-mtv-movie-awards-I533548, accessed 25 July, 2022.

Kay, P. & Kempton, W. (1984) 'What is the Sapir–Whorf hypothesis?', *American Anthropologist*, 86(1): 65–79. doi:10.1525/aa.1984.86.1.02a00050, S2CID 15144601

Keen, S. (1982) 'Chapter 6: Commentaries on the holographic theory (multiple authors)', in Wilber, K. (ed.) *The Holographic Paradigm and Other Paradoxes: Exploring the Leading Edge of Science*, Boulder, Colorado: Shambhala.

Kennedy, W. (1961) 'The nocebo reaction', *Medical World*, 95: 203–205. PMID 13752532.

Kiesley, C., Mathog, R., Pool, P., & Howenstine, R. (1971) 'Commitment and the boomerang effect', in Kiesley, C. (ed.) *The Psychology of Commitment: Experiments Linking Behavior to Belief* (pp. 66–73), New York: Academic Press.

Kinnaman, T. (2022) 'Johann Georg Hamann (1730—1788)' https://iep.utm.edu/hamann/, accessed 4 December, 2022.

Knights, D. & Willmott, H. (2002) Autonomy as utopia or dystopia', in Parker, M. (ed.) *Utopia and Organization* (pp. 59–81), Oxford: Blackwell.

Knowles, J. (Ed.) (1977) *Doing Better and Feeling Worse*, New York: W.W. Norton & Co.

Kropotkin, P. [1902] (1976) *Mutual Aid: A Factor of Evolution*, Manchester, NH: Extending Horizon Books.

Kvale, S. (2006) 'Dominance Through Interviews and Dialogues', *Qualitative Inquiry*, 12(3): 480–500. doi:10.1177/1077800406286235

Lacan, J. (1977) *Écrits*, London: Tavistock.

Lakoff, G. (2004) *Don't Think of an Elephant: Know Your Values and Frame the Debate*, Chelsea, VT: Chelsea Green Publishing. ISBN 978-1-931498-71-5.

Larsen, M. (2015) '16 Paradoxes Created By Technology: Byting off More than We Can Chew', *The Book Designer* www.thebookdesigner.com/16-technology-paradoxes, accessed 18 May, 2022.

Larsen, S. (2020) 'Are You Impressed? An Exploration of the Pressure to Perform and Impress from the Perspective of an Organisational Development Consultant', Thesis submitted for DMan at the University of Hertfordshire, UK.

Latouche, D. (1995) 'Democratie et nationalisme à l'heure de la mondialisation', *Cahiers de recherche sociologique*, 25: 59–78.

Learmonth, M. & Humphries, M. (2012) 'Autoethnography and academic identity: Glimpsing business school doppelgängers', *Organization*, 19(1): 99–117.

Le Fanu, J. (1999) *The Rise and Fall of Modern Medicine*, London: Little Brown.

Le Guin, U. (1976) 'The ones who walk away from Omelas', in *The Wind's Twelve Quarters* (pp. 275–284), New York: Harper & Row.

Levenson, E.A. (1976) A holographic model of psychoanalytic change, *Contemporary Psychoanalysis*, 12(1): 1–20. doi:10.1080/00107530.1976.10745411

Liamputtong, P. (2009) *Qualitative Research Methods* (3rd edn.), Oxford: Oxford University Press.

Lieberman, S. (1956) 'The effects of changes in roles on the attitudes of role occupants', *Human Relations*, 9: 385–402.

Logan, G. & Adams, R. [1516] (1998) 'Introduction', in More, T. (ed.) *Utopia* (pp xi–xxviii), Cambridge: University of Cambridge Press.

Lokgariwar, C. (2011) 'Changing with the seasons: How Himalayan communities cope with climate change', *Case study presented to University of Essex*, Colchester, UK.

Longhurst, R. (2006) 'Plots, plants and paradoxes: Contemporary domestic gardens in Aotearoa/New Zealand', *Social & Cultural Geography*, 7(4): 581–593.

Magagna, J. (ed.) (2015) *Creativity and Psychotic States in Exceptional People: The Work of Murray Jackson*, London: Routledge.

Mairet, P. (1989) 'Introduction', in Sartre, J. (ed.) *Existentialism and Humanism* (pp. 5–19), London: Methuen.

Mannheim, K. [1936] (1955) *Ideology and Utopia: An introduction to the sociology of knowledge*, New York: Harvest.

Manolică, A., Guţă, A.S., Roman, T., & Dragăn, L.M. (2021). 'Is consumer overchoice a reason for decision paralysis?'. *Sustainability*, 13(11): 1–16.

Mansell, S., Ferguson, J., Gindis, D. & Pasternak, A. (2019) 'Rethinking corporate agency in business, philosophy, and law', *Journal of Business Ethics*, 154: 893–899. doi:10.1007/s10551-018-3895-1

Manz, C., Vikas, A., Joshi, M., & Manz, K. (2008) 'Emerging paradoxes in executive leadership: A theoretical interpretation of the tensions between corruption and virtuous values', *Leadership Quarterly*, 19: 385–392.

March, J. & Simon, H. [1958] (1984) 'The Dysfunctions of Bureaucracy', in Pugh, D. (ed.) *Organization Theory: Selected Readings* (pp. 28–39), London: Penguin.

Marsden, J. (2002) *After Nietzsche: Notes Towards a Philosophy of Ecstasy*, Hampshire: Palgrave Macmillan.

Marsden, R. (1993) 'The politics of organizational analysis', *Organization Studies*, 14(1): 93–124.

Marsh, J. (2016) "Unboxing' videos: Co-construction of the child as cyberflâneur', *Discourse: Studies in the Cultural Politics of Education*, 37(3): 369–380. doi:10.1080/01596306.2015.1041457

Mascarenhas-Keyes, S. (1987) 'The native anthropologist: Constraints and strategies in research', in Jackson, A. (ed.) *Anthropology at Home* (pp. 180–195), London: Tavistock.

Maylor, H. (2010) *Project Management* (4th edn.), London: FT Prentice Hall.

McGregor, K. (2015) 'The labour-saving paradox', Shift Magazine https://shift-magazine.net/2015/11/18/the-labour-saving-paradox/, accessed 23 February, 2023.

McLennan, G. (2010) 'The postsecular turn', *Theory, Culture & Society*, 27(4): 3–20.

Merton, R.K. (1949) *Social Theory and Social Structure*, New York: Free Press.

Milano, M. (2022) 'The reason why the Apple Lisa computer failed', www.slashgear.com/796249/the-reason-why-the-apple-lisa-computer-failed/, accessed 12 October, 2022.

Minca, C. (2007) 'The tourist landscape paradox', *Social & Cultural Geography*, 8(3): 433–453.

Mintzberg, H. (1973) *The Nature of Managerial Work*, Hoboken, NJ: Prentice Hall.

Mintzberg, H. (1979) 'An emerging strategy of "direct" research', *Administrative Science Quarterly*, 24: 582–589.

Moffett, M. (2019) *The Human Swarm: How Our Societies Arise, Thrive, and Fall.* London: Zeus.

Moncel, B. (2019) www.thespruceeats.com/what-is-bitterness-1328482, accessed 25 July, 2022.

More, T. [1516] (1998) *Utopia*, Cambridge: Cambridge University Press.

Morgenthau, H. (1948) *Politics Among Nations: The Struggle for Power and Peace*, New York: Alfred A. Knopf.

Morris, G. & Salamone, C. (2011) *Rescue America: Our Best America Is Only One Generation Away.* Shipley: Greenleaf.

Mosley, I. (2003) *Democracy, Fascism, and The New World Order*, Exeter: Imprint Academic.

Mosley, N. (2009) *Paradoxes of Peace*, London: Dalkey Archive Press.

Mowles, C. (2015) *Managing in Uncertainty: Complexity and the Paradoxes of Everyday Organizational Life.* London: Routledge.

Mustonen, T., Shadrin, V., Mustonen, K., & Vasiliev, V. (2011) 'Songs of the Kolyma Tundra': Co-production and perpetuation of knowledge concerning ecology and weather in the Indigenous Communities of Nizhnikolyma, Republic of Sakha (Yakutia), Russian Federation', *Case study presented to the University of Essex*, Colchester, UK.

Nietzsche, F. [1878] (1984) *Human, All Too Human*, London: Penguin.

Nietzsche, F. [1883–1885] (1976) *Thus Spoke Zarathustra*, Middlesex: Penguin Classics.

Nietzsche, F. [1883–1885] (1997) *Thus Spake Zarathustra*, Hertfordshire: Wordsworth.

Nietzsche, F. [1886] (1989) *Beyond Good and Evil*, New York: Vintage.

Nietzsche, F. [1887] (1989) *On the Genealogy of Morals*, New York: Vintage.

Nietzsche, F. [1888] (1989) *Ecce Homo*, New York: Vintage.

Nietzsche, F. [1901] (2019) *The Will to Power*, New York: Dover.

Norton, R. (2008) 'Unintended Consequences', in Henderson, David R. (ed.) *Concise Encyclopedia of Economics* (2nd ed.). Indianapolis: Library of Economics and Liberty. ISBN 978-0865976658. OCLC 237794267. www.econlib.org/library/Enc1/UnintendedConsequences.html

Novak, M. (1996) *Business as a Calling: Work and the Examined Life*, New York: Free Press.

Nowotny, H. (2005) 'The increased complexity and its reduction: emergent interfaces between the natural sciences, humanities and social sciences', *Theory, Culture & Society*, 22(5): 15–31.

Oakes, T. (1997) 'Place and the paradox of modernity', *Annals of the Association of American Geographers*, 87(3): 509–531.

Olson, R. (2005). 'The Rise of 'Radical Middle' Politics, *The Futurist*, 39(1): 45–47.

Orwell, G. [1949] (1999) *Nineteen Eighty-Four*, London: Secker & Warburg.

Osterloh, M. & Frey, B. (2020) 'How to avoid borrowed plumes in academia', *Research Policy*, 49(1): 1–9. ISSN 0048-7333, doi:10.1016/j.respol.2019.103831

Pahl, R. (1995) *After Success: Fin-de-Siecle Anxiety and Identity*, Cambridge: Polity Press.

Pellauer, D. (2007) *Ricoeur: A Guide for the Perplexed.* London: Continuum International Publishing Group.

Pelletier, K. (1982) 'Chapter 6: Commentaries on the holographic theory' (Multiple authors), in Wilber, K. (ed.) *The Holographic Paradigm and Other*

Paradoxes: Exploring the Leading Edge of Science (pp. 118–120), Boulder, Colorado: Shambhala.

Perel, E. (2007) *Mating in Captivity: Unlocking Erotic Intelligence*, New York: Harper & Row.

Peters, T. & Waterman, R. (1982) *In Search of Excellence: Lessons from America's Best-Run Companies*. New York: Harper & Row.

Pfeffer, J. (1972) 'Organizational ecology: A system resource approach', PhD Dissertation, Stanford University.

Pfeffer, J. (1973) 'Size, composition and function of hospital boards of directors: a study of organization-environment linkage, *Administrative Science Quarterly*, 18: 349–364.

Pfeffer, J. (1977) 'Power and resource allocation in organizations', in Staw, B. & Salancik, G. (eds.) *New Directions in Organizational Behaviour* (pp. 235–266), Chicago, IL: St Clair Press.

Pignatiello, G., Martin, R., & Hickman, R. (2020) 'Decision fatigue: A conceptual analysis', *Journal of Health Psychology*, 25(1): 123–135. doi:10.1177/1359105318763510

Pilgrim, S. (2011) 'Resilience and ecocultures: concept note and further study', *Case study presented to University of Essex*, Colchester, UK.

Porter, M. (1985) *Competitive Advantage*, New York: Free Press.

Powers, J. (1982) *Philosophy and the New Physics*, London: Methuen.

Pradies, C., Aust, I., Bednarek, R., Brandl, J., Carmine, S., Cheal, J., Pina e Cunha, M., Gaim, M., Keegan, A., Lê, J.K., & Miron-Spektor, E. (2021) 'The lived experience of paradox: How individuals navigate tensions during the pandemic crisis', *Journal of Management Inquiry*, 30(2): 154–167.

Pretty, J. (2011) 'Interdisciplinary progress in approaches to address social-ecological and ecocultural systems', *Case study presented to University of Essex*, Colchester, UK.

Pribram, K. (1982) 'Chapter 3: What is all 'the fuss about?', in Wilber, K. (ed.) *The Holographic Paradigm and Other Paradoxes: Exploring the Leading Edge of Science* (pp. 27–34), Boulder, Colorado: Shambhala.

Prince, R. & Riches, D. (2000) *The New Age in Glastonbury: The Construction of Religious Movements*, Oxford: Berghahn.

Punch, K. (2005) *Introduction to Social Research*, London: Sage.

Punch, K. (2014) *Introduction to Social Research: Quantitative and Qualitative Approaches* (3rd edn.), London: Sage.

Quine, W. (1976) *The Ways of Paradox and Other Essays*. Cambridge: Cambridge University Press.

Rand, A. [1957] (2007) *Atlas Shrugged*, London: Penguin.

Rappaport, J. (1981) 'In praise of paradox: A social policy of empowerment over prevention', *American Journal of Community Psychology*, 9(1): 1–25.

Regibeau, P. & Rockett, K. (2011) Economic Analysis of Resilience: A Framework for Local Policy Response Based on New Case Studies, Centre for Research in Economic Sociology and Innovation (CRESI) Working Paper, University of Essex: Colchester.

Ricoeur, P. (1992) *Oneself as Another*, Chicago, IL: University of Chicago Press.

Ricoeur, P. (2005) *The Course of Recognition*, Cambridge, MA: Harvard University Press.

Rieff, P. (1959) *Freud: The Mind of a Moralist*, New York: Viking Press.

Rieff, P. (1966) *The Triumph of the Therapeutic*, New York: Harper & Row.

Riggio, R. (2012) 'Why time flies as you age', www.psychologytoday.com/us/blog/cutting-edge-leadership/201212/why-time-flies-you-age, accessed 17 December, 2022.

Rizzi, B. [1939] (1985) *The Bureaucratization of the World*, translated and with an introduction by Adam Westoby, London: Tavistock.

Robinson, A. (2006) *The Last Man Who Knew Everything*, London: Oneworld Publications.

Robinson, D. & Zarate, O. (2006) *Introducing Kierkegaard*, Cambridge: Icon.

Rose, D. (1990) *Living the Ethnographic Life*, London: Sage.

Rosenthal, R. & Jacobson, L. (2003) *Pygmalion in the Classroom*. Bancyfelin, Carmarthen: Crown House. ISBN 9781904424062.

Rousseau, D. (1998) 'Why workers still identity with organizations', *Journal of Organizational Behavior*, 19(3): 217–233.

Rousseau, J. [1762] (1998) *The Social Contract*, London: Wordsworth Classics.

Rubin, E. (1915). Synsoplevede figurer: Studier i psykologisk analyse [Perceived figures: Studies in psychological analysis]. Copenhagen: Gyldendal, Nordisk Forlag.

Russell, B. (1986) *The Philosophy of Logical Atomism*, reprinted in *The Collected Papers of Bertrand Russell, 1914–19*, Vol. 8. London: Routledge.

Russell, B. (1990) 'On some difficulties of continuous quantity', in *The Collected Papers of Bertrand Russell*, Vol. 2. London: Routledge.

Russell, B. (1994) *The Collected Papers of Bertrand Russell*, Vol. 3. London: Routledge.

Sainsbury, R. (1995) *Paradoxes*. Cambridge: Cambridge University Press.

Salancik, G. (1977) 'Commitment and the control of organizational behavior and belief', in Staw, B. & Salancik, G. (eds.) *New Directions in Organizational Behaviour* (pp. 1–54), Chicago, IL: St Clair Press.

Sarra, N., Solsø, K., & Mowles, C. (Eds.). (2023) *The Complexity of Consultancy: Exploring Breakdowns Within Consultancy Practice* (1st ed.). London: Routledge. https://doi.org/10.4324/9781003095941

Sauerborn, E., Sökefeld, N., & Neckel, S. (2022) 'Paradoxes of mindfulness: The specious promises of a contemporary practice'. *The Sociological Review*, 70(5): 1044–1061

Schema, S. (2018) 'In Civilisations: Second moment of creation', *BBC*.

Schippers, T. (2013) 'A history of paradoxes: Anthropologies of Europe', in *Fieldwork and Footnotes* (pp. 248–260). London: Routledge.

Schkade, D. & Kahneman, D. (1998) 'Does living in California make people happy? A focusing illusion in judgments of life satisfaction', *Psychological Science*, 9(5): 340–346.

Schlesinger, A. (1991) *The Disuniting of America: Reflections on a Multicultural Society*. TN: Whittle Books.

Schlich, E. & Fleissner, U. (2004) 'The ecology of scale: Assessment of regional energy turnover and comparison with global food', *International Journal of Life Cycle Assessment*, 10(3): 219–223.

Schopenhauer, A. [1819] (1966) *The World as Will and Representation*, Vol. I, translated by E.F. Payne, New York: Dover Publications.

Schumacher, E. (1973) *Small Is Beautiful: A Study of Economics as if People Mattered*, London: Abacus.

Schumacher, E. (1977) *A Guide for the Perplexed*, New York: Harper & Row.

Schwartz, B. (2004) *The Paradox of Choice: Why More is Less*, New York: HarperCollins.

Scorcese, M. (1976) *Taxi Driver*, Culver: Columbia Pictures.

Sedlmayr, A. & Boehm, S. (2011) 'Agricultural agri-food networks in the Colchester (UK) area and their contribution to developing local resilience', *Case study presented to University of Essex*, Colchester, UK.

Selznick, P. (1949) *TVA and the grass roots: A study in the sociology of formal organization*, Berkeley, CA: University of California Press.

Shealy, J., Geyer, L., & Hayden, R. (1974) 'Epidemiology of ski injuries: Effect of method of skill acquisition and release binding on accident rates', *Human Factors*, 16: 459–473.

Sidgwick, H. (2001) *The Methods of Ethics*. BookSurge Publishing.

Silver, R.L. (1982) 'Coping with an undesirable life event: A study of early reactions to physical disability'. *Doctoral dissertation at Northwestern University*, Evanston, IL.

Silverman, D. (2007) *A Very Short, Fairly Interesting and Reasonably Cheap Book about Qualitative Research*, London: Sage.

Simmel, G. (1904) 'Fashion', *International Quarterly*, 10(1): 130–155.

Simmel, G. [1922] (1955). *Conflict and the Web of Group Affiliations*, Glencoe, IL: Free Press.

Singer, I. (2009) *Philosophy of Love: A Partial Summing-Up*, Cambridge, MA: MIT Press.

Slovic, P. (1994) 'Perceptions of risk: Paradox and challenge', in Brehmer, B. & Sahlin, N.E. (eds.) *Future Risks and Risk Management. Technology, Risk, and Society* (An International Series in Risk Analysis) (Vol. 9, pp. 63–78). Springer, Dordrecht. https://doi.org/10.1007/978-94-015-8388-6_3

Smith, A. [1776] (1900) *The Wealth of Nations*. London: Routledge.

Smith, B. & Waldner, D. (2021). *Rethinking the Resource Curse*, Cambridge: Cambridge University Press. doi:10.1017/9781108776837. ISBN 9781108776837. S2CID 233539488.

Smith, M. (2007) *Fundamentals of Management*, London: McGraw Hill.

Solbakk, J.H. (1995) *Medisinen som møtested og markedsplass*, Oslo: Forum.

Solomon, R. (2004) 'Aristotle, Ethics and Business Organizations', *Organization Studies*, 25(6): 1021–1042.

Solso, R. (2001) *Cognitive Psychology* (6th ed.), Boston: Allyn & Bacon. ISBN 0-205-30937-2.

Sorensen, R. (2003) *A Brief History of Paradox: Philosophy and the Labyrinths of the Mind*, Oxford: Oxford University Press.

Stafford, T. (2013) 'Why money can't buy you happiness', *BBC*, www.bbc.com/future/article/20130326-why-money-cant-buy-you-happiness, accessed 27 July, 2022.

Standing Conference on Organizational Symbolism (2018) 'Wabi-sabi (侘寂): Imperfection, incompleteness and impermanence in organizational life', www.scos.org/conference-2018/, accessed 30 June, 2022.

Stanley, L. & Wise. S. (1993) *Breaking out Again: Feminist Ontology and Epistemology*, London and New York: Routledge.

Starobinski, J. (1975) 'The inside and the outside', *The Hudson Review*, 28: 33–351.

Stedman-Jones, S. (1988) 'Relativism/absolutism', in Jenks, C. (ed.) *Core Sociological Dichotomies* (pp. 123–137), London: Sage.

Stent, G. (1978) *Paradoxes of Progress*, San Francisco: WH Freeman and Company.

Stent, G. (2002) *Paradoxes of Free Will*, Philadelphia: American Philosophical Society.

Stern, C. & Deimler, M. (2006). *The Boston Consulting Group On Strategy: Classic Concepts and New Perspectives* (2nd edn.), New Jersey: John Wiley.

Stogdill, R. (1974) *Handbook of Leadership: A Survey of Theory and Research*, New York: Free Press.

Strachan, D. (1989) Hay fever, hygiene, and household size, *BMJ: British Medical Journal*, 299(6710): 1259.

Stratton, L. (2022) *Personal communication*, 29 September.

Streatfield, P. (2001) *The Paradox of Control in Organizations*, London: Routledge.

Strudwick, R. (2018) Discussion and collaboration in diagnostic radiography. In: Vine, T., Clark, J., Richards, S., Weir, D. (eds.) *Ethnographic Research and Analysis* (pp. 97–112), Palgrave Macmillan, London. https://doi.org/10.1057/978-1-137-58555-4_6

Styhre, A. (2007) *The Innovative Bureaucracy: Bureaucracy in an Age of Fluidity*, London: Routledge.

Šubrt, J. (2019) *Individualism, Holism and The Central Dilemma of Sociological Theory*, Bingley: Emerald.

Suh, E., Diener, E., & Fujita, F. (1996) 'Events and subjective life satisfaction: Only recent events matter', *Journal of Personality and Social Psychology*, 70: 1091–1102.

Symon, G. & Pritchard, K. (2014) 'Performing the responsive and committed employee through the sociomaterial mangle of connection', *Organization Studies*, 36(2): 241–263.

Symonds, M. & Pudsey, J. (2008) 'The Concept of 'Paradox' in the work of Max Weber', *Sociology*, 42(2): 223–241.

Ten Dyke, E. [2001] (2014) *Dresden: Paradoxes of Memory in History*, London: Routledge.

Tett, G. (2009). The lessons: The dangers of silo thinking. [online] Ft.com. Available at: www.ft.com/content/0ea1c4d4-e843-11de-

The Guardian Newspaper (2007) 'The relativity of time', www.theguardian.com/lifeandstyle/2007/sep/29/healthandwellbeing.features2, accessed 20 July, 2022.

The Onion (2018) 'God admits there was probably a better way of giving humans taste of heavenly bliss than opioids' (www.theonion.com/god-admits-there-was-probably-a-better-way-of-giving-hu-1829492107), accessed 27 July, 2022.

The Telegraph Newspaper (2011) 'Belgium to have new government after world record 541 days', www.telegraph.co.uk/news/worldnews/europe/belgium/8936857/Belgium-to-have-new-government-after-world-record-541-days.html), accessed 23 February, 2023.

Thomas, J. (1957) *Subjectivity and Paradox*, Oxford: Basil Blackwood.

Thomas, W. & Southwell, M. (2018) 'Hate the results? Blame the Methods: An Autoethnography of Contract Research', in Vine, T., Clark, J., Richards, S., & Weir, D. (eds.) *Ethnographic Research and Analysis: Anxiety, Identity and Self* (pp. 233–252), London: Palgrave Macmillan.

Tilly, C. (1981) *As Sociology Meets History*, New York: Academic Press.

Toffler, A. (1970) *Future Shock*, London: Pan Books.

Tranøy, K.E. (1998) *Det åpne sinn. Moral og etikk mot et nytt årtusen*, Oslo: Universitetsforlaget.

Tsoukas, H. (2005) *Complex Knowledge: Studies in Organizational Epistemology*, Oxford: Oxford University Press.

Van Maanen, J. (1988) *Tales of the field*, Chicago, IL: Chicago University Press.

Vine, T. (2010) 'Book review: Organizational Ethnography: Studying the Complexities of Everyday Life', in Ybema, S., Yanow, D., Wels, H., & Kamsteeg, F. (eds.), London: Sage (2009), *Organization*, 17(5): 645–649.

Vine, T. (2011) 'Searching for sanctuary in alternative organizations: An Ethnography of a New Age intentional community', PhD Thesis, University of Essex.

Vine, T. (2016) 'Strong leadership: Does it really make any difference?', *Professional Manager: The Chartered Management Institute Magazine*, Autumn 2016 www.managers.org.uk/insights/news/2016/december/strong-leadership-does-it-really-make-a-difference

Vine, T. (2017) 'Ecology, resilience and food production: Challenging discursive closure', presented at the *12th Organization Studies Summer Workshop: Food organizing matters: Paradoxes, problems and potentialities*, 17th–20th May, 2017.

Vine, T (2018a) 'Home-grown exoticism: Ethnographic tales from a Scottish New Age intentional community', in Vine, T., Clark, J., Richards, S., & Weir, D. (eds.) *Ethnographic Research and Analysis: Anxiety, Identity and Self* (pp. 13–36), London: Palgrave Macmillan.

Vine, T. (2018b) 'Methodology: From paradigm to paradox', in Vine, T., Clark, J., Richards, S., & Weir, D. (eds.) *Ethnographic Research and Analysis: Anxiety, Identity and* Self (pp. 273–300), London: Palgrave Macmillan.

Vine, T. (2018c) 'The sociology of things: A response to Peter Cochrane', University of Suffolk Research Blog: www.uos.ac.uk/content/sociology-things-response-peter-cochrane

Vine, T. (2020) 'Brexit, Trumpism and paradox: Epistemological lessons for the critical consensus', *Organization*, 27(3): 466–482. doi:10.1177/1350508419855706

Vine, T. (2021) *Bureaucracy: A Key Idea for Business and Society*, Oxon: Routledge.

Vine, T., Clark, J., Richards, S., & Weir, D. (Eds.) (2018) *Ethnographic Research and Analysis: Anxiety, Identity and Self*, London: Palgrave Macmillan.

Vonnegut, K. [1952] (2006) *Player Piano*, New York: Random House.

Vonnegut, K. [1969] (2000) *Slaughterhouse 5*, New York: Random House.

Wachtel, P. (1989) *The Poverty of Affluence: A Psychological Portrait of the American Way of Life*, Philadelphia: New Society.

Wallace, M. (2002) 'The summoned self', in Wall, J., Schweiker, W., & Hall, D. (eds.), *Paul Ricoeur and Contemporary Moral Thought* (pp. 80–93), London: Routledge.

Ward, S. & Chapman, C. (2003) 'Transforming project risk management into project uncertainty management', *International Journal of Project Management*, 21(2): 97–105.

Warner, M. (2001) *Complex Problems–Negotiated Solutions: The Practical Applications of Chaos and Complexity Theory to Community-based Natural Resource Management* (Working Paper No. 146). London: Overseas Development Institute.

Watson, T. (2006) *Organising and Managing Work: Organisational, managerial and strategic behaviour in theory and practice*, Financial Times Prentice Hall.

Weick, K. (1977) 'Enactment processes in organizations', in Staw, B. & Salancik, G. (Eds.) *New Directions in Organizational Behaviour*, Chicago, IL: St Clair Press.

Weil, S. [1962] (2020) *The Power of Words*, London: Penguin.

Weir, D., & Clarke, D. (2018) What makes the autoethnographic analysis authentic? In: Vine, T., Clark, J., Richards, S., & Weir, D. (eds.) *Ethnographic Research and*

Analysis (pp. 127–154), Palgrave Macmillan, London. https://doi.org/10.1057/978-1-137-58555-4_8

Whyte, W. (1943) *Street Corner Society*, Chicago, IL: University of Chicago Press.

Wilber, K. (ed.) (1982a) *The Holographic Paradigm and Other Paradoxes: Exploring the Leading Edge of Science*, Colorado: Shambhala.

Wilber, K. (1982b) 'Chapter 7: Physics, Mysticism, and the New Holographic Paradigm', in Wilber, K. (ed.) *The Holographic Paradigm and Other Paradoxes: Exploring the Leading Edge of Science* (pp. 249–294), Boulder, Colorado: Shambhala.

Wilber, K. (1982c) 'Chapter 10: Reflections on the New-Age paradigm: A conversation with Ken Wilber', in Wilber, K. (ed.) *The Holographic Paradigm and Other Paradoxes: Exploring the Leading Edge of Science*, Boulder, Colorado: Shambhala.

Wilde, O. [1894] (2000) 'A Few Maxims for the instruction of the over-educated', in Wilde, O. (ed.). *The Complete Works of Oscar Wilde*, Oxford: Oxford University Press.

Willmott, H. (2011) 'Chapter 11: Back to the future: What does studying bureaucracy tell us?', in Clegg, S., Harris, M. and Höpfl, H. (eds.) *Managing Modernity: Beyond Bureaucracy* (pp. 257–293), Oxford: Oxford University Press.

Winnicott, D. (1973) *The Child, the Family, and the Outside World*, London: Penguin.

Wirth, L. [1936] (1955) 'Preface', in Mannheim, K. (ed.) *Ideology and Utopia: An Introduction to the Sociology of Knowledge* (p. x–xxx), New York: Harvest.

Wolfe, G. (1972) *The Fifth Head of Cerberus*, New York: Charles Scribner's Sons.

Wortman, C. & Linsenmeier, J. (1977) 'Interpersonal attraction and techniques of ingratiation in organizational settings', in Staw, B. & Salancik, G. (eds.) *New Directions in Organizational Behaviour* (pp. 133–178), Chicago, IL: St Clair Press.

Yanow, D. (2010) Review essay: Studying organizations ethnographically: Is 'organizational' ethnography distinctive? *Organization Studies*, 31(9–10): 1397–1410.

Young, T. (1804). 'The Bakerian lecture. Experiments and calculation relative to physical optics', *Philosophical Transactions of the Royal Society of London*, 94: 1–16.

Zuckermann, G. (2003). *Language Contact and Lexical Enrichment in Israeli Hebrew*. London: Palgrave Macmillan.

Zimbardo, P. (1991) *The Psychology of Attitude Change and Social Influence*, New York: McGraw-Hill.

INDEX

about-turns, 156
Abraham, I., 164
abrasion, 219
abstract paradoxes, 12
Adams, Tony, 213
aesthetics, paradox of, 172–3
agency, 184–6
agency–structure dynamic, 186
aggressive, 139–40
AI (Artificial Intelligence), 3, 190–1
AI sociology, 190
all-too-human paradox, 140–1
Alvesson, M., 129–30
ambiguous images, 22–3
analytical engagement, paradox, 12
analytical potential of paradox, 66–7
The Anatomy of Melancholy (Burton), 210
android epistemology, 190
anecdotes, paradoxical, 218
antimony contra paradox, 4
antioxidants, oxygen and, 112–13
anxiety, psychology, 73
apeiron contra paradox, 4–5
aporia contra paradox, 4
Apple inc., 100
Apple Lisa, 100–1
argument, salience of, 8
Aristotle, 212, lifecraft, 14
Armitage, John, 210, 211
art, 19–43; science *vs.*, 121–7 *see also* cinema; literature; visual arts

Artificial Intelligence (AI), 3, 190–1
Asimov, Isaac, 156
assumptions, paradox of, 11–12
Atkinson, P., 135, 137–8, 148
Atlas Shrugged (Rand), 40
Atwood, Margaret, 67
Augustine, 157
Australian aboriginal rights, 67, 70
authenticity paradox, 96
authoritarianism, satire and, 39–40
autoethnography; 11, 187; paradox of, 144–5
autonomous actions, 185
autonomy growth, 72
awareness of patterning, 200

Baartman, Sarah, 158
Bajou, 121
Bakhtin, M., 188
balance: complexity, 211–17; dynamic understanding, 212; epistemology of, 211–12; tempo and paradox, 211
Banksy, 101, 102f
Barbour, J., 106, 107, 109–10, 128
Barnes, S., 136
Bartle, J, 46
Bastiat, Claude-Frédéric, 55–6
Bauman, Zygmunt, 50, 78, 175–6
Beardwell, I., 99
beauty, visual arts, 29–30
Beauty of Creation, 207
Becker, H., 132

Beckett, Samuel, 3
beginning-middle-end, 1
behaviourists, 211
being, concept of, 128, 189
being-in-the-world, 2
belief, study of, 48–9
Bell, E, 136–7, 139
Belvedere (Escher), 24, 25f
Bennett, William J., 179
Benvenuto, S., 70
Berger, P., 185, 197
Bergson, H., 202
Berlin, Isaiah, 69
Best, K., 143, 145
betrayal, 139–40
Beyond Good and Evil (Nietzsche), 159,
    174–5, 207
The Big Bang Theory, 58–9, 74
binary ethics, 158
binary mortality, 157–9
Bindi, 30
biological compulsions, patterns, 199
biology, 110–16
*Bittersweetness: How Sorrow and
    Longingness Make Us Whole* (Cain),
    32
bittersweet story, literature, 31–2
"Black Lives Matter," 155–6
blockbuster movies, 157
Bochner, A., 11, 145, 153, 158
Boggis, A., 136
Bohr, Niels, 160
Boncori, I., 135–6
Boston matrix, 146
Bowie, M., 67
Brave New World (Huxley), 39–40
Brexit, 45–6, 50–1
Briggs, J., 60–1, 110, 114–15, 122–3,
    133–4
British Chartered Management Institute,
    89–90
Brockmann, J., 92
Bronowski, J., 10, 108, 116–17, 194
Bryman, A., 139
Buddha/Buddhism, 195, 199; The
    Middle Way, 214
Bureaucracy: critique of, 180–1;
    organization control, 82–5; paradox
    of, 82, 83f
bureaucratic flexibility, paradox of, 84
buried objects, paradox of, 65
Burke, Edmund, 196
Burkitt, I., 10

Burrell, G., 135, 142, 212
Burton, Robert, 210
business, tension of, 163

Cain, Susan, 32
Calder, B., 89
Camus, A., 33, 35–7, 173, 177
Cantor, Georg, 104
capitalism, 166
Capra, F., 124, 125
Carter, P., 67, 85–6
Catch-22 (Heller), 35–8
Catullus, 173
Caulkin, S., 163
causality, ontology, 132–4
cause-and-effect, 1, 12
certainty paradox, 141–2
Challenger Shuttle Disaster (1986), 97
Chandler, J., 86–7
chaos, order *vs.*, 114
Chaplin, S., 100
character, paradox of, 65
Charlton, W., 4–5
chemistry, 110–16
child sexual abuse, 67
choice: economics, 56–7; paradox of, 56
Christie, L., 68
chronic fatigue syndrome, 115–16
chronology of research methods, 135
cinema, 41–3
Civilization and it's Discontents (Freud),
    65, 75, 164, 176
Clarke, D., 144
*The Clash of Civilisation and
    the Remaking of World Order*
    (Huntington), 51
cleanliness, disease and, 113–14
Clifton, J., 118–19
climate change, 116
Clinton, Bill, 121
Cochrane, J., 190
cognitive behavioural therapy
    (CBT), 68
cognitive dissonance, paradox of, 71
Cohen, Leonard, 173
collective identity, individual identity
    vs., 69
commitment: organization control,
    93–5; study of, 48–9
compatibilists, 211
competition, 60–1; pervasive paradox
    of, 198
complementary colours, 28–9

complexity: balance, 212–13; paradox, 195
compromise, 214
concept of being, 128, 189
conflict, paradoxes of, 164–8
conflict-consensus paradox, 97
consciousness, 187–90; understanding of, 3
consensus, organizational group dynamics, 97
conservatism, 49
conspiracy of nature, 111
constructive approach, pain, 180
constructivism, 197
consumption trends, paradox of, 59
contradiction contra paradox, 5
control: conundrum, 82; organization, 81–95; paradox of, 82
Cooper, R., 80–1, 139
Crawford, Cindy, 30
Creative and psychotic states in exceptional people (Magagna), 73
creative destruction, 51, 54–5
critical thinking, 10
Cronenberg, David, 41
crux of life, paradox at, 114
Cullen-Unsworth, L., 118, 119–20
cultural nuance paradox, 77
Curry, P., 122, 167, 182

Dale, K., 142, 212
Dali, Salvador, 123–4
The Dancing Wu Li Masters (Zukav), 124
Darwinian evolution, paradox of, 114
Davey, N., 201
Dead Lagoon (Dibdin), 51
Deakin, Roger, 179, 207
deceptive, 139–40
decision fatigue, 77
Deetz, S., 129–30
definition of paradox, 1–2, 4–7, 8
definitive methodological paradox, 130; ontology, 129–34
Delamont, S., 144
delegation, paradox of, 87–8
Deleuze, Giles, 65–6, 178–9
Deloria, V., 146
Denzin, N., 135
departmentalization, 9
dependency, 71–3
depression, 73
dialectics contra paradox, 5–6

Dibdin, Michael, 51
dichotomies contra paradox, 6
Dickson, A., 65
Diderot, Denis, 30
Difference and repetition (Deleuze), 178–9
disability, 158
disease: cleanliness and, 113–14; prevention, paradox of, 113
disorder, lifeworld and, 129
dissolution, paradoxes to, 199
The Disuniting of America: Reflections on a Multicultural Society (Schlesinger), 77
diversity: ethical status quo, 95–6; sociology, 76–9
division of labour, 53; paradox of, 52
Donnie Darko (2001), 41
Don't Let's Start, 43
Dostoevsky, F., 14–15, 33–4, 187–8, 213
Do They Know It's Christmas, 155
dualisms contra paradox, 6
Duckrabbit (anon), 20–1, 20f
Durkheim, E., 213
dynamics: balance understanding, 212; post-linear, 203
dystopia, 38

Ecce Homo (Nietzsche), 163
ecology, 116–21; resilience and social resilience, 119; scale of, 120
economics, 51–64; ideology, 62–4; paradox of deregulation, 64; Veblen effect, 201–2; vulnerability, 120
economic success, paradox of, 61
Eco, Umberto, 29–30, 47, 90, 131, 207, 213, 214–15
education, paradox of, 68
effect, leadership vs., 89–90
egalitarian inertia, 2–3, 169–83
egalitarian rhetoric, 138
EGOS (European Group of Organization Studies), 173
Einspahr, J., 69
Einstein, Albert, 1, 10, 107, 108, 109–10, 111, 131, 191
Elias, N., 185, 197
Elliott, Tony, 41
Ellis, C., 11, 145, 153, 158
emotion, psychology, 74
The Empty Raincoat (Handy), 53
enablers of understanding, 13

The End of History and the Last Man
(Fukuyama), 164
environment, shaping of, 117
environmental resilience, 121
epicaricacy, 174
Epimenides, 2
epistemic duality, 160
epistemology of balance, 211–12
equality, freedom *vs.*, 48
Eriugena, John Scotus, 207
Escher, M. C., 23, 24–5, 25f, 106
eternal recurrence, 201
Ethnographic Research Methods:
Anxiety, Identity and Self (Vine et
al.), 141
Ethnography: observation, 136;
ontology, 134–43; researchers in, 131;
writing, 143
ethnomasochism, 139
European Group of Organization
Studies (EGOS), 173
evening out of experience, 175–9
exclusivity, 57
existential pattern, paradox and, 13–14
existential predicament, literature, 33–8
experience, 187; paradox of, 11–12
extrinsically curved lines, 106–7

Fair Trade, 119
fallacies contra paradox, 6–7
familiarization paradox, ethnographic
research, 136–7
Family Guy, 76
fatigue, decision, 77
fault, paradoxes and, 8
feminism, 77
Feyerabend, Paul, 130
figuration, 197
Findhorn Foundation, 124, 139, 140–1
Fine, G., 142
Fleissner, U., 120
Fluoxetine, 68
Forster, E., 40
Foucault, Michel, 13, 185, 197
Foucault's Pendulum (Eco), 47
Four Antinomies (Kant), 196f
Frankl, Viktor, 183
freedom: equality *vs.*, 48; peculiarities
of, 162
free will, paradoxes and, 159–62
Freud, Sigmund, 13, 65, 75, 164,
173–4, 176, 178, 222
Frey, B., 92

Frost, J., 92
Fukuyama, Francis, 164
fun, 171–2
fundamental paradox, 166
Fundamentals of Management (Smith),
98
Futurism (Toffler), 212

Galileo, 108
Ganga, D., 138
gardener's paradox, 116
Gastin, J., 31
Gates, J., 219
Gauss, Carl, 106, 107
Genealogy of Morals (Nietzsche), 174
generalizability, ontology, 131–2
genetic theory, 115
genocide, paradox of, 78–9
geography, paradox of, 106–7
geometry, 103–11
Gephart, R., 146
Giddens, A., 185, 197, 212
Giffen goods, 57
Gilbert, W. S., 42–3
Glastonbury, 140
GNP (gross national product), 54
von Goethe, Wolfgang, 133
Golden Mean (Aristotle), 212
Goldstein, L., 23–5
Gompertz, Will, 20
Goodall, Jane, 134–5
good enough mother, 64–5
Govan, M., 26
Graeber, David, 46, 63–4
Graham-Dixon, Andrew, 20
gratitude for suffering, 180
Grayling, A., 6
Grimm's Fairy Tales, 33
Grint, Keith, 85
gross national product (GNP), 54
group dynamics, organizations,
95–102
group effectiveness, paradox of, 95
guesswork, interpretation as, 209
guiltless indulgence, pain, 179–81

Hamann, Johann Georg, 126
Hamilton, Peter F., 170
Hammersley, M., 135, 137–8, 148
Handy, Charles, 53, 55, 80, 81, 99,
114, 201–3, 214
Hansen, Marcus Lee, 47
Hansen's law, 47

Harari, Yuval Noah, 59, 71, 107
hard currency, 59
Hardy, Françoise Madeleine, 47
harmony, 214–15
haute couture, 57
Hayashi, N., 119
Hegel, G., 167–8
Heisenberg's Uncertainty Principle,
    108–9, 160, 198
helicopter parents, 35
Heller, Joseph, 35–7
heterophily, 115
hierarchy, organizations, 87
Hill, W., 20, 21–2
Hirsch, P., 78
History of Beauty (Eco), 29–30, 207,
    214–15
Hofmann, B., 4, 220, 222
Hogensen, G. B., 199
Holden, L., 99
holidaying, 181
Holliday, R., 138, 142
The Holographic Paradigm (Wilber),
    126
Homans, P., 71–2
homeostasis, 215–16
Homo economicus, 51–64
homophily, 115
Homo politicus, 44–51
Homo psychologicus, 64–74
Homo sociologicus, 74–9
honesty paradox, 139–40
Horney, Karen, 91, 171–2, 181–2
House (Whiteread), 27, 28f
Hughes, Robert, 20
Hühn, M. P., 129
Human, All-too-human (Nietzsche), 181
human paradox, 140
The Human Swarm (Moffett), 13–14,
    70
Humphreys, M., 145
Huntington, S., 50–1
Huxley, Aldous, 39–40

Ibarra, Hermina, 96
identity: paradox of, 70; pervasive
    paradox of, 197
ideology; closure, paradox thwarting,
    153–68; paradox of, 45, 49; role and,
    93–4
Ideology and Utopia (Mannheim), 130,
    189
illusions, 20–8

Immaculate Conception, 73–4
immaterialists, 211
Imponderable Questions (Buddha), 195,
    195f
imposter syndrome, 138
inbreeding depression, 115
indigenous peoples, ecology and,
    118–19
individual identity, collective identity
    vs., 69
*Individualism, Holism and The Central
    Dilemma of Sociological Theory*
    (Šubrt), 185–6
inertia, egalitarian *see* egalitarian inertia
Inland Empire (2006), 41
In Search of Excellence (Peters &
    Waterman), 90
insider–outsider paradox, 137–9
intellectual curiosity, 10–11
intellectual traction, philosophy, 8
intention, paradox of, 112, 113
interdependency, 165
international division of labour, 52
interpretation, 147; guesswork as, 209
intersubjectivity: objective attention
    change, 147; ontology, 145–8
intimacy, paradox of, 73–4
intrinsic straight lines, 106–7
investment escalation, 57
Irises (Van Gogh), 29
Irreversible (2003), 41

Jackson, Murray, 73, 85–6
Jackson, N., 67, 136
Jacobson, L., 32
Jantsch, Erich, 114–15
Januszczak, Waldemar, 20
Jobs, Steve, 100–1
Judas Unchained (Hamilton), 170
Jung, Carl, 67
Just-In-Time Manufacturing, 99

Kallinkos, J., 84
Kant, Immanuel, 160, 195, 196f,
    206
Kardashian, Kim, 158
Kelley, Richard, 41
Kierkegaard, Søren, 11, 70, 125–6,
    171–2, 193–4
Knights, D., 69
Krishna, 33
Kropotkin, Peter, 61
Kuhn, Thomas, 130, 135

labour: division of, 53; international
   division of, 52
Lacan, J., 67
Lakoff, G., 50
language, mechanics of, 31
Larsen, S., 101
Law, J., 80–1, 139
leadership, 89, 90; effect *vs*., 89–90;
   organization control, 88–90
Lean Manufacturing, 99
Learmonth, M., 145
Le Guin, Ursula, 174
Levenson, Edgar, 200
LGBTQ+ culture, 77, 219
Liamputtong, P., 143
liar paradox (Epimenides), 2
liberal democracy, 164
liberalism, 49–50
libertarians, 211
Lieberman, S., 93
life, transcendent aspect of, 9–10
Life of Brian (Monty Python), 204
lifeworld, 14; disorder and, 129
Liman, Doug, 41
Lincoln, Y., 135
linguistic construction paradox, 143–4
Linsenmeier, J., 92–3
literature, 30–40; existential
   predicament, 33–8; mechanics of
   language, 31; self-fulfilling prophecy,
   32–3; utopian circularity, 38–40
lived experience of paradox, 2, 19
Lokgariwar, C., 121
Lost Highway (1997), 41
love–hate relationship, 173
The Lucifer Effect (Zimbardo), 72
Luckmann, T., 185, 197
Lynch, David, 41, 147–8

Macbeth (Shakespeare), 33
Machievelli, Niccoló, 40
machine design, 52
The Machine Stops (Forster), 40
Magagna, J., 73
magic, science *vs*., 121–7
The Magpie on the Gallows (Bruegel),
   26f
Magritte, René, 26, 27f
Maguire, S., 99
*Man at Play: Nine Centuries of Pleasure
   Making* (Armitage), 210
Mannheim, K., 129, 130, 189
Mann, Thomas, 8

Man's Search for Meaning (Frankl), 183
Marsden, Jill, 1, 61, 122, 132–3,
   179–80, 187, 188–9, 200, 204, 206
Marxism, 166, 199
Marx, Karl, 5, 13
mathematics, 103–11; paradox and, 104
Matthews, Gareth, 161
McGregor, K., 101
mechanics of language, 31
mechanics of paradox, 181–2
mediating effects of paradox, 221
medication, paradox of, 111–12
medicine, 110–16
melody, pattern of paradox, 210
Messer, Laura, 219
metabolism, paradox of, 112–13
"Me Too," 155
The Middle Way, Buddha, 214
might makes right, 154–7
mind, dualist solution to, 160
mindfulness, paradox of, 65
minority representation, paradox of,
   77
Minsky, Hyman, 167
Mintzberg, Henry, 142
Mobile Lovers (Banksy), 101, 102f
Mobius strip, 201, 203–4, 203f
moderation, 213–14
Moffett, Mark, 13–14, 53, 70, 76, 88,
   156, 165–6, 215–16
money, paradox of, 59
moral closure, paradox thwarting,
   153–68
Moravec's paradox, 191
More, T., 39
Morgan, G., 135
Morgenthau, Hans, 165
Morrisette, Alanis, 43
Mosley, Ivo, 46–7
Mosley, Nicholas, 103
Mosley, Oswald, 46–7
motion, non-existence of, 107
Mullholland Drive (2001), 41
musical metaphors, patterns of paradox,
   205–7
Mutual Aid: A Factor of Evolution
   (Kropotkin), 61
mysinglefriend.com, 144
My Wife and my Mother-in-Law (Hill),
   20, 21–2, 22f

The Name of the Rose (Eco), 131
Nash, Ogden, 206

nature, 103–27; conspiracy of, 111;
    nurture and, 159
The Nature of Managerial Work
    (Mintzberg), 142
von Neuman, John, 190
New Age philosophy, 53
Newtonian physics, 131
Newton, Isaac, 108
Newton's Law of Politics, 46, 81
Nietzsche, F., 35, 54–5, 61, 131, 144,
    155, 159, 163, 168, 171–2, 174, 180,
    181, 182, 187, 194, 206, 207
The Night Café (Van Gogh), 29
nihilism, 198–9
Nineteen Eighty-Four (Orwell), 39–40
Notes from the Underground
    (Dostoevsky), 14–15, 33–8
Nowotny, H., 133
nurture, 159

objective, intersubjective attention
    change, 147
objectivity, 131; ethnography, 147;
    science, 125
observation, ethnography, 136
observation, pervasive paradox of, 198
observer effects, physics, 136
Occam's razor, 146
Oedipus, 33
*The Ones Who Walk Away From
    Omelas* (Le Guin), 174
ontology, 128–49; definition, 128;
    definitive methodological paradox,
    129–34; ethnographic research,
    134–43; intersubjective research
    agenda, 145–8; U-shaped patterns,
    201–3
operations: division of labour, 53;
    organizational group dynamics, 97
order, chaos *vs.*, 114
organizational Darwinism, 90
organizations, 80–102; control, 81–95;
    ethnography, 10–11, 138; group
    dynamics, 95–102; norms paradox,
    92; paradoxes of structure, 85;
    sociological paradigms, 146
organograms, 85
Orwell, George, 39–40
Oryx and Crake (Atwood), 67
Osterloh, M., 92
other, validation of, 72
outbreeding, 115
The Outsider (Camus), 33, 35–7, 177

overchoice, 56
overcoming adversity, 62
oxygen, antioxidants and, 112–13

Pagel, Mark, 31
Pahl, R., 91
pain, 170–5; constructive approach to,
    179–81; guiltless indulgence, 179–81;
    love–hate relationship, 173; paradox
    of aesthetics, 172–3; sadomasochism,
    173–5
paradox at crux of life, 114
paradoxes of conflict, 164–8
Paradoxes of Peace (Mosley), 103
Paradoxes of Progress (Stent), 145
paradoxes, solutions to, 14–15, 199
paradoxical anecdotes, 218
paradoxical intention, 112
paradoxical nature of connectivity in
    respect of smartphones, 101
paradox of aesthetics, 172–3
paradox of bureaucracy, 82, 83f
paradox of bureaucratic flexibility, 84
paradox of buried objects, 65
paradox of character, 65
paradox of choice, 56
paradox of cognitive dissonance, 71
paradox of competition, 60–1
paradox of consumption trends, 59
paradox of Darwinian evolution, 114
paradox of delegation, 87–8
paradox of dependency, 71–3
paradox of disease prevention, 113
paradox of division of labour, 52
paradox of economic deregulation, 64
paradox of economic success, 61
paradox of education, 68
paradox of free will, 159–62
paradox of genocide, 78–9
paradox of geography, 106–7
paradox of group effectiveness, 95
paradox of identity, 70
paradox of ideology, 45
paradox of intention, 113
paradox of intimacy, 73–4
paradox of labour-saving techniques,
    101
paradox of medication, 111–12
paradox of metabolism, 112–13
paradox of mindfulness, 65
paradox of minority representation, 77
paradox of plenty (resource curse), 56
paradox of populist uprisings, 50

paradox of progressive thought, 77
paradox of prosperity, 62
paradox of proximity, 75–6
paradox of psychiatric medication, 113
paradox of quality management, 98
paradox of rationality, 51
paradox of routine, 86
paradox of selfishness, 162–4
paradox of self-revelation, 144
paradox of specialization, 51–3
paradox of stability, 167
paradox of straight line travel, 107
paradox of support, 67
paradox of theft, 51
paradox of time-as-resource, 53
paradox of unanticipated consequences, 82
paradox of voluntarism, 72
paradox of working-class politics, 50
Pareto, Vilfredo, 46
Parmenides, 107
Parsons, Talcott, 216
participant-observer paradox, 135–6
Parton, Dolly, 30
patterned worldview, 198
patterning, awareness of, 200
patterns: biological compulsions, 199; paradoxes, 198–211; paradox of, musical metaphors, 205–7
Pax Americana, 88
Pax Brittanica, 88, 165
Peat, D., 60–1, 101, 114–15, 122–3, 133–4
pedagogical potential for paradox, 217–19
pedagogical technique, enhancement of, 2
Pelletier, Kenneth, 160–1
pendulum, 204–5, 205f, 206; equilibrium of, 216–17
Pepys, Samuel, 186
Perel, Esther, 73
perfect lives, 200
performance: organization control, 90–3; paradox of, 91–2
persuasive paradox, pleasure, 197
pervasive paradox, 195–8; competition, 198; identity, 197; observations, 198; unintended consequences, 196–7
Peters, Tom, 90
Pfeffer, J., 94
philosophy: intellectual traction, 8; paradoxes and, 7–8
physicists, 211

physics, 103–11
The Pirates of Penzance (Gilbert and Sullivan), 42–3
plagiarism paradox, 142–3
Plato, 154
Player Piano (Vonnegut), 40
pleasure, 170–5; love–hate relationship, 173; new dynamics of, 181–3; paradox of aesthetics, 172–3; sadomasochism, 173–5
plenty, paradox of, 56
political horseshoe, 45, 45f
Political Left–Right continuum, 201
politics, 44–51
Pompeii, 208–9, 208f
Pope, Alexander, 213–14
populist uprisings, paradox of, 50
Porter's Generic Competitive Strategy Framework, 146
post-linear dynamics, 203
post-structuralism, 197
The Potato Eaters (Van Gogh), 29
The Poverty of Affluence (Wachtel), 48
The Prague Cemetery (Eco), 90
preoccupations, paradox solving, 14–15
The presence of infinity (Mosley), 103
pretence paradox, 92
price, economics, 57–60
Prigogine, Ilya, 122–3
Prince, R., 140
professional practice, psychology, 68–9
progress, paradox and, 10
progressive thought, paradox of, 77
progressivism, 223
promotion paradox, 88
prospective satisfaction, 60
prosperity: economics, 61–2; paradox of, 62
proximity: paradox of, 75–6; sociology, 75–6
proximity thinking, 103
psychiatric medication, paradox of, 113
psychoanalysis, 65–8
Pulp Fiction (1994), 41
Punch, K., 136
punks, 44
Pygmalion Effect, 32–3
Pythagoras, 205–6, 214–15

quality, 57; organizational group dynamics, 98–9; paradox of management, 98
quantum theory, 131

questions, paradoxes as, 8
Quine, W., 8

race, 158
racism, paradox and, 76
Rand, Ayn, 40
Rappaport, J., 2, 4, 48, 220
rationality, paradox of, 51
Reagan, Ronald, 47
recurrence, eternal, 201
re-examination of paradox, 7–9
Regibeau, P., 121
Relativity (Escher), 23, 25f
relativity of simultaneity, 110
religion: foundation of, 123; science vs.,
    121–7
Republic (Plato), 154
researcher-cum-employee, 138
resilience, 117–18; environmental, 121
resilience initiatives, 120
resolution: de-emphasization, 6;
    paradoxes to, 199
resolution of paradox, 219–22
resource curse (paradox of plenty), 56
resources, 53–6, 100
rhetoric: egalitarian, 138; structureless,
    85
rhythm, pattern of paradox, 207–11
Riches, D., 140
riddles, paradoxes as, 8
risk: organizational group dynamics,
    99–101; threats and, 100
Rizzi, Bruno, 45
Robinson, A., 123
Rockett, K., 121
role, ideology and, 93–4
Romulus and Remus, 33
Rose, D., 136, 138
Rosenthal, R., 32
Rousseau, J., 69–70
routine, paradox of, 86
Rowling, J. K., 156
Rubin's Vase (Rubin), 20, 21, 21f
Russell, Bertrand, 104
Russell's Paradox, 105–6
Russia, Ukraine conflict, 209–10

sadomasochism, pleasure and pain
    game, 173–5
Sainsbury, R., 8
Salancik, G., 49, 58, 93, 94
Sapiens (Harari), 107
Sapir–Whorf hypothesis, 11, 31

schadenfreude, 174
Schema, S., 199
Schlesinger, Arthur M., 77, 95
Schlich, E., 120
Schopenhauer, Arthur, 132–3, 188–9
Schumacher, F., 119
Schwartz, B., 56–7
Schwarzenegger, Arnold, 180
science, art/magic/religion vs., 121–7
Scorsese, Martin, 184–5
SCOS (Standing Conference on
    Organizational Symbolism), 172–3
the search for glory, 91
Selective Serotonin Reuptake Inhibitors
    (SSRIs), 68, 112, 197
self, psychology, 69–71
self-contradiction, 5
self-fulfilling prophecy, literature, 32–3
selfishness, paradox of, 162–4
Self-portrait (Van Gogh), 29
self-revelation, paradox of, 144
Selznick, P., 49
semantic paradoxes, 12
sensorium, 2, 37, 148, 194
Shakespeare, William, 33, 146
Shealy, J., 217
Shulman, D., 142
Simmel, George, 2
simultaneity, relativity of, 110
Slaughterhouse Five (Vonnegut), 170
Slovic, P., 100
Small is Beautiful (Schumacher), 119
small-scale activities, ecology and,
    119–20
smartphones, paradoxical nature of
    connectivity, 101
Smith, Adam, 52, 62–3, 86, 110, 196
Smith, Christopher, 42
Smith, Mike, 98
The Social Contract (Rousseau), 69–70
socialism, 50
social resilience, ecological resilience
    and, 119
society, 44–79; Homo economicus,
    51–64; Homo politicus, 44–51;
    Homo psychologicus, 64–74; Homo
    sociologicus, 74–9; psychology, 68–9
sociology, organizational analysis, 146
Sorensen, R., 2, 105–6, 162, 218,
    220–1; fallacies contra paradox, 6–7;
    re-examination of paradox, 7–8
Southwell, M., 131–2
specialization, paradox of, 51–3

SSRIs (Selective Serotonin Reuptake Inhibitors), 68, 112, 197
stability, paradox of, 167
Standing Conference on Organizational Symbolism (SCOS), 172–3
Stanford Prison Experiment, 72–3, 93–4
Stanislavski, Konstantin, 146
Stanley, L., 147
Starobinski, J., 139
Stent, Gunther, 46, 107–8, 109, 111, 130, 145, 147, 157, 159, 160, 200–1
Stockholm Syndrome, 64–5
Stogdill, Ralph, 88–9
story of Adam and Eve, 157
Strachan, D., 113
straight lines, 106–7; paradox of, 107
The Stranger (Camus), 173
Stratton, L., 161
Streatfield, P., 81–2
Street Corner Society (Whyte), 145
strength of weak ties, 75
structuration, 197
structure, organization control, 85–8
structure–agency dynamic, 186
structureless rhetoric, 85
Strudwick, R., 141
Styhre, A., 84–5, 133, 202–3
subjectivity, ethnography, 147
Subjectivity and Paradox (Kierkegaard), 125–6
Šubrt, Jiří, 71, 75, 185–6, 200, 216
Sullivan, A. S., 42–3
Sumner, William, 165
support, paradox of, 67
sustainability, 117; environmental, 116–21
symmetry, 106
symmetry contra paradox, 7

Taoism, 214
The Tao of Physics (Capra), 124
Taxi Driver (Scorsese), 184–5
technology, organizational group dynamics, 101
television sets, 176–7
tempo, pattern of paradox, 210–11
tension of business, 163
Tett, G., 9
Thatcher, Margaret, 46
theft, paradox of, 51
theodicy, 157
theory of relativity (Einstein), 108, 109–10

They Might be Giants, 43
The Third Way (Giddens), 212
Thomas, W., 131–2, 218
threats, risk and, 100
Thus Spake Zarathustra (Nietzsche), 174
Tilly, Charles, 166
time-as-resource, paradox of, 53
time paradoxes, 110
Toffler, A., 47, 212
Tolkien, J. R. R., 167
totalitarian countries, 221–2
Total Quality Management (TQM), 98–9
Tranøy, K. E., 222
transcendent aspect of life, paradoxes as, 9–10
transgender rights, 156
The Treachery of Images (This is Not a Pipe) (Magritte), 26, 27f
tree of knowledge of good and evil, 157
Triangle (2009), 42
Trump, Donald, 45–6, 50–1
truth, ontology, 130–1
Tsoukas, H., 133
Twin Peaks (1990s), 41

unanticipated consequences, paradox of, 82
Uncanny Valley Model, 191, 192f
understanding, enables of *see* enablers of understanding
uniform motion, pendulum, 205
unintended consequences, pervasive paradox of, 196–7
universal resilience, ecology and, 120–1
U-shaped ontological patterns, 201–3, 202f
Utopia (More), 39
utopian circularity, literature, 38–40
The Utopia of Rules: On Technology, Stupidity, and the Secret Joys of Bureaucracy (Graeber), 63–4

vaccinations, 113
Van Gogh, Vincent, 29
Van Orman Quine, Willard, 193
Veblen effect, economics, 201–2
Veblen goods, 57
Veblen, Thorstein, 57
visual arts, 20–30; beauty, 29–30; colour, 28–9; illusions, 20–8
vocabulary, 143–4

Voltaire, 165
voluntarism, 185; paradox of, 72
Vonnegut, Kurt, 40, 170, 171f
voting behaviour, 46

Wachtel, Paul L., 47–8, 54
Waddington, C. H., 115
Wagner, Richard, 42
Waiting for Godot (Beckett), 3
Wallace, M., 118, 119–20
Walver, Michael, 50
war, 166–7, 221–2
Ward, S., 100
Warner, M., 119
Waterlog (Deakin), 179, 207
Waterman, Robert, 90
Watson, T., 180–1
wave-particle duality, 108
weak ties, strength of, 75
The Wealth of Nations (Smith), 62–3, 86
Weil, S., 49

Weir, D., 144
Whyte, William, 145, 207
wicked problems contra paradox, 7
Wilber, K., 124–5, 126, 161, 200
Wild at Heart (1990), 41
Wilde, Oscar, 213, 217
Willmott, K., 69
The Will to Power (Nietzsche), 174, 206
Winckelmann, Johann Joachim, 30
Wirth, L., 130, 189, 199
Wise, S., 147
working-class politics, paradox of, 50
world co-construction, 66
Wortman, C., 92–3

Yanow, D., 148
Young, Thomas, 108–9

Zarate, O., 123
Zeno's paradox, 6, 7, 103–4, 218
Zimbardo, Philip, 72, 93–4

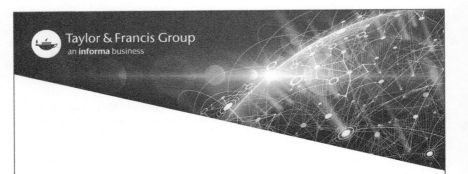